# Forty Years in the Wilderness

One woman's adventures and struggles
Homesteading in the Alaska wilderness

## dolly faulkner

Copyright © 2012
by Dolly Faulkner

All rights reserved. No part of the material protected by this copyright notice may be reproduced or utilized in any form or by any means, electronic or mechanical, including photocopying, recording or by any informational storage and retrieval system without written permission from the copyright owner.

ISBN: 978-0-615-70153-0

Printed and bound in the United States of America by
Maverick Publications ● Bend, Oregon

For my daughter

# PREFACE

The events described in this story are told from my perspective to the best of my knowledge and memory. Most names have been changed. After years of being told, "You should write a book!", I finally decided to share my life's trials and triumphs with total strangers. I do this in hope that one of you can help me in my battle to save the home I have put my life's efforts into. If you have any suggestions, please feel free to share them with me.

        Dolly Faulkner
        White Bear homestead
        c/o P.O. Box 1307
        Bethel, AK 99559

# Chapter One

**October, 1971**

"SHIT!!" Harry yelled as our small Cessna cartwheeled on the frozen Alaskan tundra. In a single terrifying instant, the earth and the sky exchanged places. I hung suspended by my seat belt, disoriented, struggling to grasp what had just happened. Where was I? The cabin filled with the strong scent of aviation fuel. The sounds of crunching metal mingled with the wail of the emergency locator transmitter. Where was Harry? Terror rose inside. The plane could explode at any moment. I had to get out, get out now, but which way was out? I choked on the thick smoke and groped around wildly for the door handle, fighting back panic.

Just a few hours ago, I had sat in the office of Harry's air charter business in Bethel, dispatching the charters and trying to catch up on the paperwork. It was my birthday. Harry had forgotten. Oh well. I finished the billing and went on to the scheduling for next week. Harry was flying a charter to Tuluksak and should be back soon. The kids were in school and the office was quiet. Suddenly the marine radio crackled and I jumped up to answer it. "Get your stuff ready and meet me, I'm 15 minutes out. "

"Where are we going?" I asked, and my heart filled with hope.

The radio crackled again. "Home."

My heart soared and I did a happy little dance. But, was it too good to be true?

"What about the rest of the charters? There's a couple wanting to go to Kasigluk in an hour."

"Joe can fly the rest of the charters."

"What about the kids?" I wanted to know. Harry's three children were all in school. Who would pick them up, and who would watch them while we were gone?

"Linda can babysit. Dammit Dolly, just get ready, OK?"

Ohhhh goody!!! I gave a squeal of delight and tore around the room frantically trying to gather what we needed. I was going home!! It was the best birthday present in the world!

Home was nearly 100 miles away, the remote wilderness homestead Harry and I had carved out in a rugged mountain valley. The only access into our home was the small airstrip Harry had made in a tiny clearing between the mountains. It was 45 miles from the nearest river and just as far to the nearest neighbor. It was so beautiful and serene. I wanted so much to live there the rest of my life and raise my family there.

The radio crackled again. "White Bear, KYH6." Harry was calling the homestead. We had named it White Bear, after a big white grizzly we had seen nearby. KYH6 was the radio call sign of our air charter business.

"Go ahead." Buzzy Wheeler answered. Harry had flown Buzzy and Dan Charles up the week before to finish the new rooms we were adding to the cabin.

"What's the weather doing up there?" Harry asked.

There was a short pause. "Overcast, good visibility, and light south wind." Buzzy replied.

"Get any snow?" Harry wanted to know. It had rained most of the week in Bethel, but with the higher elevation, it could have snowed at White Bear.

"Yeah."

"How much snow is on the strip?" Harry prompted.

"Uh, about three inches." Buzzy said.

"Are you sure that's all?"

"Yeah."

"OK. Dolly and I are coming up, and I will take you guys back tomorrow and come back next week for Dolly. We will be there in about an hour."

I gave another shriek of delight. This would be my best birthday ever! A whole week of staying at home! I missed my two husky dogs,

Tengupak and Freckles. I wondered how the cabin looked now with the new addition. I was so excited it was hard to concentrate on packing. Let's see, I could bring my sewing, some books, food, and better not forget toilet paper, and oh yes, my long johns....

The Cessna 180's engine had purred as we turned the corner of the mountain range and started up the narrow valley. The small opening in the trees came into view and Harry throttled back the power.

"Seat belt on?" He asked. It was something he always asked his passengers, both on take-off and landings.

"Yes." I smiled back at him as I strained my eyes to see the cabin. But it was too far away and tucked back into the last stand of trees at the edge of the timberline. The plane glided softly through the air over the treetops. I felt as though I could reach down and touch them if I tried. Harry was an excellent pilot, skilled and competent, although a bit impatient at times. We had flown all over Alaska during the first years we had been together. I trusted him entirely. In just a few moments I would be home! I looked out at the mountains and was surprised to see how much snow was on the ground. Buzzy had said three inches. It looked like more. Maybe it would snow again while I was home and maybe I would get snowed in for a month! I smiled at the thought.

There would be so much to do at the cabin. Firewood to split, shelves to build, water to haul, laundry to scrub... I wondered if I would have time to read the novel I had brought. I loved to read, there just never seemed to be time at the office.

The plane flared gently and settled onto the soft white field of snow. And then, the wheels had grabbed suddenly in the deep powder and the plane had flipped. The snow was well over a foot deep, and far beyond the safe landing capabilities of a wheel-equipped Cessna. Instead of rolling out to a smooth stop, we had gone from 60 miles an hour to an almost instant halt. The cargo had been thrown violently forward. I had felt a hard thump to the back of my head as an oil can hit me.

"SHIT!!" Harry yelled. "DAMMIT!"

I felt an enormous relief. Harry was still alive!

"We have to get out of here! Hurry up, Dolly, take off your seat belt!" Harry shouted. I fumbled with the latch on the seat belt as Harry struggled with the door.

"Dammit!" Harry swore again, and said something about the door being stuck.

Oh no, oh no! Waves of panic hit again. We had to get out NOW! I choked back the fear and clawed at the seat belt. Suddenly the latch gave away and I tumbled to the roof of the airplane, which was on the ground. I laid there a second, stunned, trying to grasp that concept.

"Dammit Dolly, help me with this door! Give me that fire extinguisher!"

I saw the fire extinguisher above me, dangling from its bracket on what had been the floor of the plane. I reached for it, tugging at the rusted bracket that held it there.

"Hurry up!" Harry shouted.

My head throbbed, and I felt muddled and confused. The rusted latch seemed far away and foreign.

"HURRY UP!" Harry yelled again.

I ripped the bracket loose and handed him the fire extinguisher. He snatched it up and pushed at the door. It opened partway. I felt hope rushing into me as I shifted groceries, boxes, and other cargo.

"Get out!" Harry shifted his body to let me pass. I squeezed through the door, my thick parka snagging and stopping me abruptly. Oh no! I was stuck! My face and upper body were out of the plane, in a puddle of aviation fuel from the wing tank. The rest of my body was inside. I felt nauseas from the gasoline fumes. Oh man! Why hadn't I taken off my parka? The sight of freedom had overpowered my senses. I should have known I would not fit through such a tight squeeze with all my heavy winter gear. I struggled futilely, clawing like a wild animal at the smooth metal surface of the wing. I gasped when I felt a huge boot on my rear, shoving hard. My coat tore and then gave way. I tumbled out into the snow, gasping for air.

"Come on, Dolly, help me out!" Harry shouted, bringing me back to my senses.

He had gotten his head and one arm out and was stuck also. I sat in the puddle of fuel, grabbed his arm and pushed with my feet against the fuselage of the airplane. Harry strained and swore. Suddenly two pairs of strong hands reached down and grabbed Harry's shoulders. I was so relieved to see Dan and Buzzy. Together we heaved until he slid out of the plane into safety. No sooner than Harry had gotten his breath back, he tore into the two men. Dan and Buzzy hung their heads in shame.

"Three inches!!! This snow is more like three FEET deep! We could have been killed! Look at my plane!" He went on for a bit, using some pretty descriptive words to tell the men what he thought of them .Then he remembered I was standing there.

"Dolly, are you OK?" He asked, concerned.

I was looking at the damage to my parka. "Yes." I said. I was still shaking. "Are you?" I asked.

"I'm alright." He walked over. "Quite a happy birthday, huh?" Harry said dryly.

He gave me a hug. We both laughed, relieved that we weren't injured. But we were 45 miles from the nearest town, with a broken plane in the middle of the airstrip, upside down, smoke and steam still coiling up in the cold mountain air. Harry had a business to run, Buzzy and Dan wanted to go back to Bethel, and there were the kids to worry about while we were gone. The oldest, Tara, had been getting into a lot of trouble lately.

"It will be OK. We will make this work out somehow." I said hopefully.

Harry swore again. "What a mess!" He paced a bit.

The men stood there uncomfortably shifting their weight from foot to foot and avoiding eye contact. He always paid them well for odd jobs. They both had a drinking problem and had difficulty holding a job elsewhere. They were excellent carpenters, but not entirely reliable. They knew when to keep their mouths shut around Harry, and that was why Harry liked to hire them.

I reexamined my parka and wondered if I had brought the right color of thread to match it. Any dark color would probably do…I felt a wet nose against my hand. I reached down and stroked Tengupak's big black head and looked around for Freckles. She hung back timidly, but crept up to me when I called her. She did not like men. I did not know anything about her past. Both dogs had been starving strays in Bethel. They loved the homestead nearly as much as I did. There were rabbits to chase and all the room they wanted to run and play.

"Alright," Harry said. "Here's what we do. Dolly, you get on the radio and tell Joe what happened. Dan, is there any lumber left over?" He had flown in the lumber for the cabin that summer, cutting it into lengths short enough to fit inside a Cessna.

"Uh, yeah, there's some." Dan offered.

"What do you want me to tell Joe?" I asked. The marine radio frequency was public and anyone who monitored it could hear a conversation. Harry had a business and a reputation to uphold and couldn't afford to make the accident public knowledge. Most bush pilots carefully covered their mistakes to avoid the paperwork. Since no one was hurt, no one needed to be informed.

"Hell, Dolly! I don't know! Figure something out!" Harry snapped, irritated.

I started to walk toward the cabin.

"Wait," Harry said. "OK. Tell Joe we had a little problem with the plane, and we need him to put the other 180 on the wheel-skis and pick me up tomorrow if the weather is good. Have him call back tomorrow at noon for the weather."

"But, this plane is in the way...." It was heavy. I didn't think the four of us could lift it.

"Geez, will you just go call Joe and I will worry about that!" Harry went back to instructing Dan and Buzzy on building something to help lift the plane.

I started off for the cabin, trudging through the deep snow, Tengupak dancing ahead and shy Freckles trailing in the shadows behind. I was aware of every step and every breath, grateful my body was intact and I was alive. I had some lumps and bumps and scratches, but it was nothing to complain about. What if we had gotten seriously hurt? It could have been days or even weeks before we could get help. Or we could have died. I shook off the thought and unhooked the latch to the cabin door. I stepped inside and was greeted with a strong odor of stale whiskey. My eyes became adjusted to the dimming light filtering through the cabin windows. The place was a mess. Broken dishes, empty whiskey bottles, and someone had urinated on the floor.

Harry would be livid. He did not allow anyone to drink while they were working for him. They must have smuggled the whiskey in one of their personal bags. I had to clean up the mess, fast! There was enough tension about the wrecked plane. I shuddered to think of spending the night around three angry men. I waded through the carnage toward the wood stove. It was a simple design, an old 55 gallon oil barrel with legs and a flat cooking surface welded on, and a stovepipe rising out of the roof. First, I would heat some water... wait, I had to call Joe! But what if Harry came in and saw the mess? I hesitated, torn between what to do next. In the distance, I could hear Harry instructing the men on something they were building. I ran back outside, nearly tripping over Tengupak, who had followed me into the house. I snatched up the snow shovel near the doorstep and darted back inside, quickly shoveling the mess into one corner and throwing a blanket over the heap. I turned to the wall where the radio sat on its little shelf. Turning it on, I was greeted with the familiar static and squelchy squeals. Joe answered quickly, and I relayed the message. He asked if there was anything he needed to bring.

I hesitated. "I will ask Harry and let you know when you call back at noon tomorrow."

OK, so that was done, now let's get this mess cleaned up. But back at the stove again, I found that the men had burned up all the firewood and had not replaced it. I rushed outside again and tramped through the woods looking for dead branches. Freckles gave a little yip. I looked up to see a large snowshoe hare racing by, mottled brown and white as it changed into its winter coat. Both dogs took off in hot pursuit. Arms full of branches, I headed back and soon had a roaring fire going and snow melting in a pot to boil. In short order the cabin was scrubbed clean. I took the empty whisky bottles and food tins out to the pit we put our trash in, stamping it into the snow so Harry wouldn't see. I found a half bottle of Pine Sol in the corner of the cabin by the bucket we used as a latrine. Hoping to disguise the still-lingering whiskey scent, I doused the whole area liberally. It was nearly dark. The men would be hungry. We had brought boxes of food. It was still in the plane. I heard hammering, and wondered what the men were up to.

As I approached the wreckage, I was astounded at the structure the men had quickly erected over the plane. It was a huge tripod. A cable with a pulley hung over the tripod and attached to the tail spring of the plane. They were going to try to pull it over gently to minimize the damage to the plane. Harry had an ever expanding fleet of small Cessnas, but each one was vital to the business.

"What are you going to use to pull it over?" I asked.

Harry wiped sweat from his brow and waved at the ancient Dodge power wagon sitting near the end of the airfield. It was old and cantankerous. Sometimes it started and sometimes it didn't. Harry had it flown into a small clearing several miles away, replacing the tires with giant DC3 cargo plane tires. The little Case he flew in a piece at a time needed repairs. The two Ski-doo snowmachines were too light for the task.

"Will it start?" I asked.

Harry sighed. It was a long day for him and he was tired. "We'll see tomorrow. We have to heat it up, it's too cold for it to start." Then he asked, "How were the new rooms?"

I gasped. I hadn't even noticed! I had been so frantically trying to clean up Dan and Buzzy's mess, I hadn't even looked at the new rooms! What if they were messy too? I had to go back before Harry did.

"Nice." I said. "I'm going to go start dinner."

"OK," Harry said," We are almost done here for the night. We will flip it over tomorrow. We are going to siphon the rest of the gas out of the wing tanks into jerry cans and unload what we can from the plane. Dan, can you help Dolly get what she needs out of the plane?"

Dan reached as far as he could into the plane and started pulling out the supplies. I had to get back to the cabin. I grabbed a chunk of frozen moose meat and a sack of potatoes and carrots. "You left a mess!" I hissed at Dan.

He looked up at me, dark eyes wide with surprise. "I'm sorry." He did look sorry, about everything.

I rushed back to the cabin, Freckles and Tengupak at my heels, hopefully eyeballing the chunk of meat. They were thin. Did Dan forget to feed them? The rabbit hunt must not have been successful. The rabbit, light weight and big-footed, could fly across the deep snow, but the dogs sunk in every step.

Back at the cabin, I set the food down on a shelf out of reach of the dogs and stepped into the addition. I gasped, not because it was filthy (and it was), but because the rooms were wonderful! Suddenly the cabin had transformed into a house. There was a room for Harry and I, and two for the kids. And then the rest of the house could be a kitchen/dining room area. It was so new and nice with the fresh lumber and doors that closed! I instantly forgave the mess. The mess! I scrambled to clean it up. Between boiling water for cleaning, I threw together a moose stew in another big pot, trimming two little chunks of meat off for the dogs. They scarfed it down like they were starved. Where did the two sacks of dog food go that Harry had brought up last week? I would have to look around. I rinsed the dish rag, and then noticed with shock that I had rinsed it in the pot of stew instead of my cleaning pot! I was horrified. It was too late to make dinner over. What should I do?

"Something smells really good!" Harry said as he stomped the snow off his boots. "How long until we eat? I'm starving!"

"Uh, about, uh, five minutes." The stew would have to do. I threw in some more black pepper.

The men chattered nervously as they went into the addition and Harry inspected their work. "What the hell?" Harry said. "A flat roof! Why did you guys make a flat roof?! We get a lot of snow in these mountains!"

"Yeah, uh, see, we didn't quite have enough lumber to make the roof sloped, uh, we can do it over in the spring, we just wanted to get it done before it snowed."

Harry snorted. He would have done it himself if he were not so busy flying. The men had needed money and had been bugging him for work, so he thought he could let them finish the building.

"Dinner's done!" I hollered from what was now my kitchen. The men sat down on stumps of wood arranged around the small card table as I ladled the hot stew into assorted mismatched bowls. It smelled OK. I served the men and retreated back to the kitchen. I was so hungry I felt faint. I realized I hadn't eaten all day. I sipped at the stew. It was very, very good. That thought was confirmed by the compliments that came from the men at the table. There wasn't much room at the table so I sat in the kitchen and smiled secretly at my new stew recipe.

Later, lying in sleeping bags on the floor of our new room, listening to Harry snore, and the other men snoring in the next room, and a crackling of fire from the barrel stove, I though back on the day. It hadn't been that bad after all. No one was hurt. We were home! There was still so much work to do tomorrow. But for now I was grateful to be home, and to be alive.

The next morning was a bustle of activity. While I fried up some bacon and flapjacks and made a big pot of coffee, the men went out to the power wagon, taking along the small gasoline generator and diesel space heater we used to heat aircraft engines on cold days. They took turns watching it to make sure it wouldn't catch on fire, trickling in one at a time to grab some coffee or breakfast. I heard the generator, then as I was finishing the dishes, the power wagon started, stalled and started again, amongst the men cursing. There wasn't much I could do to help, so I tidied up a bit and looked at my watch. Joe would be calling on the radio soon. What should I tell him? I pulled on my boots and threw on my torn parka. Hopefully I would have time to patch it tonight.

*Cessna 185 flipped over in deep snow*

Dan was hooking the cable to the power wagon as I walked up. Harry, in the Dodge, waved at me to get back. The cable could snap and swing back with enough force to cut someone in half. I scurried back into the trees. I worried for the safety of the men. What would happen if one of them were to get hurt? How would a plane land to pick them up? The airstrip was blocked by the wrecked plane. I pressed my forehead against the scratchy bark of the spruce I was leaning against, and listened to the clanking of the tire chains, the creak of aluminum, Freckles whining nervously nearby, and then a solid thunk and the men whooping as the plane righted itself. I looked up. They were all grinning as Harry towed the plane off the strip and shut off the power wagon. It backfired loudly and Freckles jumped, and bolted for cover. I walked over.

"Joe's going to call soon. What do I tell him? Do we need anything?" I asked.

"Just tell him to come and get Dan and Buzzy and come back tomorrow for me." Harry said. He was pleased their plan had worked.

Joe landed that afternoon, picked up Buzzy and Dan, and left. As I was helping load their things into the plane, Dan leaned over and said softly, "Thank you. You are a good woman, Dolly, and I'm sorry for everything." Buzzy squeezed my hand gently and they were gone. The rest of the day, Harry tinkered with the wrecked plane, taking inventory of the damage, listing the parts he needed. I sewed my parka and cooked up a big pot of beans. I did not rinse the dish rag in it this time. It still tasted very good.

The next morning was foggy. The fog hung in until afternoon and then slowly lifted. Joe called every hour for a weather update. Just before dark, the fog lifted and he was able to pick Harry up. At last, I was alone and could unwind and enjoy my new house and my novel!

## Chapter Two

GRRRRRROWWRRRRR!!! I bolted out of a sound sleep, the hair standing on the back of my neck. The cabin was pitch black. For a second I sat stark still, wondering if I had dreamt the sound. The wind shrieked outside and the window panes rattled. Then it came again, a deep blood-curdling growl, seeming to be right beneath me where moments ago I had so peacefully slept, wrapped in my sleeping bag on the cabin floor. What the hell was that?! I felt around the floor for my flashlight. The cabin shook and the floorboards under me heaved. Freckles screamed. I was wide awake now. The two dogs usually slept under the cabin. Something was under the house, something big! It had already killed my dogs! My hand brushed against the flashlight and I snatched it up and turned it on. It flickered dimly and went out. I cursed under my breath. The spare batteries were across the room on the shelf I had built a week ago. And, in the next room, hanging from the wall near the door, was the battered old 30-06 rifle. It might as well have been on another continent, it seemed so far away. I sat still, afraid to breathe, terrified that the monster would tear through the floor boards and dismember me next.

I was completely alone in the middle of the Alaskan wilderness. I shivered, but not from the cold. The monster snuffled, then I heard the gristly crunch of bones snapping as it devoured its prey. The dogs! Suddenly I was angry with the creature. I leaped to my feet yelling and cursing loudly as I threw everything I could get my hands on at the floor. I bumped around in the dark shouting and throwing things until I reached the gun at the door.

"Come and get this, you evil beast!" I snarled, no doubt sounding like an evil beast myself. I threw open the window and fired off a shot. The gun recoiled solidly against my shoulder, and suddenly I did not feel helpless. I lit the kerosene hurricane lantern and continued to shout and bang the broom against the floor until the handle broke.

Gasping for air, I paused to listen. I was ready for anything. The large windows had thin glass and the thing could smash through them easily. The kerosene lantern threw distorted shadows. Everything looked like a monster. Outside, the trees creaked and groaned and the windows shuddered. Just the wind, I thought. I started the fire in the barrel stove and got dressed. I found my watch amongst the debris on the floor. It was two in the morning. Harry would call on the radio at seven. No one would be monitoring the radio at this hour of the night. It would be a waste of batteries to turn it on. I changed the batteries in the flashlight and made a mental note to bring twice as many batteries next time.

I huddled in the corner of the cabin next to the stove and listened to the sounds of the night. Sometime later, I must have dozed off. I awoke with a start. It was already daylight, and I had missed the seven a.m. call-in time! The next call-in would be at seven tonight. Harry would not be concerned. Sometimes the radio signals were weak and we could not hear each other. The events of the night seemed blurred. Was it real? Perhaps it was just the wind, or the dogs fighting over a rabbit. Or was it all a dream?

I had been home a little over two weeks. It had seemed to fly by. There had been so much to do. Wood to chop, the shelves to build, water to haul from the creek, rabbit snares to check, food to prepare, patching and mending mittens and snowshoes. It was real living, and at the end of the day, I felt like I had accomplished something. It was not like sitting in an office and drawing a paycheck. But Harry had worried that I might not be able to handle being completely alone.

"Some people can't hack it," he had explained. "It makes them go 'stir-crazy'. They see things and hear things that aren't there, just go bonkers. You read about it all the time in the papers."

I didn't think I was one of those people. I loved it here. This was my ideal dream. From the moment I had laid eyes on this beautiful valley, I had wanted to live here. It was Harry's dream, too. Building the place together had formed a deep bond between us.

Outside, the wind had subsided. I put on my parka, putting an extra box of ammunition in my pocket. Gripping the gun tight, I went outside. I had to find out if the monster was real. It would have left tracks. It could not be a bear. It was well into November, and Harry had assured me they were all hibernating. We had made several trips home since the plane wreck, and had not seen any fresh sign in the snow.

I thought back to a time I was in the office. The weather had been bad for a few days and flights were backed up. Our passengers were mostly Yup'ik Eskimos, traveling to and from their villages. Most of the time, they spoke amongst themselves in their own language, laughing and telling stories as they waited patiently. They were friendly and easy to accommodate, as they understood the weather and delays it caused better than the white people. They were telling a story and the younger people were listening raptly.

"What are they saying?" I had asked Elena. She and her husband travelled a lot with us and we became good friends.

"It's an old story about the Hairy Man." She said after listening a bit.

"The Hairy Man?"

"Yeah. The Hairy Man is really big, maybe ten, twelve feet tall, and hairy, and walks like a man."

"Oh!" I said. "Like Bigfoot?"

"Well, sort of, yes, but he is real. My uncle said he saw one once when he was lost in the fog. The elders say, if you see big footprints, never follow them because on the other end, it could be the Hairy Man." Elena explained.

"Why? Is he bad?" I asked.

"They say sometimes he eats people, but mostly he just eats dogs." Elena laughed then. "There's a lot of old stories and people who say they saw him, but you know, people did eat a lot of rotten food back then."

I shuddered, thinking of the unknown monster that had eaten my dogs. Maybe my mind was playing tricks on me, the same as the people before me who swore they saw the Hairy Man. For an instant, I almost hoped the monster was real, so I could assure myself I was not going crazy. I called loudly out to the dogs, hoping beyond hope that one had survived. I walked to the back of the cabin, where there was a piece of plywood missing in the skirting around the cabin. I had cut and dried armfuls of hay and put it under the house for the dogs. Their food dishes sat just inside the opening. It was a big cozy nest, and the two huskies loved it, far better than being chained in the yard in Bethel. I called loudly as I neared the opening. There were no tracks in the snow. I almost wept with relief and confusion. It wasn't real. Unless the creature was still under the house, lurking in the dark shadows! Stop it, Dolly! It's not real, I told myself firmly.

Where were the dogs? Probably off chasing rabbits. Hopefully they would not get to my snares before I did and eat anything I caught. Everything was confusing to me now. Maybe the growling and thrashing I had heard last night was the dogs fighting. Maybe I was going nuts. I didn't feel nuts. I put on my snowshoes and checked the snares. I was still on edge and jumped when I saw a shadow move in the bushes. It was Tengupak! I cried out with joy. He came to me and I hugged him close, surprised once again how thin he was. Dan and Buzzy had gone through two bags of dog food in a week.

"Those dogs eat a lot!" Buzzy had complained. "They must have worms."

And I had gone through nearly as much myself, practically shoveling food into their bowls under the house.

"Where's Freckles? Did you guys have a fight?" It was odd. They had always gotten along so well. She was an old dog when she first showed up, and Tengupak was a pup. They were inseparable. Just then, another shadow crept out of the bushes. Freckles!!! I whooped and rushed to her. She was limping and trembling but licked my face while I gently felt her leg. Nothing seemed broken.

"You be nice to this old lady!" I sternly admonished Tengupak. He squirmed and licked her face. Whatever argument they had had was over, and they seemed to be best friends again.

As I snowshoed back, I thought back to the first time I had laid eyes on the valley. I had just started working for Harry in the office. He walked in one day, and I overheard him telling Larry to finish his shift for him, he was taking the rest of the day off. And then he turned to me and told me, "Come on, I'm taking you someplace very special."

Having no idea where we were going, I ran upstairs and changed into the new short dress I had just sewed, pulled on a pair of very stylish, tight, high-heeled leather boots, quickly fixed my hair, and grabbed my purse. Harry was waiting impatiently at the plane. He laughed when he saw me.

"Are you sure you can walk in those?"

"Of course!" I said confidently.

We took off in the small two-seater plane and flew across the vast expanse of the tundra delta. After about an hour, the terrain began to rise sharply and the rivers diminished into small creeks trickling down from the mountains. We had not seen any sign of humans since we had left the river after Bethel. It was early summer and the higher peaks still had snow. Harry banked the plane steeply and flew up a narrow valley. It was breathtakingly beautiful, steep mountains rising out and seeming to enfold us. Harry yelled, "There she is!" and banked again, even steeper. I looked out the window as my stomach churned. A white bear looked up at us and ambled into the bushes. It was like an omen.

"A polar bear? This far from the coast?!"

"No," Harry shouted over the engine, "it's a white grizzly. I'll tell you about it after we land."

"Land?" I didn't see where. There was a small gap in the trees with a beaver dam on the other end. I clung to the door post in horror as Harry lined up for it and throttled back. Then, we were bumping along the ground, and stopped just short of the dam.

"It's a little short," Harry stated." Miners cleared this out back in the early 1900's and nobody has used it for a long, long time. It's going to be a long walk to where we are going. Are you sure those boots are ok?"

"Yes." I said excitedly. "Tell me about the bear!"

"I saw her around here a few years ago. I thought polar bear, too, but it looked wrong. I brought my biologist friend Ray Baxter up here and we saw her again. He said it is a very, very rare mutant gene of the grizzly, not an albino, but a true white grizzly."

"Oh! I hope nobody shoots her!"

"We didn't let too many people know. Ray wants to make this valley part of the Wildlife Refuge, or maybe a National Park."

It's lovely, I thought to myself as I followed Harry through the brush, across the creeks and over the tundra. My boots were soaked and chafing. Walking on the tundra was like walking on a sopping wet mattress covered in loose cabbages. Add tight high-heeled boots and a short dress that kept riding up, and it was downright uncomfortable. But I had my pride, and I wasn't about to let Harry think he was right about the boots. I strode ahead purposefully, and then looked back. Harry was no doubt enjoying the view. He laughed.

"Want some bug spray?" He asked.

I looked down and my bare legs were covered with mosquitoes. Then they were swarming everywhere, and it was hard to breathe without choking on them, so we trudged on in silence. I sprayed my arms and legs and it helped a bit. We broke out of the timber and started across a small creek.

"Wait," I said. "I'm thirsty."

We stopped there and drank deeply from the cold mountain spring. Since then, that creek has always been called "Dolly's Drinking Spring." We continued on, and several miles later, I began to smell a strong odor of rotten eggs.

*Dolly's drinking spring*

"Did you fart?" I asked Harry.

He laughed. "You'll see."

We climbed the gently rising terrain and fought through the thick brush. Suddenly we popped out, and at our feet was a tiny trickle of tepid water covered in thick green algae. It looked toxic.

"It's a hotsprings," Harry said, "It needs a lot of work, but I think we can get it running better. There's a few more scattered around this part of the country, but I like this place best. I built a little cabin right over here, but the wind gets really strong here and it looks like it blew away. Let's look around for it."

We beat through the brush again and Harry spotted the cabin, upside down, 100 yards from where he had built it. Uphill! The wind must be very, very strong here, I thought.

"How did you get this here?" I asked. It was in the middle of nowhere.

"See the top of that mountain over there? I landed there on skis and brought everything here a board at a time, and snowshoed it down here and built it."

"I want to live here." I said longingly.

Harry grinned. "Well, you're in luck. This area was open for homesteading, and I filed for it. We will fix the hotsprings up and use it to heat the house. And, there's another adjoining parcel I filed for as a Trade and Manufacturing site. I was thinking we could run a little lodge."

Ever since I was a little girl I had dreamed of living on a homestead in Alaska! My dreams were coming true, and the white grizzly was truly an omen. We trudged back to the plane, my mind full of possibilities and excitement. The miles seemed to fly and I hardly noticed the discomfort of my bad choice of clothing. By the time we got to the plane my legs were scratched and bleeding from the thick brush and my feet were blistered and sore, but my heart was light and happy.

Now here I was, in the place I had always wanted to live, and I was freaking out about Bigfoot! I laughed to myself as I went back to the cabin to start breakfast. Better feed the dogs first. I went inside and got the empty coffee can and filled it with dog food. As I walked around to the opening, I noticed the dogs had not followed me, but hung back in the trees. Probably hunting, I thought. I knelt down and filled their bowls. Suddenly, the skin on the back of my neck began to crawl and I got the odd sense something was watching me. I took a deep breath and stepped back carefully. I had left the gun inside. Stop being paranoid, Dolly, I told myself firmly. You're just tired. I snorted at my silliness and went back inside. I made a big pot of tea and a bowl of oatmeal. I can't say anything to Harry when he calls, I thought. He will think I'm going bonkers and come and get me. I want to stay here right forever.

Harry called that night and the radio signals were bad, so I couldn't have told him if I wanted to. I put food out for the dogs again, and turned in early. I fell asleep almost at once.

I awakened to a chill that filled the room. I had slept soundly well into the morning. The fire was out. Oh my god! The door was open! I was sure I had closed it as I always did. But then, it didn't always latch properly, since the building had shifted as the ground froze. It probably had just blown open at some point in the night. I tiptoed nervously toward the door. A little drift of snow had crossed the door sill. It must have been open all night! My heart stopped. In the center of the snow drift was a huge footprint. Oh! The monster had been in the house! I snatched up the gun and forced myself to go for a second look. The tracks came from under the house and onto the porch. Silly me! It was probably just my snowshoe tracks from when I had gone to feed the dogs. In the deep powder tracks didn't take a definite shape.

When Harry called that morning the radio signals were good and he asked for the weather. My heart sank. He was going to come to pick me up. He needed help at the office. Be ready by two, he said. I tidied up and wondered when I could come home again. Better leave lots of food for the dogs. Harry had brought a few extra sacks last time he came. I carried two bags of dog food out to their nest, ripped the tops off and placed them under the siding, crawling partway inside to find a flat spot to set them down. I caught a sharp whiff of a pungent odor and my skin started to prickle again. Come on, Dolly, I chided myself, it's probably just the latrine, or as we call it here, the "honey-bucket". Better bring more Pine Sol next time.

Harry landed and picked me up an hour late. He was having a rough day. Planes were needing repair, flights were backed up, and the kids were acting up. It wasn't until the next day that I told him about the monster. He howled with laughter.

"A little case of the cabin fever, huh?" He went downstairs and told all the guys. Soon everybody was laughing at me. I was mortified! I shouldn't have said anything! Now everybody was laughing and making jokes about "Dolly's monster".

Elena looked up from her knitting, eyes wide. "I told you the Hairy Man was real! There's 'little people', too! The elders say the 'little people' live in holes in the ground and they steal children, or travelers who are lost. They live in the mountains. That's why our people don't go to the mountains often. Dolly, you shouldn't stay there alone! It's too dangerous."

The next few weeks were a blur. Everyone was travelling back home for Thanksgiving. Our planes seemed to be flying non-stop. Harry and I made a few quick day trips home to put more food out for the dogs and shovel snow from the flat roof of the house.

The first part of December, Harry and Alexie went up to White Bear to spend a few days working on the wrecked plane. Most people called Alexie "Dummy" because he was deaf and mute, but he certainly was no dummy. He could change an airplane engine with just a few tools in a matter of hours. He was smart and extremely strong. I had seen him lift full drums of stove oil. He was one of Harry's right-hand men. Harry treated him with respect. They communicated well with each other, although I don't think either of them knew official sign language.

The day after they left for the homestead, Harry called me on the radio with some news. "Dolly, I shot your monster! Call Ray Baxter and see if he is busy! Send him up with Joe if he isn't busy!"

Through the crackling radio and Harry's excitement, I pieced together the story. They had heard the monster under the house that night. Alexie held the flashlight and Harry held the gun. It had come out from under the cabin toward them and Harry had shot it. It was a very, very big old grizzly bear. Ray Baxter later recorded it as being a state record. It was so old and thin it was unable to build the fat reserves it needed to hibernate. Its teeth were worn down and its face was covered in porcupine quills. It had been living under the cabin, eating the dog food we had set out. Ray went on to say it was a good thing Harry had shot it, as it probably would have taken advantage of an easy meal, like for instance, a certain young lady who handed food to it under the house.

*Harry bagged Dolly's "monster".*

# Chapter Three

"Is anyone on the radio? I need some help!" It was Vern's voice, laced with urgency. Oh no! What could be wrong? Vern had just flown a load of passengers to Nunapitchak and was returning to Bethel. The village had no airstrip back then, so he was operating the plane on skis, landing on the frozen lake near the village. I was in the office, listening for the radio and the phone. I jumped up to answer.

"This is KYH6, go ahead." I hoped it was nothing serious.

"Dolly, is Harry there? I broke a ski cable on takeoff." Vern sounded anxious.

Oh shit! What should I say? Harry was gone flying himself. I knew the broken rigging could seriously affect the flight of the aircraft, and make it nearly impossible to land safely. I didn't know what to tell him or where to get help for him. The office was empty.

Just then Harry's voice crackled over the radio. "Hear you got some problems, Vern. Want to tell me what's going on?"

I was enormously relieved. Most of our fleet was equipped with radios, and Harry had overheard.

"The cable snapped on the left ski." Vern also sounded relieved to hear Harry's voice. "The ski is hitting the side of the fuselage."

"How is it flying right now? Can you control it?"

"Yeah, it's pulling hard to the left, but I can keep it flying."

"Good." Harry said calmly. "Do you have passengers?"

"One."

"OK. Tell him to throw everything else out of the plane. You need to get it really light for the landing."

"The ski is hanging down. It's going to flip over when I touch down!" Vern sounded pretty nervous again.

"Just do what I tell you. It won't flip," Harry said soothingly. He proceeded to explain to Vern how he was to land on the river in front of Bethel just like he always did, except all on one ski, the good ski. "Just like you are doing a really strong crosswind landing."

I paced the office. I didn't want to interrupt the critical conversation. Nunapitchak was close, and Vern would be attempting to land soon. Should I do something to prepare for the landing, or call someone? There wasn't time. Vern was making his final approach now, and looking up, I could see Harry's plane circling overhead as he patiently instructed Vern. I realized then, looking out the window at the river, a small crowd had assembled. Many households had citizen's band radios to communicate and to listen to the local gossip. I sure hoped everyone would stay out of the way! I snatched up the first aid kit and the fire extinguisher and ran out the door.

Vern's plane banked sharply, wingtip nearly touching the ground as he carefully eased the plane down, settling all the weight on the good ski. Everyone held their breath as it slid along crisply over the hard river ice. As the plane lost momentum, it started to wobble, and then slowly sank onto the dangling ski. The tip caught the ice, and the tail lifted sharply off the ground. For a second, I thought it was going to flip over. Vern added a quick burst of power, and the tail came back down, but the plane swerved sharply, right toward the crowd! Everyone scattered. Vern somehow managed to herd the runaway plane into a tight circle and pull to a grinding halt. The crowd converged on the plane, myself still clutching the rescue gear, as Vern and his passenger climbed out of the plane, unscathed. Harry landed soon afterwards. He walked over.

"Good job, Vern." Harry said, shaking Vern's hand. "You're a hell of a pilot!"

Vern glowed from the compliment. Praise from Harry not common. "Couldn't have done it without you!" He smiled back.

The passenger was unruffled. If anything, he seemed to be pleased to be part of all the excitement and to have such a great story to tell. The plane was undamaged. After Alexie replaced the ski, Vern was back to flying it again the next day. It was just a typical day in the charter business. Long hours of monotonous labor punctuated by moments of heart-stopping fear.

Preparing the fleet for the day's flying was sometimes a lengthy task. The engines needed to be preheated for at least one hour, and ice had to be scraped from the wings. We used a small generator and a big Herman-Nelson space heater with a section of stovepipe transferring the heat to the cowling of the plane. Sometimes we used the smaller Coleman firepots. The plane could never be left unattended while it was preheating. Any spark from the heater could ignite a fire and destroy the plane. In addition to my tasks of preparing the planes for the morning, I also refueled, sometimes hoisting full jerry cans onto the wing, and then climbing the ladder to pour it into the wing tanks. I loaded cargo and passengers, balanced the accounts, did the scheduling, paid the bills, answered the phone and the radio. It was a full day's work, but I had grown up on a farm and was accustomed to physical labor. Harry had only given me one paycheck at the beginning, but I didn't mind. The money that slowly trickled in from the business went to building our homestead.

It was expensive just to get to White Bear. The only way to get there was by airplane and fuel was costly. Everything we needed to build our home had to be flown in. The hotsprings was several miles beyond the treeline and where the trees did grow, they were small and stunted from the extreme climate of the rugged valley. We bought all the lumber we needed from Swanson's and Guinn's stores in Bethel, and then cut it into sizes that would fit in a small Cessna to take it to the homestead. It was very costly.

Harry had built the first cabin next to the hotsprings in the mid 1960s, landing his ski plane on the top of a mountain, and snowshoeing the lumber down, a board at a time. The cabin was small, about 16x18. There were no trails or any sign of humans anywhere near the hotsprings, and he had beat through thick alder brush and rough tundra to get to the springs. It was an incredible amount of physical effort, and Harry loved his little cabin in the mountains. He spent as much time as he could there, whenever he could get away from work. He wanted to make an airstrip, closer than the old overgrown clearing we had landed in when he had first brought me to White Bear. That was nearly seven miles away and rapidly becoming unusable due to the brush and beaver dams. He needed somewhere closer he could land any time of the year. The best option was nearly two miles away, at the edge of the treeline, where the valley widened slightly. In the late 1960s, he bought a small dozer from some miners for an exorbitant amount of money, and after the ground had frozen enough, he had driven it nearly 30 miles across a mountain range to the homestead. Once he got there, he started clearing a flat area on the tundra for the airstrip. Partway through the process, the cantankerous old dozer had quit, right in the middle of the clearing. Joe, who had flown over to check on Harry, had landed on the top of the mountain with the ski plane. Harry hiked up to meet him and they flew back to Bethel. Harry was discouraged but not defeated.

Harry worked long days, saving up money. He had ordered parts for the dozer, but they wouldn't be here until summer. He needed to do the plowing in the winter while the ground was still frozen or the dozer would sink into the spongy tundra and get stuck. He bought a small backhoe with a blade and, with Alexie's help, disassembled the entire thing. Then he put it inside the ski plane, and flew it to the top of the mountain in many trips. He also flew in a small snowmachine, a plow, and lumber which he used to build another small cabin at the proposed airstrip site. He covered everything with tarps. Spring was coming and he was running out of time, fast.

Last year in late April Harry had been on the phone a lot that day, and I could tell he was hatching up a plan. The snow had mostly melted in Bethel, and he hadn't been to White Bear in a few weeks, since dropping off the last load of dozer parts. He walked into the office.

"Can you arrange things so we can leave for a few days? The Burgess workers have Sunday off. They are really good heavy equipment mechanics. I'm going to take them up to help me put the Case backhoe together. They have to be back to work Monday morning." Harry sounded excited. His plan might just come together after all!

"Sure," I said. I called the pilots in to divide up the charters between them.

I threw on my parka and headed out the door to help Harry put a few more seats in the plane. He drove off to pick up the mechanics and was back by the time I had the seats carried down to the plane.

"I hope this cool weather stays a few more days," Harry said as he installed the seats. "The ice is really melting fast."

I felt a chill of fear, envisioning the deep swirling water just beneath the ice upon which we were standing. We all loaded up into the plane and flew toward White Bear. The wind-swept tundra was already showing brown patches. Harry set the plane down on the mountaintop and we stepped out. It was an instant scurry of activity as they began to assemble the parts.

I took the little MotoSki snowmachine down to the cabin to prepare lunch. On the way down, I became disoriented after breaking out of a thicket of brush. Which way to go?! I followed the edge of the clearing, and then thankfully ran into tracks from our last trip. Things looked different now that the deep snow was melting. I started the fire in the barrel stove and fried up some Spam sandwiches and made coffee.

By the time I got back to the mountaintop, carefully following my tracks this time, the men had nearly finished the assembly. The little Case backhoe had transformed from a scattered pile of parts into a nearly completed piece of equipment. They ate and went right back to work. Meanwhile, I walked along the area where we had landed and threw the stones that were just starting to emerge from the snow off to the side. Catching a stone with the ski could cause the plane to swerve uncontrollably.

Right before dark, they were done. Harry took off with the men, the plane roaring across the patch of snow and then disappearing out of sight on the far edge of the ridge. It rose up again in the distance, tipped its wings, and vanished into the dimming light. I took the snowmachine back to the cabin and waited for Harry to call on the radio to let me know he had landed safely.

Over the next several days, Harry made several trips, flying in supplies and food, and a total of seven men. I was terribly disappointed when, on the last trip, he told me to get into the plane.

"I need you in Bethel, to run the office while I'm gone. I'm coming back out here to finish the airstrip." He said.

I got in, crestfallen. The plane gathered momentum and surged across the improvised short mountaintop airstrip. Suddenly the terrain fell sharply away, and I gasped as I clutched the door post. Then I realized we were flying already, and soon we climbed, tall mountains rising up on each side of the wings. Harry dropped me off on

*Harry and mechanics reassembling Case backhoe on mountaintop*

the ice in Bethel, threw in a few jerry cans of diesel and more lumber, and turned to me.

"One of the guys has to be back by Monday to make their flight to Anchorage on Wien," Harry explained. "So, we will have to hustle, as the snow is melting fast. I think we have all the tools we need. We should be back Sunday."

"OK," I said, giving him a quick hug goodbye.

"If we aren't back by noon on Sunday, send someone up to check on us." There was a radio at the cabin, but sometimes the reception was bad in the mountains. Harry got into the plane and flew off toward White Bear.

The next day it rained hard. The Kuskokwim river ice was breaking up and the resulting ice jams created dangerous floods in the upriver villages. Tuning in to the public radio station, I heard that the National Guard was helping to evacuate the residents of several villages, using a huge Sikorsky helicopter.

I remembered the first time I had seen the river ice break up. I had been sound asleep in the room Harry and I shared, when I had been awakened by an unusually loud noise. I sat bolt upright.

"What was that?!"

"Shhhhh. It's just the ice. Go back to sleep." Harry rolled over and immediately went back to sleep. It was nearly five in the morning, but despite the early hour, daylight filtered in the window. The strange creaking groan continued. There was no way I could go back to sleep! I had to see this for myself. I put on my clothes quickly and went out to the river. For a second, I just stared, not recognizing what I saw. The smooth, well packed snow where we had parked the ski planes just a week before had shifted into unrecognizable jagged chunks. No wonder Harry had been in such a hurry last week to change all the planes to wheels and take them to the Bethel airport. As I watched, the entire surface of the river seemed to shift. The strange sounds were other-worldly. Loud pops, creaking groans, grinding, scraping, and deafening roars emitted from the ice floe. Suddenly an entire sheet of thick ice shot up right in front of me and crashed down with enough force to shake nearby houses. Instantly, the space it had left was filled with dark rushing water, and then the gap closed again as uncountable tons of water and ice from upriver were driven along.

A wooden skiff that had been trapped in the winter's ice pack was snapped into splinters like a child's toy. I stood there a long time that morning watching the tremendous forces of Mother Nature at work. It was both magnificent and destructible and almost indescribable. By the next day, most of the ice had gone. Occasional large chunks of ice, along with whole trees, ripped out of the river bank by the strong current, bobbed along in the deep, silty water. The water had risen alarmingly, and I had to wade across knee-deep water to get to Swanson's store across the street.

"Nothing to worry about," Harry had said. "It will go down again as soon as the ice jam breaks downriver." And it did, leaving behind huge puddles that slowly drained, and a various array of garbage from other peoples' yards.

It rained again the following day. I waited until noon, pacing nervously. No word yet from Harry. What could have happened? I knew White Bear was too high in the mountains and too far from the river to be affected by the flooding. Harry could have crashed somewhere along the way back, or maybe he had never even gotten there. Or he could have gotten hurt building the strip, or even moving the equipment. Maybe they had problems with the plane. At 12:30, I sent Larry to check on them. Then I waited nervously almost two hours, for him to return.

"Good news and bad news," Larry said when he returned. "The good news is, they are all ok, got the backhoe down to the cabin, and the strip is done. The radio signals were bad, that's why you didn't hear them check in."

"What's the bad news?" I asked cautiously.

"Well," Larry said. "They are stuck there for at least a month and those boys are going to miss their Wien flight."

"You're kidding!"

"No, I'm not. After they got the backhoe off the mountain and finished the strip, Harry flew the plane down off the mountain last night onto a patch of snow on the tundra and changed to wheels. The snow up there was almost all melted and he couldn't wait a moment longer. He was planning to leave early this morning and bring those guys back here to Bethel, but it had rained hard last night."

"So?" I said. "The weather is fine. You made it there and back with no problems. Is the plane OK?"

"Yeah, the plane is fine, the mud is just too deep to take off."

"What do you mean? I thought they plowed it." I was confused.

Larry went on to explain that the ground had still been frozen beneath the tundra when they had made the strip. It was froze hard when Harry took off from the last lingering snow patch. It had been getting dark and the men had all been tired, so they decided to wait until the morning to depart for Bethel. But it had rained all night, and the next morning the new airstrip was a muddy mess. The deep mud caused impossible flying conditions. They were literally stuck.

"How long do you think it will be until the ground dries out enough for them to take off?" I asked.

Larry sighed. "Shit, I don't know. A month, at least. When you plow up tundra, all that permafrost underneath has to melt. And the way it has been raining lately, it might be longer."

I gasped. I could just imagine Harry cursing his luck. "What did Harry say to do next?"

"He didn't really say. He was going to wait a few days and hope it would freeze again, but I don't think it's going to. He said come back and check on him in a few days and air-drop some food."

I went back to work, refueling Larry's plane as he looked over the manifest for the next load of passengers he was taking to Kasigluk. This was the last flight he would be able to make to Kasigluk before the lake ice became too thin to land on safely. Soon we would transition the planes to floats after breakup and land on the rivers near the villages. There were few villages in those days that had airstrips, and they usually got pretty muddy in the spring. On the bright side of things, Harry wouldn't be missing out on too much flying in the next week or so, I thought, as I helped Larry load the cargo and passengers into the plane. I went back to the office to write down Larry's departure time and call the village of Kasigluk on the radio, so they would know when to meet the plane. There were two passengers returning. The public radio announcer chattered about the flood upriver, and gave the advisory for all residents to evacuate for higher ground. The National Guard was sending a helicopter to Red Devil to shuttle the residents of that village across the river to higher ground. And then it hit me! It was out of the way, but perhaps the helicopter could swing over and pick the guys up at White Bear on its way back to Bethel? Harry could go back later in the summer and pick up the plane. Harry had some friends in the Guard. I tried to remember their names. I was excited now. I picked up the phone and dialed the National Guard.

"Hello," I said tentatively, "this is Dolly down at West Air. We have eight guys stranded in the mountains, and I was wondering if you could pick them up?"

The lady that answered the phone was less than sympathetic. "We don't pick people up unless it is an emergency." She hung up.

I sat there a second, listening to the dial tone, and then suddenly I remembered the name of Harry's friend. I called back. "Can I speak to Don Shantz?"

There was a long pause, and then a man's voice answered. "Can I help you?"

"Yes," I said. "It's Dolly. Harry and seven guys are stranded in the mountains, and they are out of food. Do you think you could pick them up on the way back to Bethel? I know it's a bit out of the way but...."

"Dolly, this line has a bad connection. I think I heard you say there are eight men stranded in the mountains, and maybe Harry had a broken leg or something. Sounds like we can help. Yes, we can divert the chopper on the way down, it will be empty anyway." Don was a shrewd man, and he knew how to manipulate the rules. Besides, he owed Harry a favor.

"Thank you," I whispered into the phone, relieved.

"Sure thing, Dolly. We will have them out of there in no time. The helicopter should be back in Bethel around seven tonight. I will call the pilots up and let them know right now. Can you tell me how to find them?'

I hesitated. I couldn't exactly describe how to get there. I wasn't good with directions. I thought fast. "Um, when Larry gets back, he will call you and tell you, in pilot talk, how to get there."

"Sounds good. No problem. And when Harry gets back, tell him we were grateful for the rescue he did for our lieutenant last year."

That was how things worked in those days. People were more apt to help each other out, and they loved to barter and trade favors.

Larry landed about fifteen minutes later, and I had him call Don back to relay the directions how to get to White Bear. Don then transferred those directions to the helicopter pilots who realized it was basically on their way to Bethel. I felt a bit inefficient that I couldn't tell them the directions myself, but oh well, it had gotten done anyway, in a roundabout sort of way.

I waited with bated breath that evening for the helicopter to show up. It just seemed the plan was too good to be true. At 7:15, the phone rang. It was Harry.

"Hey, come pick us up at the airport!" He sounded excited.

When I got there he couldn't wait to tell me his story. "You'll never guess what happened! A helicopter came to pick us up! I knew the one pilot, but the other guy was a little kooky! He kept asking which one of us had the broken leg! I don't know what that was all about. He could see we were all walking around fine. I think they were actually supposed to pick up someone else, but we weren't about to turn down the ride. Man, what great luck! Just this morning I thought we would be stuck there for a long time and these guys would miss their flight tomorrow." Then he noticed I was smiling. "You knew about this, didn't you?"

## Chapter Four

"NOOOOO!" I screamed at Harry. "He is just a child! He will drown! Let him go!" I frantically tugged at the terrified little boy that Harry held with an iron grip as he strode toward the cold, swift Kuskokwim river.

"Get back, Dolly!" Harry snarled. "He's MY son, and I know what I'm doing! I'm going to teach this little brat never to wet his bed again!"

"He's only eight years old! He didn't do it on purpose!" I pleaded. I had never seen this side of Harry and it frightened me. I blocked his path to the float plane dock. He threw me aside with such force the wind was knocked out of me. Then he dropped little Henry into the icy waters, turned on his heel and stomped off back toward the house. As he passed me where I sat, shocked from the unexpected violence, he said coldly, "You're next if you don't stop coddling him!"

I leaped to my feet, stumbling over myself in the rush to reach Henry. He was clinging to the dock, still partly submerged, sobbing his little heart out. I reached down and pulled the sodden little boy into my arms. He held onto me tightly, shivering and sobbing. I rushed up the steep river bank to the room above the office, dried him off and started a pot of hot chocolate.

Henry stopped crying and had the hiccups. "I'm sorry, Mama. I, I didn't mean to…"

My heart melted. He had just called me Mama! "I know, honey." I said soothingly. "I'll tell you a little secret. I wet the bed once too. I was nine years old, way older than you!"

"Did your daddy throw you in the river?" He asked.

"No, he didn't. What your daddy did was very mean. Here, drink this cocoa, it will warm you up."

"Why does Daddy hate me?" Henry asked mournfully.

"Oh sweetie," I said, kneeling down and putting my arms around the sad child, "he doesn't hate you. He just doesn't know how to treat a child. His father probably did the same thing to him. Let's just not tell him when you have a little accident, OK? You can come and tell me instead."

"I didn't tell him! Tara did!" Tara was the oldest, an angry child who would stop at nothing to make everyone as unhappy as she was.

"Oh. Don't tell Tara either. It can be our secret. Here, let me show you where I put the clean sheets. When you have an accident, you can change them yourself, put them in the laundry, and no one will know but you, OK?"

Henry looked up at me. "Is that why my mommy left me? Because I was bad?"

"No, no, honey! She loves you very, very much! And you aren't bad at all. I love you very much, too, and so does your daddy even if he doesn't always show it." Henry's mother, Evalyn, had divorced Harry when Henry was just a baby. I didn't know much about the circumstances, but Harry had gotten custody, and she hadn't seen her kids since the divorce. I had spoken to her once on the phone. She had called me as soon as she heard the kids were coming to live with us.

"Please take care of my babies," she had whispered into the phone. She sounded as if she had been crying.

"I will," I promised. I didn't know what I was in for.

It was the summer of 1970 when Harry had sent for the kids. They had been bouncing around between friends, relatives, and foster homes. Harry had three children with Evalyn. He had married again, had another child, but at the end of that marriage, the mother got custody.

Harry had left me to answer the phones when he went to the airport to pick up the kids. I tidied nervously. I was excited and anxious. I would have a little family of my own while Harry was away on his many business trips. Harry had been travelling a lot lately, purchasing new airplanes and getting his Airline Transport Pilot's training. I hoped the kids liked me! We could have lots of fun together. I envisioned games and movies and a house full of giggling children.

When I met them, I loved little Henry at first sight. He was a thin, quiet boy with big blue eyes and a sweet innocence about him. He was the youngest of the children. Lisa was the middle child, a gentle, plain little girl with droopy eyes and light brown hair. Tara was the oldest, a stunningly beautiful young lady with dark hair and blue eyes, but her beauty belied her angry soul. She had decided she hated me before she had ever met me, and there was no changing her mind. I don't think it was especially me that she hated, it was the idea of me, another woman, replacing her desire or plans to get her mother and father back together. She was determined to make me leave. Tara was bold and bossy and overshadowed the other children, and it soon became obvious that they were used to her manipulating them. Lisa followed on her every footstep. Henry clung close to me and avoided the girls when he could. I think that only made them more jealous.

I tried hard to win over the hearts of my new family. I bought them ice cream, took them to movies at the new Swanson's theater, sewed the girls new dresses and braided Lisa's hair. I told them stories and read them books and played games. I cooked for them, cleaned, did the laundry, and hoped they would decide to like me. I did all of this in addition to my work with the air charter business. I tried to give them each a household chore, because I believed a child should have some chores. Henry was to bring meat in from the freezer for dinner, Lisa to help with the dishes, Tara was supposed to sweep the floor. Of course, she rebelled.

"You're not my mother! You can't make me do your work like a slave!" she shrieked, throwing the broom at me and stomping out to tell her dad how mean I was.

Harry sided with Tara. HIS children did not need to have chores. And I did not have the right to give them chores or discipline or love. In a way, I think it was partly because he felt so guilty about abandoning them for so long. So the kids were allowed to do whatever they pleased, and I tried not to impose my rules, just to keep the peace. Little Henry would sometimes sit in the kitchen with me while I cooked dinner, to get away from the tormenting of the girls. I would sneak him an extra cookie or piece of pie. The girls resented it, but they rejected any affection I tried to give them. Harry resented it even more. I just hoped things would get better before winter. We were building the homestead and planned to spend a lot of time there that winter. Maybe the following winter we could live there permanently, and I could home-school the kids.

There was much work to do in the first years of building. The first cabin at the hotsprings had blown over in the wind. After the new airstrip that Harry had built dried out enough, we flew in supplies to add on to our small cabin at the airport. Sometimes, in the endless days of the summer, Harry would fly three or four trips to the homestead, shuttling in the needed materials. He would do this in addition to his daily work at the charter business. I would come along often to help unload the plane, and help with the construction of our home. Sometimes it would get dark, or the weather would close in on us and we would have to spend the night. These were much needed breaks for all of us, as tensions between the girls had us all on edge. While we were gone, our neighbor Linda would watch them.

Harry had grand plans for the lodge. He would try to obtain a liquor license and a guiding license. He wanted to make a bathhouse and a swimming pool, and heat the house with the hotsprings water. Then we could live there permanently, and it would pay for itself. We would have a greenhouse and a hydroelectric generator. The kids could run and play outside, and I could sew and read, and Harry could tinker with his latest projects. It sounded like a marvelous goal.

The hotsprings was nearly grown over with brush, and the thick algae choked the tiny trickle. It was a very old springs, sunk deep into the ground. It had a very strong odor. Harry and I spent days removing the algae, and using picks and shovels to unearth large rocks and sod that had collapsed over the source of the spring. After much muddy, grueling labor in the smelly water, we managed to increase the flow minutely.

"Not enough to run the hydroelectric generator," Harry had said, disappointed. He had already flown it in. The cold water creeks were too small and shallow, also they would freeze up the generator in the winter. But the hotsprings would still work for the heating. We built a small wooden dam, about a foot wide and three feet long, and got the water to rise about six inches inside the dam. Then he funneled the water into fire hose, connecting hundreds of rolls together to form a line to our cabin at the airstrip, nearly two miles away. The system was wrought with problems. The distance was too great and the water was cold by the time it got to the end of the line. We patched endless leaks, before realizing they were caused by a bear chewing the hose. Once again, Harry was disappointed. He had erected a full sized swimming pool at the airport, a huge metal frame lined with a thick, tough plastic liner. He had even constructed a building to cover the pool.

"Well, that's not going to work," Harry sighed. Next he built a small bathhouse right at the hotsprings. He put in a deep tub and piped hot water in one side, and cold water in the other side. We would sit in the bathhouse soaking after a long days labor, talking about hopes and dreams and plans for the future. Often, during the course of building, Harry would hire men to help. He usually hired Natives and paid them well. We would invite them to use the bathhouse, but none of them cared to.

"That's white man's steam," laughed Johnny. "Us Natives do it differently." He proceeded to tell us how the traditional way to steam was to build a hot fire over some rocks and then throw cold water on the rocks.

"There's another hotsprings over by Tuluksak," Johnny continued, "and another one by Bogus Creek. Long ago people used to bathe in it, but it closed up and only the really old people know where it was. People just didn't care anymore, I guess."

I knew all too much how easily these fragile old relic hotsprings could close up forever. This was later confirmed by the many geologists who visited the White Bear hotsprings, and had praised us for keeping it flowing.

The bathhouse was short-lived. The Bureau of Land Management caught wind of it and ordered us to remove it. They also claimed, citing the Geothermal Act of 1970, that we could not build anything, or own land within a quarter mile of the hotsprings. The upside down first cabin had to be removed. Harry used the little dozer and a heavy iron sled to pull it the distance he paced off to be exactly one quarter mile away. The BLM also demanded we apply for water permits, and

*First homestead cabin blew over and uphill in 100-knot winds*

a Right of Way permit for transferring the hotsprings water to the edge of the homestead, a quarter mile away.

Rather than giving up, Harry took on the challenge. He filed for the necessary paperwork, the Right of Way, and a lease on the hotsprings itself. People thought he was nuts for dumping all his time and money into the place, but Harry was no quitter. Even when the lab samples came back that the hotsprings water was "unsuitable for human bathing" and we knew we wouldn't be able to pass health codes to run a lodge, Harry did not give up.

"We can still live here, just looks like the lodge might not be the best idea." He said.

I was fine with that. Secretly I hadn't been that thrilled about sharing my home with a bunch of drunken strangers. I wanted to raise the kids in a safe environment. Besides, we were beginning to see that transportation might be an issue. Although we had built a short airstrip, it was so muddy it was unusable in the spring. In the winter, the snow could be three feet deep on the strip, and blow bare the next day. The weather was extreme, with winds frequently reaching over one hundred knots. Fog hung in the mountains, sometimes for weeks, and the temperatures plummeted dangerously low in the winter. There were no navigable rivers for forty miles in any direction.

It was the summer of 1971. School was out and Harry had dropped myself and the kids off at White Bear. We had been home a few weeks, and things were finally beginning to smooth out with the kids. Harry called us on the radio twice a day. Then Harry had an odd request.

"Hey Dolly," he crackled over the radio. "'I want you to walk to the biggest lake out on the edge of the tundra, and I will meet you with the float plane."

"Why?" I asked. We didn't need anything from town, and the nearest lake would be at nearly 20 miles away, across mountains, over the tundra, and through thick brush. Besides, I didn't want to leave the kids alone. Tara, the oldest, was nearly 15, but she could be quite the troublemaker.

"Just do it." Harry made it sound urgent. "I only have planes on floats right now, and want to see if you can do it, and how long it will take. The kids will be fine for the day. I want to know if this will be a good option for coming in springtime."

"I might take a whole day, or even two," I said hesitantly, "I don't think it's a good idea to leave the kids alone."

"Dammit, they aren't babies anymore! They will be fine. If they need anything they can call on the radio twice a day, and there should be plenty of food. Just try it, OK?"

"OK. I will get started tomorrow morning. It will be late when I get there."

"Good. Now let me talk to Tara."

I called Tara. The kids were playing in the other room. She threw down what she was doing with a slam and stomped in.

"What do you want!? I'm busy! Whatever it is, do it yourself!" she snarled.

"Your Dad wants to talk to you." I held out the microphone. "Do you want me to tell him what you just said?" Tara was daddy's girl, and he doted on her.

"No!" she quickly rushed over and grabbed the mic from me. "Hi Daddy." She said sweetly.

Harry proceeded to tell her the plan, and that she was to be a good girl and keep the kids in the house until I got back. "I'm depending on you." He told her. She glowed with pride.

I spent the rest of the day preparing for the trip. I baked extra muffins and made a big pot of stew, made sure the latrine was empty and the water barrel was full, and there was extra firewood cut and stacked next to the stove. There shouldn't be anything else the kids needed. They had books and games and cards. And, as Harry had said, they weren't babies anymore!

"What if a bear breaks down the door?" Lisa asked.

"That's why Daddy wants you to stay in the house. Tengupak will stay with you, and he won't let anything happen to you." I assured her.

"But what if the bear eats Tengupak?" Lisa wailed.

"I will leave the pistol, and Tara will shoot it." Harry had taught the kids to shoot already, but they were still so young, and he had only let Tara shoot the big .44 magnum.

Tara, overhearing, glowed with pride. She was in charge! I put the loaded pistol and a box of shells on the shelf and told her where it was.

"You are the only one who knows where this is. Don't touch it unless you are getting eaten by a bear." I instructed her as I pulled on my boots.

"Yeah, yeah. Just hurry up and leave already."

I picked up the old 30-06 rifle, the map, and a small sack with some cookies. Slipping out the door quickly with Freckles, I set out on my new adventure. It was about five in the morning, a crisp new day, sun already rising and birds were telling the world about it. Freckles danced ahead, and behind me, I could hear poor Tengupak crying out his indignation at being left behind with the kids. The miles seemed to fall behind rapidly. Although the terrain was rough and there were many creeks to cross and thick brush to beat through, I was in good physical strength from the rigorous toils of building and maintaining the homestead. I was ever watchful for bears, but trusted Freckles to give me a warning if she encountered one.

I passed the small clearing where Harry and I had first landed, remembering how Harry had sent me up to White Bear that first year with Sam Gant in a chartered Wien Sky Van. Although I had only been there a few times and was poor with directions, Harry had asked me to go along to show Sam where to land in the small clearing. On the way up, I had gotten lost, and had directed Sam up the wrong canyon! We had managed to find the clearing eventually, after circling and exploring another valley. Our cargo had been some lumber, and an old Dodge Power Wagon. Harry had later assembled it and mounted huge DC-3 aircraft tires on it. Although he also put chains around the tires, and the beast was equipped with a sturdy winch, it had been an exhausting ordeal transporting it to where our current airstrip was located. We had gotten stuck so many times we could not even count them. Each time, Harry and I would shovel and pick and clear brush and saw logs to throw under the wheels as we looked around for something to winch the beast out of the soggy tundra. I had worked hard right alongside Harry, although I had thought the whole ordeal had been a bit silly. Men! They always had to have some tool or vehicle although it was twice as much work as just doing things without it. It was so much easier to just carry things in backpacks or pull toboggans. But Harry had bigger plans, and if he wanted his toys, he usually got them.

Thinking back on that incident, I felt a pang of fear. What if I got lost? It was a long way. No one would ever find me. I would starve or be eaten by bears. But no, I had Freckles, and she would find the way back home. So really, all I had to do is find the big lake. As I strolled along, I felt the stress and anxiety begin to lift. The rush to build our home, the incredible obstacles we already faced in just our first few years, the relations with the children, Harry's sometimes frightening temper, the stresses of working in the office, aircraft accidents, and loneliness of missing my parents and siblings thousands of miles away. It had all built up within me, and I had pushed it down and kept up the outside appearances of a normal existence. Now here I was, finally with free time all to myself, here alone deep within the wilderness, hiking through the brush and across the tundra on a nonsense mission, but peace flowed up inside me. I felt free and happy, and a great sense of relief. Things would be fine. Everything good came with a price. I sang as I strolled along and Freckles wagged her bushy tail happily.

After about eight or nine miles, I passed an old log cabin. It was small and old, built in the late 1920's, and already growing over with brush and tall grass. It had been built during a short-lived gold rush that had passed through the area, by a black woman named Natalie Crosby. Her nickname was Tootsie, and the rumor was, she had been a prostitute in Fairbanks, but had moved to this area, spending a few years panning for gold. She had been a large woman, but very pretty. Knowing how men sometimes talk, I wondered if she had really been a prostitute, or if she was a just a strong woman, working a mine, alone in the wilderness. Passing her cabin, with the roof already beginning to cave in, I suddenly felt a connection to her and wished I could have met her. It was rumored the she had passed away in a nursing home in Fairbanks. How sad, I thought, and promised myself to honor her legacy as a fellow adventurous spirit.

Glancing at the map occasionally, and double-checking the old cracked compass in my pocket, I found the lake without too much difficulty. It had taken a little over 8 hours, and I was already beginning to feel the strain. I still had to hike all the way back. I sat at the edge of the lake and waited for Harry. I took off my boots and soaked my feet and ate some cookies. Freckles splashed over, lapping at the water, and I gave her a cookie. It was nice to sit and relax. There was a gentle breeze and the mosquitoes weren't bad. I was a little earlier than the proposed rendezvous time. I wondered if Harry would come on time. I closed my eyes.

The idea of a nap was short-lived, as the sky vibrated with the sound of the plane's engine. Soon it roared overhead as Harry steered the plane in the general direction I had taken on my hike, looking for me. I stood up and waved. He saw me, and circling again, landed on the smooth lake with a splash. The plane turned and started taxiing towards me, but stopped about a hundred feet out into the lake and the engine shut off. Harry got out and began waving to me. He was yelling something but I couldn't hear. I left my boots on the bank and started wading out toward him. The water was very clear and shallow. Then I understood why the plane had stopped so far out. It would have gotten stuck if he had come any closer. I reached the plane and Harry leaned down and pulled me up onto the float.

"Hey, you're early!" He sounded pleased.

"I left at five," I said. "I've still got a long way to walk back."

"Well, you had better get started then," he said. "I just wanted to know if it could be an option in case there was an emergency and you had to get out, or if we had guests who had to leave when the strip was too muddy or it was too windy."

"If it had been an emergency, I probably wouldn't have been able to walk, and definitely not that fast! And not every guest would be in good shape."

"I see that now," Harry said. "I have to get back to flying. How are the kids doing?"

"They are fine. I left Tengupak with them and Tara knows where the .44 is." I gave Harry a quick hug and started wading back toward the bank. I put my boots back on as I watched the plane take off, circle once, and disappear off into the distance, the sound fading shortly afterward. I was a bit disappointed Harry hadn't brought me anything, even though I knew he was on his way back from a charter.

Earlier, on the walk down, it had crossed my mind that Harry might propose to me there at the lake, away from the kids, in the middle of the wilderness. We had been dating for several years now. I wasn't sure what I would have said. In a way, I was relieved that Harry hadn't handed me a ring there at the lake. He hadn't thought to bring anything. A candy bar would have been nice, I thought. Well, I couldn't expect too much, Harry was so busy lately. I felt fortunate to have had the time to myself. I called to Freckles and started back home. Surprisingly, I had little trouble finding the way. Freckles started off with her tail high and she seemed to be going in the right direction.

As we crashed through a particularly thick stand of brush, I heard an equally loud crashing just ahead. Freckles growled. I stopped in the very awkward position I was in, and tried to untangle the rifle that I had slung on my back. Oh shit, I thought as I fumbled for the gun, if this bear is serious about eating me he would have done it already! And then, I saw it, a large black bear, finally fighting free off the alders and loping out onto the tundra. He was running as fast as he could away from me, with Freckles right on his heels.

"Freckles, come back!" I shouted after her, but she paid no heed, and soon they disappeared into the next thicket. Not much I can do, and she will probably find her own way home, I thought. I just hoped I could find my way back too. I felt a quick stir of doubt as I looked at the map. Which valley was it, now? Should I stay right or go left? I tried to think back to that particular junction on the way down, but I had not been paying attention, lost in my thoughts. I pulled out the compass again, and as I was looking at it, I saw a footprint in the mud. Relief washed over me. It was my footprint from walking down just a few hours earlier. I back-tracked my old footprints, and did not have any more trouble finding my way back. Soon Freckles caught up and I scolded her for leaving me. She was tired now, and lagged behind, panting heavily. Good thing I didn't have to rely on her now to take me home!

My legs were tired and every step seemed like a tremendous effort. I tried counting steps for awhile. I stopped at Dolly's Drinking Springs and drank. I had to force myself to get up and keep going. It was only a few miles farther. By the time I waded across the last creek and headed toward the cabin, I was totally exhausted. I had been walking almost 20 hours, and it was just starting to get dark. I felt a little bit of sadness that it was all over. Now it was back to reality and trying to get along with the kids.

When I stepped through the door, I instantly knew something was wrong, as only a mother can know when something was wrong. The kids stared at me with big round eyes. My pain was forgotten.

"Is everything OK here?" I asked Tara, who lingered in the corner.

"Yeah," she mumbled, but I knew something was up. And then I saw the bullet hole in the wall.

"What happened here?!" I gasped, and all the kids tried to answer me at once.

"Henry did it! He was playing with the gun." Tara said.

"No I didn't! You tried to shoot me!" Henry wailed.

"I didn't know it was loaded!" Tara whined.

"Lisa," I said sternly," you tell me what happened. Remember big girls don't tell lies."

Lisa looked doubtfully from Henry to Tara, struggling with the dilemma. Should she tell the truth, or stand behind her sister, whom she worshiped? Henry hid behind me, calling Tara a liar. It was up to

Lisa now. Whose side would she take? I was almost too tired to deal with it. I knew Tara was lying. What was I going to do about it?

Lisa stepped over to stand behind me for protection. "Tara pointed it at Henry and it went off." She looked frightened.

Tara looked frightened and unsure of herself for the first time. The tables had turned, and no one was backing her up.

"What do you think we should do about this?" I asked the kids, as I pulled off my boots. I was trembling, thinking with horror of what had almost happened while I was gone. "This should not have happened! Tara, you are almost grown up, and you need to start acting like it! What is your father going to say when he hears about this?!"

Tara started to cry. "Please, please, don't tell Daddy!! I will be very good! I won't cause any more problems, I promise!" She pleaded between sobs.

I hesitated. This was serious. On the other hand, now I had some leverage over Tara. What had happened could not be undone, but the promise of a peaceful future was tantalizing. "I will have to think about this." I said. I was extremely tired, and I didn't want to make any decisions.

The next day I called a family meeting, and amongst us, we decided the incident was to be kept a secret from Harry. IF Tara behaved. The next few months were blissful, the kids got along great and treated me with respect. If Tara as much as insulted anyone whenever Harry was around, Henry or Lisa would say to her, "Hold onto yer guns, little missy!" and she would instantly apologize.

## Chapter Five

What should I do?! I felt the panic rising. It wasn't a question of SHOULD I tell Harry, it was WHEN should I tell Harry. And how would he react? I had a feeling he would not be very happy. I took a deep breath and tried to calm myself. It wasn't something I needed to rush into. I had some time to think about it.

I had just found out I was pregnant. I was already nearly two months along. That would explain the queasiness I had been feeling. I had attributed my illness to the cargo I had been helping Harry load in the planes. In the summer of 1971, we had been contracted by the City of Bethel to spray the city and surrounding areas with an experimental mosquito repellant. Harry had converted the Cessna 180 for the task, and I had helped load the smelly chemicals . Often, the toxins would drip in the cargo bay, and I would scrub up the mess. I was glad when the City finally called a halt to the spraying. So were Dave and Susie, who traveled with us frequently. They did not care for the smell of the chemicals in the plane. As hard as I scrubbed, nothing seemed to get rid of the lingering odor. I couldn't imagine how Harry could fly the plane like that. No wonder he had been so cranky lately.

I went over it again and again in my head, how I would tell Harry he was going to be a father again. And then something would come up, and I would postpone my dreaded task. I wasn't sure what I wanted to do. I loved the homestead with every ounce of my being, I wanted to spend my life there, and yes, I did want children of my own, but I wasn't sure I still wanted to be with Harry. Sometimes things were wonderful and it was just like when we had first gotten together. But more and more often now, another side of Harry was starting to show, and I wasn't sure I liked it at all. He could be very controlling and often insulting. He had shoved me once already. His ex-wife Evalyn had warned me to be careful of his temper. I did not like the way he treated little Henry or the way he had started becoming jealous of any friends I spoke with. But, I kept reminding myself, things would be better once we made enough money to move out to the homestead for good. Right now we were still building and shuttling supplies. Although I did get to spend the majority of my time at White Bear, Harry would often bring me back to Bethel to help with the business. He had invested nearly every penny into the homestead and the charter business was suffering. Payments were late and he was constantly borrowing money.

I thought back just a few weeks to late November, when the planes had gotten impounded and the business was temporarily shut down by the Internal Revenue Service. I had been in the office that morning finishing the manifest for a charter Harry was about to fly. Harry was out on the river ice preheating the aircraft engine and doing his preflight inspection. Four men walked into the office. I looked up from my work.

"Can I help you?" I asked. They all looked so professional. But then, we did fly a lot of school officials and businessmen around. On closer inspection, I saw two of the men were Alaska State Troopers.

"We are looking for Harry Faulkner. Can you tell us where we might find him?"

"He should be back shortly. I do the scheduling here. Where do you want to go?"

The two businessmen looked at me as if I were beneath their dignity. The troopers stood by the door impatiently.

"We are from the Internal Revenue Service, and we need to talk to Harry. It is a confidential matter." The taller man said haughtily.

I froze. This could not be good! What would Harry want me to do? I guessed he would want to avoid them. Harry was down on the river and would be coming inside at any time to pick up the manifest. If I could somehow warn him....

But it was too late. The door swung open and Harry started inside saying, "Hey Dolly, do you remember how many passengers I have to pick up in Akiak? I might have to put another seat..."

He was instantly cut short as he became aware of the men. They stepped up with all the pomp they could muster, and identified themselves as IRS agents.

Harry regained his composure quickly. "Let's discuss this inside my office. Dolly, can you make these men some coffee?" They all crammed into the tiny office and shut the door.

I dipped the water out of the barrel and began making coffee. Harry would handle things. He always did. But I couldn't help but eavesdrop. It seemed that Harry owed money on back employment taxes, and the IRS intended to collect it. Right now. I wondered if Harry had received any notices for this bill. Most likely he had. He tended to ignore bills. I hoped our business and our homestead wasn't in jeopardy! Were they going to arrest Harry? Why had the troopers come along if they weren't?

After what seemed a long time the men came out of the office. I offered them coffee but they kept moving right out the door, Harry at their heels, begging for more time.

"You can't do this. I need to make a living. If you shut down my business, how will I pay you?"

The men kept walking, all the way down to where the planes sat on the ice. One of the IRS agents had pulled a heavy suitcase out of his truck and carried it along. Oh no, I thought, are they going to destroy the planes?

Harry was getting irate, and the troopers kept warning him to stand back. From the window of the office of our now-defunct business, I watched as the IRS agents placed chains with padlocks around the airplane props. How the hell were we supposed to pay the bills now?! And then, just like that, with a final ultimatum, they left.

Harry came back and sat in the old sofa, shoulders drooping from defeat. He had put his entire life's efforts into this business. What was he going to do now? He couldn't get the planes back until he paid the IRS a little over $10,000, plus penalties and interest. It was a lot of money, much more than we could hope to borrow. And he only had 30 days until the planes went up for auction.

The next day, Harry was on the phone for hours. He was not going to give up. He gave his pilots a short vacation without telling details. He leased a Cessna 185 from his friend George Hohman and for the next several weeks, he flew all the charters himself. We made a quick trip to the homestead right after the IRS visit, and to our dismay, found the cabin door was padlocked and there was a notice posted from the IRS. Asking around, Harry later learned that they had chartered Samuelson's Flying Service to take them to the homestead, covering all their bases and making sure all of Harry's possessions were at stake. I was frightened and angry. I had worked very, very hard for the home I was making at White Bear, and I wasn't about to give up either!

Harry came back from a charter. I could tell he had an idea. Sometimes Harry's ideas didn't make sense at first but they usually worked out in the end.

"Come on, get ready. We are going out to Nunapitchuk. You have to ask the village leaders there for money."

"Me?! I don't know anyone in Nunapitchuk! How am I going to ask for money?" I was aghast.

"I know someone there. Nick O. Nick. He owns a store. You should ask him."

"Why don't YOU ask him? I don't know what to say!"

"Dolly, you have to! I have charters all day, and another meeting with the IRS tomorrow. If we don't get this money we lose everything! You have to do this!" Harry insisted.

I had learned that arguing with Harry never really worked. Besides, he was right. It was just that, well, I didn't feel comfortable going to a village, being the only stranger there, begging for money from someone I didn't even know. Time to swallow my pride. I got into the plane with Harry and we made the short flight to Nunapitchuk.

"I will be back tomorrow. Make sure you strike a good bargain, we can pay back a loan with flying passengers. You can stay with George and Martha Keene at Kasigluk. Good luck." He kissed me goodbye and left. I stood staring after the plane, wishing I didn't have to beg for money from total strangers. This was going to be awkward. I did know Martha, and she had invited me to stay with her if I was ever in Kasigluk.

I had accumulated quite the following of village children. Nunapitchuk was a small village, and strangers were always the talk of the town. The children were curious. I didn't mind at all. They were very helpful, pointing out Nick O. Nick's store. After I walked around a bit, I went to his store.

Nick O. Nick chartered to Bethel often with Harry. He was quiet and busy-looking, and I felt awkward and intimidated by my Herculean task. So I rushed into it headlong, blurting it all out, stammering and stumbling through the whole chain of events that lead me there. I was grateful that the store was empty. I felt like an idiot. Nick stood there quietly listening.

"Well," he finally said, "the elders will have to have a meeting about this."

"When?" I asked. "Harry needs the money now. The IRS is going to sell everything!"

"Tonight." He reached over to the citizens band radio that everyone had back in those days, and said something in Yup'ik. There was a lot of chatter on the radio as they set up the meeting. He turned back toward me. "It will be in the community hall around seven."

I walked nervously outside. I had hoped it would be all over with the one visit to the store. Now I would have to repeat my whole plea for money again. I had hours until the meeting, so I thought I had better make sure I could stay with Martha. As a snowmachine was passing me, I flagged it down to ask how I could get to Martha Keene's house in Kasigluk. I was told to hop on the sled, he was on the way to Kasigluk and would drop me off at the Keene's house. I knocked on her door and was warmly welcomed into her home. We drank tea and talked a bit about people we knew who were traveling with Harry's charter business.

"I made fish head soup," Martha offered. "But I can make you something else if you want."

"I would love to try your soup." I was hungry.

"Are you sure? Most Kassaqs don't care for our food." Kassaq is the word for white person. I was not about to be labeled as a picky eater just because I was a white person.

"It looks delicious!" I said, stirring the soup with my spoon. Just then an eyeball floated to the surface.

"This is the best part!" Martha exclaimed, picking an eyeball out of her soup and popping it into her mouth. "Try it!"

I didn't want to be rude, so I spooned the eyeball into my mouth and swallowed it without chewing. It really wasn't bad. Just a gelatinous blob. Martha smiled, delighted. I finished the soup, thanked her, and helped with the dishes as we chatted more about her fur sewing. Then George took me by snowmachine and sled back to Nunapitchuk. I was a bit early, but already people had started showing up at the community hall, hoping to catch a glimpse of the stranger, or even better, get a chance to talk. I waited, making idle conversation with a few locals. Then the meeting started. The hall was full so we sat on the floor. Most of the people spoke Yup'ik. I had no idea what they were saying. I could only pick out a few words. Occasionally someone would turn to me, and ask me something in English, for clarification. I felt very, very left out and awkward. I tried to explain how we needed the money to save the charter business, and we could offer fares at a reduced rate to Nunapitchuk to repay the loan. I knew Harry did a lot of business with Nick, flying in tons of supplies for his store. It was hard to judge what the people were thinking. And just like that, the meeting was over. I was confused. I had no idea what the outcome was. We went back to Kasigluk.

"How did it go?" Martha asked.

"I don't know. Nobody told me." She could see the disappointment in my face.

"We don't make decisions fast. If you didn't hear anything, that is a good thing. It means they are still deciding. They will let you know in their own time."

The next day, Harry flew in to pick me up. He was tired, but hopeful. "Did you get the money?"

I told him that I didn't know yet, they were still deciding. I got in the plane and we left. Looking down on the tiny village as I left, I wished circumstances had been different, and I could have been there to visit and go ice fishing, not beg for money.

For the next few days, we were both on pins and needles. Harry and I worked endlessly. I had just come back from picking the kids up at school. Walking in the office, I noticed Harry's door was closed, and laughter was coming out of the room. It had been long tiring days since anyone had laughed. Then the door opened and Nick O. Nick came out. Harry shook his hand, and he left, nodding politely to me.

Harry could barely contain himself. "You did it, Dolly! We got the loan!"

He sent the money off to the IRS, and within days, the troopers came over with the keys and unlocked the planes. They gave Harry the key to the cabin that was locked at the homestead. We had called the pilots back from their vacation, and went back into business full swing, trying hard to catch up.

With the recent financial struggles just behind us, I decided to wait a few days until Christmas to tell Harry and the kids that I was pregnant. I had spent a good deal of time decorating and baking. Harry had cut us a tiny straggly spruce and I had lavishly adorned it. I had wrapped gifts for the kids, and planned the big turkey dinner. Harry had told the pilots they could have Christmas Eve and Christmas Day off. I rehearsed over and over what I would say to Harry.

On Christmas Eve morning, Harry got a call from Dave Sheppard. Dave was having a hard time finding a flight down from Mountain Village. He wanted to bring his grandson to the Lower 48 for the holidays, but most of the charter businesses were closed for the holidays.

Harry turned to me. "I'm taking the 180 up to Mountain Village to pick up Dave. There's a big storm moving in from the coast, so I have to hurry. Listen for me on the radio. And be sure you give me weather updates. I will be back soon." He went through the necessary motions of preheating the plane engine, and I helped scrape the ice from the wings. The kids played inside, and would hopefully answer the phone or the radio. I should tell Harry now, I thought. But no, he is about to fly off into a storm, and I didn't want to distract him. It can wait until he gets back.

Harry took off, and I carried the heavy space heater back up to the shed, and put away the ladder and brooms. Harry would be back in a couple hours at the most. I went inside and started making another batch of cookies. Henry and Lisa came in to help me, or rather to sample the dough, so I doubled the batch. Tara had gone to visit her friend across town.

"KYH6, this is 29 Victor, how do you copy?" the radio squawked.

I rushed over to answer it. "Loud and clear."

"How's the weather there?" Harry asked.

"It's about the same as when you left, but the wind picked up a bit. It's about 10 to 15 now from the southwest and looks like it might start snowing."

"OK, just checking. It's starting to get pretty bad out this way, but I'm almost to Mountain Village. Just making sure I can get back again. I will call you on the way back."

I went back to the kitchen. Henry and Lisa were excited about Christmas and still trying to get me to give them a hint what they were getting.

"Is it big?" asked Lisa.

I smiled. The three new bikes were locked in the shed. Other gifts were wrapped under the tree, but I was sure they had already peeked at those. "Sort of." I tried to be vague.

"Come on, tell us," Henry begged. "We can still act surprised when Daddy gets home."

I gave them both a big hug. What would they think of having a little brother? I was sure it was going to be a boy. I hoped they wouldn't be jealous. Since the incident with the gun, we had been getting along fairly well. Tara was still a bit cold and angry toward me, but at least when Harry was around, she seemed to be trying to control her temper.

"KYH6, 29 Victor, I just landed in Mountain Village. I will call back again when I take off." The 180 was on skis and Harry had landed on the Yukon River ice to pick up his passengers.

Looking out the window, I was dismayed to see the weather had deteriorated rapidly and light snow was starting to fall. I passed this information along to Harry. "Perhaps you should stay there overnight." I suggested.

"No, I think I can make it back. I will call you when I take off."

His passengers were late, and it was nearly half an hour before Harry called back. By this time, the wind had picked up even more, and snow was beginning to swirl around. The visibility was probably only two miles now. I relayed that to Harry.

"It's about the same here." Harry said. "It's still flyable. I will call you if it gets any worse. I should be there in about 45 minutes."

I was really nervous now. If the weather would stay the same, Harry might make it. I tuned in to the weather station to listen to the forecast. It called for strong winds and snow, visibilities less than one quarter mile, and warned people to prepare for the storm. I put on my parka and went outside. Staring up at the sky, I willed it to hold out until Harry returned safely. A gust of wind nearly knocked me over, and I stared with horror at the solid white wall of snow that was rapidly approaching. By the time I had walked back to the office, just a few steps away, the storm had hit. It was a swirling blizzard, impossible to tell the difference between the sky and the ground. It was starting to get dark. Harry was going to fly right into this! I had to warn him. I had left Henry and Lisa to listen for the radio when I stepped out. When I walked in, to my dismay, they were playing in the other room and the radio squalled with unanswered transmissions. I rushed over and picked up the mike.

"The blizzard hit here! It's right down to the ground! Go back to Mountain Village!"

"It's out here too! I'm picking up a lot of ice on the windshield and the wings. I don't think I can get back to Mountain Village. I'm going to set it down out here and wait out the storm." The plane was on skis, but what if he hit a clump of tundra and flipped over? How could he even see the ground to land? Should I send someone out in the storm to find them?

But before I could even ask those questions, Harry came back on the radio, sounding relieved. "We're down safely. I landed on a little lake out here, and we will wait out the storm." I could hear the passenger cheering in the background. It must have been an intense few minutes.

"Should I send someone out there on a snowmachine? Is everyone OK? Where are you?" I asked.

"Yeah, we are fine, we landed just fine. No, don't risk anyone's life to come out here! The storm will pass. It's starting to get dark anyway and nobody would be able to find us. Just call me on the radio every three hours."

For the rest of that long sleepless night I paced the floor. They had landed safely, but were still not out of danger. Harry always carried extra warm clothing and sleeping bags and emergency gear in the plane. Every three hours, he would start the engine of the plane and run it to keep the engine warm. If the engine cooled off too much, he would not be able to get it started again when the storm abated. He had to conserve fuel, so he only ran it ten minutes each time. Every time he started the plane, he would check in on the radio. He assured me they were all warm enough inside the plane with extra sleeping bags, and yes, they had some frozen pilot crackers to gnaw on. I listened to the forecast, but you could never really rely on it, a forecast was, at best, just a guess. At midnight, Harry wished us all a merry Christmas. When daylight finally filtered through the window, I was disappointed to see the storm was still in full force.

Joe, stopping by to drop off a Christmas present for the kids, tried to reassure me. "Look over there. See how that part of the sky is a little bit lighter? In a few hours, it will probably be good enough to fly."

Rather than continuing to pace nervously, I started the Christmas dinner. This was the darkest time of the year, and there were only about four hours of daylight. If Harry didn't take off soon, it would be dark. Just then, the radio squealed.

"KYH6, this is 29 Victor. We just departed Sheppard Lake and we are inbound for Bethel. We will be there in 25 minutes." In the background, I could hear the passenger chuckling about having the lake named after him. Looking outside, I could see the weather had improved considerably, but was by no means good flying weather. Nevertheless, Harry did land safely. The men were in great spirits as they told me of their adventure. On Christmas day, Harry had went out into the storm and chopped down a tiny willow branch and brought it back to the plane. He stuck it in the seat back and decorated it with shredded bits of cardboard from the pilot bread wrapper. He took a spare set of socks from his emergency gear and hung them up inside the plane so the little boy would not miss his Christmas. I looked down at the little boy, still playing with the silver dollar Harry had put inside the sock, and thought, Harry will be a good father to my child. But it wasn't the right time to tell him.

And so I did not tell Harry at Christmas, nor any of the other times I thought I had worked up my courage. Sometimes he would leave me at White Bear for several weeks and I would run out of pickles. My cravings had become intense but I learned to endure them. At the homestead, I was at peace. There was so much to do. We had ordered six small prefab tin sheds from Sears and were assembling them at the homestead for guest cabins. Harry would stay in Bethel and fly, and watch the kids when they got out of school. Then he would come and pick me up whenever he needed my help in the office. I would go straight to the store and buy a jar of pickles, and inhale the whole thing.

I didn't tell Harry until I was nearly six months pregnant. He had been teasing me lately about getting fat. All my rehearsal went out the window, and I just blurted it out. Harry wasn't at all happy about it. He swore it wasn't his baby, and that I had cheated on him. I was aghast. We had been exclusively together, and I had never dreamed of cheating on him! Where was I supposed to find time to have an affair? I worked from sunup until sundown, and when I wasn't in the office, I was alone at the homestead. I was hurt and scared and very unsure of myself. What should I do? It was too late to have an abortion, and besides, I did want my own child. Should I leave Harry? I would miss White Bear and my son would grow up without a father. I was very attached to little Henry, and just starting to get along with Tara and Lisa. They needed a mother in their lives, or Harry would send them off to foster care again. Henry and Lisa didn't seem to mind about the baby, but Tara was lividly angry and had started acting out again. Fortunately, Harry would leave me at White Bear for long periods of time, giving us all time to think about how this new life within me would affect all of our lives.

## Chapter Six

My son, Eddie, was born August 8, 1972 after an exhausting 12 hours of labor. I had been working on the float plane dock, refueling planes late that night when my water broke. Harry was out of town, purchasing a big DC3 cargo plane. I waddled back into the office, made arrangements with Kathy to watch the kids, and drove myself to the hospital. I was scared and alone and in pain, but I kept reminding myself it would soon pass.

When it was finally over the next day, my relief was short-lived. The doctor who had delivered my baby had a very concerned look on his face, and I knew instantly something was wrong. I burst into tears as I saw my son had deformed feet and legs. The doctor held my hand as he assured me that my baby was normal in every other way.

"I just want my baby! Give him to me!" I wailed.

The nurse handed him over and gently placed my son in my arms. He was a large boy, 8 pounds and 12 ounces, perfect in every way, from his tiny little fingers to his adorable little nose. But his feet were twisted inward at an awkward angle.

"Will he outgrow this?" I had asked.

The doctor was new to Bethel, and didn't have much experience with birth defects. He didn't know. "He might eventually be able to walk with corrective surgery. We don't know. I will call other doctors and consult them."

They called the affliction "clubbed-type feet" for lack of a better term, but the deformation included both lower legs, and my baby was missing some critical tendons for walking normally.

My mind was aswirl. How could this have happened? I did not smoke or drink. I was strong and led a healthy lifestyle. Perhaps I had worked too hard in my last trimester. Or maybe it was the mosquito repellant chemicals I had been handling the previous summer? Or was it the time Tara had kicked me in the stomach?

I thought back to that incident. The kids and I had been at White Bear, and I had been planting the garden at the end of the airstrip while they played. I had shoveled and hoed up the rocky soil, picking what seemed like tons of rocks out and tossing them into the brush. Then I had added the bag of fertilizer and shoveled and hoed all over again. Dark clouds loomed ominously and I hurried to get the garden planted before the rain began to fall. Mosquitos swarmed, and the air was thick with their incessant buzzing. I worked late, planting potatoes, radishes, cabbage, turnips, carrots, and peas. I knew from the previous year's garden that some vegetables like corn and tomatoes would not grow here. Everything seemed to be so much harder now that I was pregnant. It was uncomfortable to bend over, and I gasped for air from the effort, inhaling countless mosquitoes. I could hear the kids laughing and playing in the cabin. I had long ago learned not to ask them for any help. Besides, since learning about the baby, Tara had been extremely rude and hostile. It was just easier to avoid conflict. It had been late when I finally finished the garden. I walked into the cabin, and changed out of my dirty clothes.

"When is dinner? I'm hungry!" whined Tara.

For a moment I just stared at her. I was hungry too. But I had been working all day and was hot and tired and pregnant.

"You know, you are nearly a grown woman! You could have started making dinner if you were hungry." I snapped.

The next moment I found myself sitting in the pile of firewood, gasping in pain and clutching my belly. Tara had kicked me and I had not even seen it coming. She shrieked obscenities loudly. Henry and Lisa hid in the other room.

"I'm going to tell your dad!" I threatened.

"Go ahead," she screamed. "You're not my mother. You can't tell me to do anything!" And then she stomped off, slamming the door loudly. I had been so worried about the baby, and relieved when I had felt him moving again the following week.

Now, here in the hospital with my tiny child, I vowed to do anything to give him a normal life. After spending the night in the hospital, I returned to work. Every spare moment between working and caring for the baby, I made phone calls and wrote letters and read everything I could about birth defects. Henry was a great help to me, seeming to be thrilled at the role of big brother. Tara shunned the baby, and Lisa followed in her footsteps. Tengupak, still mourning the loss of Freckles, (she had died of old age that winter) became very protective of Eddie. Tengupak had always had an aversion to drunks, and now he would not let anyone smelling like alcohol in the same room with HIS baby.

Harry returned, excited about his new toy, the huge twin engine DC3 that he had just flown back from Anchorage. He had grand plans for it, starting a new route flying cargo from Anchorage to Bethel. He was in a good mood, and had brought me back a beautiful gold brooch, sort of as an apology for not being there for the birth of our son. He had also brought along a little toy plane that would later be Eddie's favorite toy.

Just a few days after Eddie was born, Susie gave birth to her daughter. The little girl had a very similar birth defect. I now suspected the mosquito repellant chemical had played a large role in our children's birth defect. Susie and her husband Dave flew a lot with us, in the same plane Harry had used to spray the repellant. This was around the same time the DDT chemicals started to make the news. I called every doctor listed, but the result was the same. The damage that had been done to my child would be permanent. Eddie was given a tiny pair of stiff shoes with braces, to hopefully force the little bones into a more natural position as they grew. I was given a list of therapeutic exercises to help Eddie's muscles strengthen to compensate for the missing tendons. Walking would be very difficult for him to learn, I was told. It would not come naturally, and he would have to concentrate on every step.

Despite the uncomfortable braces and endless exercises, Eddie was a happy baby, cooing and smiling as he tugged on Tengupak's ears with his chubby little fingers. He was a good baby, and laughed far more than he cried.

On Sunday, August 13th, 1972, Harry woke up early and turned to me as I was feeding Eddie. "We might as well get married today."

"OK," I said, surprised, placing Eddie back in his crib. We had never talked about marriage. It was a blunt and practical proposal, like nothing I had ever read in my romance novels. I didn't have much time to think about it. It made sense at the time. My son needed to grow up with a father and Harry's children needed to grow up with a mother. Perhaps, if we were married, Harry would let me start acting like a mother to his children, rather than just a hired (but unpaid) servant. They needed love and discipline.

Harry called judge Nora Guinn to see if she was available to marry us. Harry went downstairs and told the kids while I tried to find something to wear. I could hear Tara swearing and stomping around and Harry trying to console her. I laid out some clothes for the kids. Henry could wear his best shirt, Tara and Lisa could wear the matching red dresses I sewed for them at Christmas. I didn't have any white dresses, so I would wear a red dress too, to match the girls' dresses.

Tara did not want to wear the dress I had made her. She picked it up and ripped a hole in it, and then threw it into the trash can. I did not want to fight with her. We were already late. I went through my closet and picked out my prettiest blue dress. Tara and I were nearly the same size, so it should fit her. I fixed Lisa's hair and sent her downstairs with the dress for Tara to wear. Tara was still throwing a fit, and throwing dishes too. Harry went downstairs and, for the first time ever, I hear him scolding her to behave herself. Now we were really late. We all crammed into the old truck and bounced down the dusty, pothole-lined road to Nora's house. Nora Guinn was the first Yup'ik Eskimo woman judge in Alaska. That was a big accomplishment for a woman back in those days, and I felt honored that she agreed to marry us, especially on such short notice, on her day off. Nora got into the truck, smiling.

"It's about time you two got married!" she admonished as we lurched along to Sue's house. By the time we got there, J.B. Haroldsen had brought over the cake his wife had made and Johnny York showed up to sign as a witness to our marriage. We all piled into the house. Tara was still pouting. Henry was excited, and offered to hold the baby for me. Lisa seemed torn between the two extremes, she did not want to miss out on the fun, but she didn't want to make her big sister angry with her. I was nervous. It didn't seem real. I had never been married before so I wasn't sure quite what I expected. We said our vows and ate cake. Harry gave Nora $20 and Johnny drove her home. Then we all went to the Wild Goose restaurant and had burgers, and went back to work as if nothing had happened. Harry, who had been married several times previously, would always joke about his $20 wedding, "The cheapest one yet!"

## CHAPTER SEVEN

"You know how to catch a polar bear?" Harry asked John, as they sat in the kitchen at White Bear watching the storm brew up over the mountains.

"Nope. How?" John asked.

"Well, first you chop a hole in the ice. And then, you take a can of peas, and sprinkle it around the hole. When the polar bear comes up to take a pea, you kick him in the icehole!" The men guffawed loudly. It was Harry's favorite joke.

John had offered to help us with building in exchange for spending time at our new lodge. His work had been done the past week and his agreed-upon time had been met, but he didn't want to return to Bethel until the next week.

I finished the dishes and started putting Eddie through his exercises. John should have left when he was offered the ride to town yesterday, I thought. This weather will not hold out until Friday, when he wants to leave. Harry should have been more firm with him. I just hoped he wouldn't get stuck here and ruin our family Christmas!

I was looking forward to celebrating Eddie's first Christmas at the homestead. He seemed to be growing and developing normally, with the exception of his lower legs. They were still twisted awkwardly inward. We had been to a few doctors in Anchorage, and the general consensus was that he was not a good candidate for surgery. Eddie's new braces looked uncomfortable. I cringed as I gently strapped the contraptions on his tiny legs and put him back in the playpen. I wondered curiously, why had John wanted to stay a longer? He was supposed to leave on the last trip when Harry brought the kids in, after they got out of school for Christmas break. But then, he had suddenly changed his mind. Was it when he saw Tara get out of the plane? She had been blatantly flirting with him as we unloaded the plane. I felt a deep discomfort. Although Tara was extremely hostile toward me, I still felt protective of her. But, Harry was here, so if John made any unwanted advances toward his oldest daughter, I was sure Harry would deal with it.

We now had the six small sheds assembled, and used these as guest cabins for the lodge. After the failed two-mile pipeline experiment from the hotsprings, we had decided to heat the cabins with stove oil flown in from Bethel. It was very costly, and we had intended to shut down the guest cabins for the winter to save heating costs. So, hopefully, John would be able to leave soon so we could close up that cabin for winter, saving the heating fuel for our own house.

In addition to the sheds, we had the main house, a large shop, and the building the swimming pool was enclosed in. Since Harry had already built the swimming pool before the pipeline experiment, he did not want to give up so easily. So he pumped water from the creek and heated the pool with a stove oil burner. We had countless problems maintaining the monstrosity for the weeks it was operational. The liner had leaked and the foundation of the pool had eroded. Permafrost had melted and the building sunk lopsidedly. It was too costly to fly fuel in to heat it, so we drained the pool for the winter, and had begun disassembling it. Perhaps it would be more feasible closer to the hotsprings.

The previous winter, Harry had walked in a huge D8 Caterpillar, trekking over 100 miles across the wilderness to White Bear, pulling two old Volkswagon vans behind. One was filled with diesel fuel, the other was sleeping quarters for the two men. He planned to start building a road from the airstrip up toward the hotsprings. And then, we would move the buildings up to the edge of the homestead tract, closest to the hotsprings, and attempt the pipeline again. But now, as winter was rapidly setting in, it was time to get our cabins ready for what the elders promised to be a long hard winter.

The snow fell softly at first, and then with increasing urgency as the big fluffy flakes seemed to race each other to the ground. By the next day, the snow was knee deep, and the following day it was over four feet deep. By the time the storm was over, snow reached the roof of the house. The wind shrieked through the trees and rattled the windows, until they were covered by the towering drifts. Each day I had to tunnel through the deep drifts to the creek for water, and to the place we dumped the honey-bucket. The following day, the tunnels were completely filled with the driving snow.

At first, the kids played outside for most of the day, building snowmen, sledding, and having snowball fights. I would bundle Eddie up warmly, and Henry would pull him around in a little sled. Tara and John would sometimes go off together, "looking for firewood," but never did return with any. I had spoken with Harry about the dangers of this inappropriate relationship, but he had scoffed at me.

"Tara's a grown woman," he reminded me, "Besides it's nice to see her happy for a change." Tara would do as she pleased. Harry had never denied her anything, except the attention and affection she so desperately craved from him. Perhaps she would find what she was seeking with John. Harry had made it clear to me that I was not to act as a mother to her.

As the days progressed, the kids barely left the house, and John seemed to have moved in permanently. Harry slept much of the time, and tinkered with the generator. He was also wiring the house for electricity so we could use the generator to light the house. The house was very dark all day since the windows were covered by the snow drifts. The ski plane was completely buried, only one antenna poked through the snow.

I would check my rabbit snares nearly every day, snowshoeing through the ever-deepening drifts. We were running low on food, not having planned for the unexpected houseguest, so the rabbits I caught became our staple. One day, snowshoeing out to shovel off the roof, I noticed a tunnel from the girls' room toward John's cabin. Had John been sneaking into our house at night? I asked Lisa later that day.

"No, Tara has been crawling out her window every night. I have to close the window for her and then open it when she wants back in. Please don't tell her I told you!" Lisa looked up at me mournfully.

I gave her a hug. "It's OK. I already figured it out. What do you think we should do?"

"I don't like it! Tara doesn't play with me anymore! All she does is hang around John."

"That's what teenagers do. Soon you will do the same thing. It's a natural course of growing up."

"I don't like it! I don't like him! I want him to go away!" Lisa threw a snowball hard at the nearest tree.

"So do I, honey," I said, hurling a snowball myself. "Daddy will take him away when the storm breaks."

The storm did not break for nearly a month. The kids were cranky, Harry was irritable, and things had gotten uncomfortable between Tara and John. The peaceful Christmas I had longed for had been a disaster of accusations and yelling. Our food supplies, and tempers were running short. The kids had to get back to school and Harry had to get back to work. I was exhausted from the constant shoveling, cleaning, and cooking. John and the kids did nothing to help. And, to top it all off, I was pregnant again.

When the weather finally broke, Harry demanded everyone help shovel out the plane. We had to drag countless sled loads of snow out of the way. Tara and John disappeared. After we dug out the plane, we had to jack it up on blocks, scrape the ski bottoms and practically fly it out of the hole it was in.

Harry cornered John late that afternoon." Get your shit together. You are leaving tomorrow."

"No," John said, "I'll stay here another week. Then my next welfare check will be in Bethel. You can take me to Bethel then."

My jaw dropped in disbelief. Who did he think he was? Telling US when we should pick him up? This was OUR home, he was eating OUR food, the cabin was heated with fuel WE had bought, and I was cleaning and cooking for him, with no thanks or help with any chores. Harry had better say something before I exploded!

It was Harry who exploded. In fact, he nearly dragged John out and threw him in the plane. Harry had been planning to leave the next day, but now he was really upset and just wanted the jerk out of our lives. Besides, he had already heated the plane when we had extracted it from the snow bank. He took off just before dark. I heaved a huge sigh of relief. Tara, however was inconsolable.

"This is all your fault, you stupid bitch!" she screamed, throwing a fit. Then she slammed the door to her room and I could hear her sobbing. This was going to be a long night, I thought sadly.

The next day it stormed again. Tara did not come out of her room at all. I remembered what it had been like to be young and in love, and tried to say a few consoling words at her door, but was met with the shuddering crash of a thrown dresser drawer. It was a relief when Harry showed up the following day and took the kids back to school. He would be back for me in a week, he needed help at the office again. The woman he had hired had to take a few weeks off. He told me John-the-freeloader had been pretty upset, and told Harry he hadn't heard the last from him. A few months later, we received a bill demanding payment from John for "work that he had done" during the time he had been snowed in and we were feeding him.

Eddie and I enjoyed a few peaceful days alone at the homestead, and then Harry returned to take us to Bethel.

"Just a couple weeks, " he promised," then we will come back."

The next few weeks were incredibly busy. It was at the height of Harry's aviation career. At this time he had no less than 12 aircraft and 8 pilots flying, and various mechanics and ground crew. He had made a place in history when he became the first (and possibly only) person to modify a twin engine Islander and fit it for skis to make travel to Alaskan villages even more economical.

With the incredible amount of flying that we did, and frequent close calls, it was only a matter of time until tragedy struck. The weather had been particularly bad that week and we had canceled many flights. But now, there was a small break in the weather, and a nurse was anxious to get to Chevak, where she was to pick up a patient with appendicitis and return to the Bethel hospital. The pilot who took the flight had been with us for less than a month, and had just gotten his instrument rating to fly in clouds. He was eager to show his skills. I listened to the radio after he took off, but never heard him call in that he had landed in Chevak. He was new, perhaps he had forgotten to check in? After another hour passed, I became concerned. He should have been back by now. I alerted Harry and the other pilots. Harry began diverting all aircraft toward the route of flight to search for the missing plane. But then the weather had worsened, so they had all turned back, narrowly missing disaster themselves. The next morning, Harry cancelled all charters and sent all our aircraft out to search. It was Harry who found the wreckage later that day, past Kasigluk. The pilot had become disoriented and flown into the ground. The occupants of the plane had died on impact. It was a brutal reminder of the stark reality of bush flying.

Shortly after the tragic airplane accident, Tara left us. She had become increasingly violent and destructive, and had been causing problems at school. I had suggested counseling once to Harry.

He had dismissed it angrily. "There's nothing wrong with Tara! This is all your fault for not being nicer to her." I didn't know how much "nicer" I could get.

Then Tara had gotten arrested a few times, and finally Harry was at his wit's end as to how to deal with the angry teenager. He sent her off to live with her mother in Idaho. Lisa, who had worshiped Tara and followed her every footstep, was struggling to adjust and no doubt felt abandoned. I tried hard to compensate by giving her extra attention. Harry resented any affection I bestowed on his kids, particularly little Henry. It was a careful balancing act, but fortunately, with the frequent trips back to the homestead, I was able to retain my sanity. The beautiful serenity of the Alaska wilderness soon made me forget my troubles. The hard toils of living in the rugged land gave a purpose to my life.

Harry was in Texas buying a pair of Lockheed Connies when our daughter Jillian was born. She was small and pink and "a perfect ten" the nurses had said. I couldn't leave the Bethel hospital soon enough. The other babies I had seen there were shockingly discolored an odd shade of yellow. There was an outbreak of jaundice, and I wasn't sure if it was contagious, but I didn't want to take the chance with my beautiful baby girl.

Right around the time Jillian was born, Martha Lott's grandmother died, so in the Yup'ik tradition, her grandmother's soul was passed on to the newborn infant. Martha and her husband Peter lived in the village of Tuluksak, and Peter ran a little store there. Harry did a lot of business with Peter, hauling freight for his store, and flying them to Bethel frequently to buy more supplies. While Peter was off shopping, Martha would wait in the office with me. She would knit and tell me stories. We became close friends. Often I would invite Martha to the homestead, but Peter would decline.

"It's too far to travel from our village, and gas is too expensive. You should fly us up sometime." Airplane gas was far more expensive than snowmachine gas even then, but Harry good-naturedly rearranged cargo trips to bring them up for visits. He would have to leave behind supplies and food in order to accommodate them, as the weight of the airplane was critical when operating off the short airstrip.

I enjoyed Martha's company, but Peter could sometimes get on one's nerves. He did little to help when he visited. He never brought food along, or offered to pay for the food he ate. And did he ever eat! He was a small man, barely five feet tall, but he sure could put away the food. He would stand up and scoop nearly the entire contents of any serving dish onto his plate, while the kids watched in shock and hunger. In the rare instance there was seconds, he would empty the entire dish onto his plate and ask, "Is there more?" When Peter was visiting, there was rarely any food left by the time I had finished serving, and I would go hungry. His table manners became a family joke, and if Harry ever thought one of the kids was taking more than their share he would say, "Are you sure you have enough there, Peter Lott?"

Harry would take Peter out to trap beaver, and would generously give Peter whatever they caught, although it was Harry who had done the trapping. Peter really wanted a black wolf pelt to hang in his store, but we rarely had wolves around in the mountains. He would eye Tengupak and make jokes about skinning him, or the condition of his pelt, and everyone would laugh. Peter did keep the kids entertained for hours telling tall tales about seven-headed monsters he had seen, or retell an event that had just occurred with lavish exaggerations. Little did we realize then how much Peter's tall tales would later threaten our lives.

*Tengupak in front of Lodge with snow nearly to the roof*

## Chapter Eight

"Get back!" I shouted at Lisa. She stood frozen in terror as the airplane careened wildly toward her. She had rushed out to meet Harry as he landed at the White Bear airstrip.

Just as he had been about to touch down, a strong gust of wind had pushed him forward, and he had landed way too fast. Now the airplane was barreling straight toward where Lisa stood in the garden at the end of the airstrip. I sprinted forward and grabbed her arm, dragging her back toward the safety of the trees as the airplane shot past us, spraying mud, brakes squealing and rocks pinging off the tail. The runaway plane charged through the garden rows, propeller chopping up the potato plants, until it came to rest on the far side of the garden.

I breathed a sigh of relief when Harry stepped out to survey the wreckage. The nose gear had collapsed and the prop was bent, the garden was ruined, but the important thing was, Harry was uninjured.

"Thought you needed help making another row," Harry joked, waving to the deep furrow the plane had left in the soil. "That ought to grow a lot of potatoes."

It wasn't the first time an airplane had an incident at our short airstrip, and it certainly wouldn't be the last. Although the strip was a whopping 900 feet long, the approaches to both ends were compromised by the terrain and the wind was always unpredictable in the narrow, rugged canyon. Sometimes the wind would be coming from the north everywhere else in the State, but south in this canyon.

Harry started to extend the airstrip later that summer, promising me a new garden site. The old garden was practically ruined anyhow after the Cessna 206 had plowed through it. I shrugged and dug up as much as I could to transplant to the new garden.

Harry brought Carl, a Native from Akiak, along to help him with the airport extension. He offered Carl a considerable amount of money, but Carl still had one condition. He wouldn't come unless he could bring his mother. It sounded silly, but she was a nice elderly lady and I did enjoy her company. She seemed afraid to leave the house, and when I asked her about it, she said, "The moose! I saw tracks outside, and I'm scared of moose!"

I thought it a bit odd that she hadn't seemed to notice the bear tracks, but was terrified of moose. The next day she insisted on leaving. Harry and Carl had to stop in the middle of the project to take her back to Akiak. Carl had decided he would also stay in Akiak, so Harry returned alone.

"I want to get this done before winter, but I can't find anyone to help," he said.

"Tell me what you need. I can do it." I offered.

"Are you sure? You know how you are with directions." Harry was referring to my frequent inability to tell him if something was straight or level.

"Let's just give it a try."

While Lisa watched the babies in the house, Harry let Henry sit on the dozer with him, and I walked ahead, trying to keep a straight line. Then I would set out a marker, and Harry would plow towards it. I would walk ahead again and set out another marker. I really hope this is straight, I thought to myself, listening to the monotonous clanking of the dozer tracks. I didn't particularly care for the noise and smell of exhaust, but if this would make access to our home safer, I could tolerate it. It certainly was a lot less work than doing it all with a pick and shovel.

Harry gunned the engine sharply, and I looked up. He was motioning me to come over.

"Hey, I think we are done. I'm just going to park this out of the way, and see what we did."

I was relieved. It had been a very long day, and my ears still rang with the sounds of heavy equipment. The kids would be hungry, and I was sure Lisa hadn't thought to start cooking, so I had better go make dinner.

Harry walked out on the new extension and surveyed his work. "Holy shit! That is really crooked! What the hell were you doing? Dolly, come here and look at how crooked this is!"

I sagged with disappointment. I had tried so hard to make it straight. I just couldn't seem to see how far I had drifted to one side, until now.

"Oh well," Harry sighed. "It's usable, and better than what it was. We don't have enough diesel left to change it. We will have to use it like this until I fly more fuel in. That's OK, we will fix it next year." He reached down and picked up a potato, unearthed from the old garden. "Here, you forgot something."

We never did straighten it, and to this day, the White Bear airstrip has a noticeable bend in it. After awhile, Harry just became used to it.

That Christmas, defying doctors' predictions that he would never walk, Eddie took his first two steps. It was the best Christmas present I could have ever asked for. Although he went back to crawling for months afterward, it gave me the glimmer of hope that my son would be able to live a normal life.

I was smiling, thinking of those two magical steps, when I hear my son scream. I dropped the pail of water I had been carrying and bolted for the house. Lisa had promised to watch the kids while I fetched the water, but she was nowhere to be seen. Eddie had crawled to the tub of scalding water that I had been preparing for his bath, and tried to pull himself in, burning his tiny hand. I snatched him up, shocked that he could have reached the tub in such short time. He wailed and sobbed, and I was horrified to see the skin blistered on his hand. I applied cold cloths, rocking him and singing softly until he finally stopped crying. I was angry with myself for not putting the tub higher out of reach, not adding the hot water last, and angry with Lisa for not watching Eddie as she had promised.

Lisa hid until Harry came home, then she raced to him and told him that I had thrown Eddie into the boiling water. I was astounded. Was she merely trying to shift the blame from herself, or did she really hate me enough to tell lies about me? Harry soothed her, told her it was an accident, not anyone's fault, but that incident had left me disturbed and distrustful of Lisa.

There was something different about Lisa lately. I just couldn't put my finger on it. She had always been a quiet, gentle child, overshadowed by her dominant sister. She had an incredible imagination and wrote beautiful poetry. But there was something else, something different, just lingering beneath the surface. I remembered an incident when she had come home from school in the middle of the day crying uncontrollably. Concerned, I tried to ask her what was wrong. But whatever had terrified her, she would not say. So I held her, told her softly, "It's OK, you don't have to tell me if you don't want to. But if you do, I'm here for you."

She had hugged me back and cried a little more, and drank the hot chocolate I made for her, but she never did tell me what was wrong. We had gotten along fine, especially when Tara wasn't around to impress, but now she was a teenager, and things were changing. She had told some pretty unbelievable tales recently.

That's why I didn't react much when she ran up to me, while I was weeding the new garden, gushing out a new story. "There was a bear! It came right up to us, and I touched it! I called it right to me, and…"

Just then Henry ran up too. "We saw a bear! It was really close, and we…"

"Where?" I interrupted. "Is it gone?" The gun was in the house.

"It was over by the swings. Me and Lisa were swinging and it came right up to us! We thought it was Tengupak and it was a bear!"

Just then Tengupak came out of the bushes where he had been napping next to where Eddie and Jillian were playing in the dirt. He sniffed the air, and then decided that yes, indeed, a bear had been nearby. He was off with a growl to find the intruder, who had probably long since departed.

We spent most of our time at the homestead now. Harry had begun building a trail up from the airport to the opposite corner of the homestead, which was one quarter mile from the hotsprings. The trail was muddy and we got stuck often. It was an extraordinary amount of effort to bring the building supplies up to the new home site. Every time the power wagon got stuck in the deep mud, we would have to unload the entire thing, and, with picks and shovels, dig ditches to drain the mud away from the tires. Then we would throw logs under the huge tires and hope for the best. Due to the terrain, the trail wound along the edge of mountains and ended several hundred yards short of our destination. We would carry heavy sheets of plywood on our backs the remaining distance to the new house site. Harry was planning to build on to his original cabin that had blown over in the windstorm. Then we would extend a pipeline from the hotsprings down to the cabin and heat our home with the hot water.

Harry made many flights to Bethel whenever the weather permitted, and now, with the extension on the airport, we were able to bring some of the lumber in with larger aircraft. He sometimes hired people to help with some of the construction. I would balance taking care of the kids, cooking and cleaning, and helping Harry with the building. It was also my duty to put away all the supplies and tools when we were done. Since I knew where everything was stored, it was my task to find any tool or part that was needed. From sunup until sundown, I was on the run, finding things, fetching things, trying to keep the kids out of trouble.

At the end of each day, we were exhausted and everyone was cranky. Harry had become increasingly mean to little Henry, ridiculing and striking him without provocation. At first, I had stood up for Henry, and demanded that Harry treat him better, but this just caused Harry to become more angry and upset, and he would take it out on Henry. Although it broke my heart to watch Harry mistreating his son, the best thing I could do for Henry was not to get involved when Harry was around, since he resented any affection I bestowed on Henry. Sometimes Harry would shove or strike at me too, when I stood in his way of assaulting his son. He more or less ignored the rest of the kids. Things will be better when the ordeal of building the new house is over, I thought. Harry is just under a lot of stress, and suddenly he wants his son, who he has ignored all these years, to be a man. Henry was used to doing pretty much whatever he pleased, and unaccustomed to having to work. Now suddenly Harry is trying to make him to pull his share of the load, and Henry doesn't know how. To compensate for Harry's cruelty, I did chores Henry was supposed to do, and hesitated to ask him for help. How Henry ever turned out to be the successful, generous person he later became despite his early hardships, still amazes me.

## Chapter Nine

The whole house shook so violently, I thought it would fly apart into a thousand pieces of plywood shrapnel. The winter storm that had descended upon us was by far the most extreme force of Mother Nature that I had ever witnessed. Outside, entire trees were uprooted and the sounds of cracking and splintering wood melded into the shrieking howl of the wind. Sleet hammered down on the roof with such force I was certain it would puncture the plywood.

"Mama, I'm scared!" whimpered Eddie.

"It's just the wind. It will be over soon," I said soothingly. I didn't like the strong wind either. It made me nervous of the house blowing apart. I kept envisioning the overturned first house, blown a hundred yards uphill from its original location.

"Don't be scared. An airplane is louder. Let's play with your airplanes." Henry suggested helpfully. Eddie was fascinated with airplanes and could already distinguish between the makes and models of planes his dad flew.

Harry was back in Bethel working and had left the kids with me. It was Henry and Lisa's spring break, so they were out of school. Harry had flown them here to White Bear the previous week.

I was about to start making dinner, but afraid to start a fire in the woodstove with the wind howling down the chimney. What should I make, that didn't require starting a fire? I looked through the cupboards at my stores of rice, noodles, and beans. Then I decided to make cold Spam sandwiches, and peanut butter on pilot bread. I started cutting the Spam and setting the table. The wooden dining table sat next to the large window in the main room of our airstrip house.

We hadn't quite finished the new house yet. I called the kids in from their rooms to eat.

"Look at that window! It's going to break!" Lisa pointed to the window, just as I sat down.

I felt a chill of unease as I turned to look at the window behind me. It bowed inward alarmingly with each shuddering gust of wind. "It's a hurricane window. It's built for this wind." I tried to reassure Lisa.

She would have none of it. "I still don't like it. It scares me. I think I'm going to eat in my room." She picked up her plate and wandered off to her room.

Henry finished eating and helped me feed Eddie while I fed Jillian. She was being fussy, and finally I decided to put the kids to bed.

"Thanks for helping me," I told Henry, giving him a quick hug. He beamed and carried the dishes to the sink without me asking. I scooped up Eddie and Jillian and carried them to their beds, one under each arm. Just as I left the room, I heard an explosive CRACK-KKKK! I ducked instinctively, covering the kids as something whizzed by my head.

"Henry!" I shouted. "Are you OK?!"

"Yeah, I'm fine," his voice came from his room. "What was that?!"

Lisa came running out of her room. "I told you that window was going to break!" She pointed to where the window had been. Now there was just a jagged hole and the storm surged into the house. Snow swirled through the dining area. Pictures were ripped from the walls. Chairs blew over with a crash. Deadly projectiles of glass broke free of the pane and hit the opposite wall. Eddie and Jillian began to wail. I stared in shock at what had been the thick double paned storm glass, now scattered across the floor, and already beginning to cover with snow. I had been sitting there next to it just moments ago.

The house was rapidly getting very cold. "Lisa, take the kids to your room and put on their coats." I instructed. "Henry, come here and help me move this table."

I took a purposeful stride toward the table, and was nearly knocked over by the next gust of wind. Staggering, I set my foot down on a sharp piece of glass, and yelped with pain.

"Henry, put your boots on first!" I shouted over the wind. It was too late for me to turn back now. I was halfway across the room and would have to walk through just as much glass to get back to where my boots were, by the door. I needed to stop the wind from damaging the house, fast, or all of our lives would be in danger. I lunged forward and caught the table, lifting one end to push it against the window. The wind caught the upended table with enough force to send me tumbling back against the opposite wall, pinned under the heavy table. I struggled for breath as I shoved the table off me and stood up. Then suddenly, Henry was there, gripping one side of the table and helping me pull it toward the window.

"Let's wait for a little lull, and then flip it up and cover the window!" I gasped, my words blown away with the wind.

The wind surged again. We clung to the table and waited for the lull. Pieces of glass still flew past us. Just then, the wind abated slightly and we heaved the table on end across the open window. I put my back to it and braced with my legs, pinning it in place.

"Hurry! Go grab a hammer and some nails!" I shouted. Henry scurried off and I held on with all my might as the next gust hit, and shook the house.

"Where is the hammer?" Henry called from the next room.

"Over on the shelf by the door. The nails are in a can next to it. Bring the biggest 16 penny nails. Hurry!" I wasn't sure how much longer I could hold on.

It seemed like an eternity while Henry was looking for the nails. I could hear the kids wailing, and then Lisa came out of the room and ran to help me hold up the table. "You should go back to the kids." I said, but my legs were quaking and I was grateful for the help.

"They're fine. I locked them in the room so they won't crawl in the glass. Tengupak is with them."

Henry ran up, and began nailing the table into the wall. Finally he said, "I think I got it. You can let go now."

Lisa stepped away, crunching through the glass with her big boots. I was almost afraid to let go, afraid the storm would enter our home again.

"You can let go." Henry said again. I took a deep breath and stepped away. I could hear the wind battering against the table, but it held strong. I let out my breath.

"Henry," I said, "You did a wonderful job. You too, Lisa! Now, can one of you bring me my boots from over by the door?" My foot was oozing blood onto the snow covered floor.

After I had cleaned up the mess, bandaged my foot, and comforted the kids, I went to bed. But I had a very hard time going to sleep. I could still hear the wind outside, and the house shuddered with each gust. I replayed the events of the evening over in my head. In an instant the evening had turned into a frightening struggle for survival. Such was life in the wilderness, I thought.

The next day, the storm was still raging, although just a bit less strong. We were nearly out of the drinking water we stored in pails next to the door.

"Henry," I said. "Can you watch the kids while I go out for water?"

"Yeah. You should tie a rope around your waist so you don't blow away." He offered helpfully.

"I think I read that in 'Little House On The Prairie,'" Lisa informed him.

"We don't have a rope that long, to reach all the way to the creek. I'm just going out for one bucket of water, I won't be gone long. It's not as windy as yesterday."

I put on my snowpants and parka, grabbed the bucket and icepick and stepped out the door. I was instantly knocked off my feet by a sharp gust of wind and the bucket went flying out of my hands. Fortunately it blew up against the side of the house, and I was able to crawl over and catch it before it flew off into oblivion. I got back up, and using the icepick to brace myself, started trudging through the deep snow for the creek. I was leaning over just inches from the ground to compensate for the wind, and when it lulled, I would almost fall down. The wind kept taking my breath away, so by the time I got to the creek, I was panting. I will be done with this soon, I thought. Then, since I have all my clothes on, I should dump the honey-bucket. It fills up fast with five of us in the house.

Pawing through the snow, I reached the ice, and chopped through about two feet to reach the water. Meanwhile, I had to hold the bucket under my foot to keep it from blowing away. I filled the bucket and started back. As soon as I stepped out of the depression I had dug in the snow, the wind hit me with full force. The water swirled in the bucket, spraying the water all over my clothes. By the time I had staggered to the house, the bucket was nearly empty. We still needed the water, so I grabbed a bucket lid, and went back out to refill it. I had better luck this time, and only lost about half of the contents. My clothes were covered with ice from the spraying water.

This will have to do, I thought. We can melt snow. As far as the honey bucket goes, that will have to wait until this wind stops! We still have another spare bucket we can use.

When the storm abated a few days later, we stepped out to survey the damage. Tar paper had torn off the roof, a piece of plywood had ripped off the shop wall, two trees were uprooted and blown across the airstrip. We repaired the buildings and removed the trees, and Harry landed the next day to pick up the kids for school. They were excited to go back to see all their friends, but I was sad to see them leave. Maybe, by the next school year I could home school them here at White Bear, I thought.

That summer was a blur of activity, finishing the new house. We coupled together 1500 feet of two inch diameter steel pipe and ran it from the hotsprings to the new house. But that pipe was weak and cracked frequently. It also didn't have enough volume to heat the house. So Harry purchased 1500 feet of four inch diameter Arctic pipe. It consisted of heavy plastic tubing wrapped in foam insulation, and covered by thick corrugated aluminum. We chartered a Wien Sky Van to fly in the twenty foot sections of pipe, then hauled them to the trail's end, and carried them the remaining way to the hotsprings. We fitted the sections together, a piece at a time, until the pipeline finally reached our house. At the house, the pipe went into several valves to regulate the pressure, then circulated through the house, and emptied back out into the creek, the same creek that the hotsprings joined a quarter mile upstream.

Harry was a brilliant engineer, and if his design did not work out, he would adjust it until it did. The system had to be vented to prevent air bubbles from creating uneven pressure, and soon we discovered that the weight of the water, traveling downhill for a quarter mile, pulled the sections of pipe apart, erupting into small geysers of steaming sulfuric water. We would hurriedly scurry into action, shutting down the flow of water into the pipe with a cap on the end of the pipe at the source. Then we would use a come-along and chain to pull the pipe back together. We staked and wired the pipeline to keep it from shifting.

During these leaks, the water would create smelly, warm, muddy puddles. Eddie and Jillian were delighted to play in them, much to my dismay. Sometimes it was just easier for me to let them play in it. At least then I knew where they were while we were working. Besides, they had so much fun, giggling and rolling in the mud, I hated to spoil it!

We were also clearing the lines for the homestead and Trade and Manufacturing site boundaries. The old lines had grown thick with brush in just a few years. In September, 1975, Harry flew Bureau of

*Jillian and Eddie playing in the mud caused by pipeline break*

Land Management's cadastral surveyor Harold Corbin flew in to survey our property. He was quiet and patient, and very good at his job. Harold would walk ahead, using his instruments to take sun sightings and the necessary readings. I followed him and tied bits of flagging on bushes where he indicated and cut brush with a hand saw. Eddie and Jillian scampered along behind, and I would have to stop often to help them across creeks or over terrain. Eddie was walking well by now, although he still had an odd gait that stayed with him for the rest of his life. Jillian was everywhere, and difficult to keep track of. Henry would follow me with the machete, whacking down brush. Harry cut some of the trees that blocked the survey line with a chainsaw. Sometimes Lisa would come along, but usually she stayed home and read or wrote poetry.

One day, while we were sitting at the kitchen table, waiting for the rain to ease up, I asked Harold Corbin to help me interpret the chemical analysis for the hotsprings water. Several years earlier, Dr. Thomas Miller had done a geothermal study on several hotsprings, and had sent me a copy of his work. I was curious about the chemical contents, and whether the water was safe for bathing.

"It has some arsenic, a lot of sulfur, and phosphorous. I definitely wouldn't drink it, but it might be OK for occasional bathing. It's hard to say. This isn't really my line of expertise." Harold had explained.

"Arsenic! Isn't that deadly poisonous? That's what Agatha Christie uses in her novels to murder people!" I said.

"I don't know that much about it." Harold had said. "You should ask someone else. I certainly wouldn't drink the water myself."

I remembered once long ago, flying to the Nyac gold mine with Harry, seeing another hotsprings steaming up out of the tundra closer to Tuluksak. Kalskag Native Sinka Williams had told me stories of the old people using that hotsprings to soak in.

"They say it's good for arthritis." He had said. "I also heard people say they drank it. But all the people who say they drank it are dead now! And they died young too."

"What about the White Bear hotsprings? Do you think I can drink it?" I had asked.

Sinka had laughed. "Depends on how long you want to live! Death is one cure for arthritis."

And then he said seriously, "Every water source is different. Even cold springs. They all have different content. Some water is not good, it has too much of certain things in it. I probably wouldn't drink that water just because you heard someone drinks water from a different hotsprings."

I had envisioned dipping a cup into the springs and making tea without building a fire. Now that didn't sound so good. Besides, the strong smell would probably overpower any tea. It would be like drinking rotten eggs. And, at 140 degrees, the hot water just wasn't hot enough to get a good brew, I was sure.

I picked up an encyclopedia and thumbed through until I reached arsenic. Before I could start reading, the sun came out, and Harold was ready to get back to work. I put in a bookmark , and set the encyclopedia to the side. I would read up on it later.

When we got home, we were all tired from a day of plodding across tundra, our feet sopping wet, and faces swollen with the bites of billions of gnats and no-see-ums. I didn't notice at first that Lisa was acting oddly. It wasn't until later, when she refused to eat dinner with us, that I was aware of her unusual behavior.

"What's wrong, Lisa?" I asked her, concerned.

"Stay away from me! You're trying to kill me! I know it! Daddy, I can prove it this time!"

It wasn't the first time Lisa had accused me in this manner. I had mentioned it several times to Harry, but he had either blown it off or made it all seem like my fault. Lisa had quite the imagination lately, and I was curious to see what "proof" she was going to show her dad.

Harry was tired, too, but looked up when she brought him the encyclopedia.

"Look, Daddy, she's planning to kill me! She's going to use arsenic!" Lisa was in quite a panic.

I just stared at her, not quite sure what she was talking about. Then I remembered the conversation from earlier in the day about arsenic. Harry had been sitting there at the table also, drinking his coffee, but Lisa had been in her room.

"No, no, sweetie, nobody was talking of poisoning you! We were talking about the hotsprings water!" Harry tried to console her.

After much cajoling and reasoning with her, Harry was able to calm Lisa down. In a way, I was glad that incident had happened while Harry was home. I hoped that now he would understand what I had been talking about when I had confided in him that Lisa had been acting differently lately. But Harry merely brushed off the incident.

So frequently now, Lisa was rushing to her dad as soon as he came home, gushing out strange accusations of things she had thought I had said or done. I couldn't understand these very personal attacks, since I had always been kind to her and didn't expect her to work at all. She honestly seemed to believe the things she said. I wondered why she wanted her dad to think these things about me. I just hoped she would outgrow these childish fantasies soon.

Harry had been busy in Bethel with the air charter business. He was now trying to shift from passengers to hauling freight. There was just getting to be too many Federal Aviation Regulations now, and the costs of maintaining compliances were draining the company. Harry had laid off most of his pilots by this time, and had been talking of selling the business to John Kupka. Harry had several rental houses in Bethel, and these were slowly bringing in money. Still, his spending exceeded his earnings, a problem he had a lifelong battle with.

Harry had decided that Henry and Lisa would not to go to school in Bethel that year. I was hoping I could teach them at home. I had set up appointments and gathered books and supplies from the school district. But the kids were not as enthusiastic as I was. Lisa was not interested in doing her homework. Henry wanted to be in Bethel where his friends were. Harry took him to town every time he left, and put him to work as ground crew at his business. He was still incredibly demeaning and cruel to the boy. Henry would come home with black eyes and bruises. And so would I. I often thought Harry liked our arrangement of me living at the homestead and himself in Bethel, so people could not see his wife's bruises. But, we had good times too, and they mostly outnumbered the bad times, so being married to Harry was tolerable. I found so much peace in the solitude of the mountains, I was able to overlook much of life's rough spots.

## Chapter Ten

"Tengupak! Come here, Tengupak!" I shouted into the darkness, but now I knew beyond the shadow of doubt that Peter Lott had killed my dog.

A few days earlier, Harry had brought Peter and Martha Lott up to White Bear for a visit. Harry had set some beaver traps out the day before Peter had come up, and the two men snowshoed out to check the traps daily. Martha and I had sat in the kitchen and sewed, and little Jillian pulled up a stool to join us. Martha doted on Jillian, as she believed the child possessed the soul of her deceased grandmother. When she came to visit, Martha would bring Jillian pretty ribbons for her hair, and teach her Yup'ik words. I handed Jillian some scraps of material and a threaded needle, and she copied what Martha and I were doing stitch for stitch, which delighted Martha.

Harry was outside working on the little Arctic Cat Kitty Kat snowmachine he had bought for Eddie. He wanted to finish, but Peter was in a hurry to check the traps that day.

"Why don't you just go by yourself?" Harry said. "I will catch up when I finish."

"OK. I want to take the snowgo." Peter had said.

"No, use the snowshoes, it's not that far. We don't have enough gas for the snowgo."

Peter had argued a bit with Harry about using the snowgo, then took off on snowshoes, calling Tengupak to follow. Eddie had chased along behind them for a few steps, then wandered back to watch his dad working on the little snowgo.

That evening, Peter had come back late, and had seemed very ill at ease. His backpack bulged, and I saw a tuft of dark hair sticking out of the flap. He hurriedly stashed the backpack under his bed, closed the door to the room, and came into the kitchen.

"I see you caught a beaver! Good! You should bring it out here to thaw, and skin it tonight." I cut some potatoes into the stew.

Peter reached out and took a huge handful of the rolls that were cooling on the countertop. "No!" He said quickly, maybe a little too anxiously. "I didn't catch anything today."

I shrugged. I had seen the fur sticking out of the backpack. If he wanted it all to himself, so be it. Harry usually gave it to him anyway. Sometimes I just couldn't understand that man.

"But I saw fur. I will skin it while Dolly is making dinner." Martha offered.

The conversation suddenly turned to Yup'ik, and became heated. I thought I heard Tengupak's name mentioned several times, but brushed off the uneasy feelings that were starting to rise within. Tengupak was the Yup'ik word for "black". Maybe they were talking about a very dark beaver. The lighting in the house was poor, and I had only gotten a fleeting glimpse of the fur.

Jillian came over, pulled up a stool, and helped me peel the carrots. My attention turned from the conversation to the very helpful mess my little daughter was creating. I didn't think about Tengupak again until much later that night when he didn't show up for his dinner.

We sat at the table that evening eating dinner, and making idle chitchat. Martha and Peter had had some sort of quarrel over the fur in his backpack, and she was silent and still upset. Peter ladled the majority of the stew onto his plate and passed the nearly empty bowl on to Henry. Henry was a growing boy and ravenous. He took a tiny spoonful and passed it on. He already knew I had hid an extra bowl of stew for him in the kitchen.

Eddie was still excited about his little snowgo.

"Go-go, snowgo, go-go," Peter teased him. Go-go had been one of Eddie's first words, his version of snowgo.

Eddie giggled and made a face.

"Don't make ugly faces." I told Eddie. "Your face could get stuck like that and you would look like that for the rest of your life."

Eddie giggled again. I got up to serve the blueberry pie I had baked. From the kitchen I could hear Peter telling a tale about herding reindeer when he was a young man.

In the early 1900's, there had been a big government project to feed the Natives and teach them a trade. Breeding stock of reindeer were imported from Russia, and Lapland reindeer herders were sent over to teach the Natives how to herd and care for the animals. Young men were recruited from the villages, and followed the herds with the Laplanders, or Sami people. The herds were grazed over nearly the entire Western part of Alaska. Unfortunately, the project was not embraced by the Native people. They did not want to travel constantly caring for the herds. It caused them to miss out on some of their traditional subsistence activities, and the young men did not want to be away from their families so long. Although the herds were usually driven along major river drainages to insure there was enough food for the herders, the Native people would slaughter too many of the reindeer, and the herds did not increase. Every time they would pass a village, the tame and easily caught animals would suffer major losses. In 1937, the government, hoping to spark more interest in the Native people to care for the herds, made it illegal for anyone other than a Native to own a reindeer herd. The Sami people, who had devoted their lives' efforts to these herds, were given the shaft, and many did not have enough money to return to their native Finland. A majority of the Sami herders settled in Alaska and married Native women.

Within just a few years, the reindeer herding industry collapsed. The Native people did not wish to commit the time and effort into the care of the animals. The animals they did not slaughter ran away to join the caribou herds, and the project was disbanded.

Dishing out the pie, I wondered how much of Peter's tale was true this time. It was hard to believe this little man had actually walked hundreds of miles herding reindeer. He had just asked Harry this morning to use the snowmachine to check the traps, a half mile down the trail!

"Most of the herding was done out of Akiak," Peter was telling Harry. "But I went all over this whole land, we camped everywhere! From Bristol Bay up to the Yukon! I still know where the old reindeer fences are, even they are falling down..."

"Where?" I asked. "Where are the closest ones to here?"

"What? Oh the fences. There was one over by Bear Creek, you know, Nyac? And one over, down there across those mountains, way over by Bogus Creek. None here. But sometimes they would come past, way down there, and go through the mountain's pass to get to the miners at Nyac. But not here, no, nothing for them to eat here. And nobody here to eat them!" He chuckled, puffed up with pride of knowing such important trivia.

"Every time the Laplanders went past the old hot water place, you know the one on the tundra, they would stop and bathe in that water! And then by the old fence, there's another. Very hot! More hot than tea kettle! Boiling! They would cook the meat in it. Just cut off a whole hind quarter and throw it in! In a few hours it would be cooked all the way done!" Peter finished his pie and looked at me. "Is there more?"

"No," I said. "I only made one pie. I didn't get many berries this year."

"Where is the really hot springs?" Harry asked. "I've only seen the other one over by Tuluksak."

Peter's chest expanded even more. He loved to feel important. "See those mountains over there? Look. See the top of that one? You go up that way, then cross those mountains, and the next ones. Go through that next little valley, and you get to the tundra edge. There's a place we call Qerrlurcaq. The fence is there and hot, hot water there. Very hot! You can cook a whole reindeer leg in it!"

"Maybe we can fly over it on the way back and you can show me." Harry said.

"It's been a long time now since it steamed. They say the earth shook once and it stopped making steam. The old people used to know where all the hot places were, but nowdays, the young ones don't remember."

"Did people drink the water?" I had asked, thinking of the chemical analysis of the White Bear hotsprings.

"Yeah, the old people said, it's good for stomachache. Makes you sleep really good."

I had laughed. Arsenic probably would make you sleep really good, forever.

"You don't believe me! It's true. The old people long ago talked about it." Peter was indignant.

I shrugged. It didn't matter. I had already decided I wasn't going to drink this hotsprings water. In the many years since we had been living here, we had never seen anyone stop by to bathe or drink it. Sure, it was a long way off the river, and not along the way to any village, but if the water was so great to drink, I was sure the hotsprings wouldn't have been totally overgrown and caved in when Harry first landed here in 1960.

I cleared the table as Peter went on to talk about "little people" he had seen on the tundra. They were well known in Yup'ik legends.

"If you are driving your snowgo fast at night, and you see a rabbit, you turn fast the other way. As soon as the lights are off him, the rabbit will turn to little person! Then you turn the light back on him, and he changes to rabbit! It's true!" Peter informed.

"Awww, bullshit, Peter! You're telling tales again!" Harry snorted.

I went in the kitchen and started the dishes. Henry crept in, and I handed him the stew I had hidden. He practically inhaled it. Poor kid, I thought, Harry doesn't feed him enough in Bethel. Maybe I can talk Harry into letting him stay here at White Bear. But Henry seemed to like going to town, and now Lisa was always bugging her dad to take her too. There wasn't much of a night life here for teenagers. Now that Lisa wasn't going to school, it was hard to keep her out of trouble during the day while he was working. So she stayed at the homestead with me, although she longed for the excitement of the city. Perhaps that explained the turmoil within her.

Back at the table, Peter had gone on to his seven-headed monsters.

"That's enough, Peter." Harry said. "We are going to bed now."

I tucked Eddie and Jillian into the makeshift cots I had set up in our room. Martha and Peter were using the kids' room while they were here. I wondered briefly again where Tengupak was, and why he hadn't come home for dinner. Then I drifted off to sleep.

Sometime in the middle of the night, I heard Eddie crying, and Peter chuckling. I jumped up, grabbed my flashlight, and went into Peter's room. Eddie was sitting on the edge of the bed, bewildered, while Peter laughed at him. Eddie had went to the bathroom during the night and, half asleep, had wandered back into his room, and crawled into his bed, not expecting to find Peter there. I soothed Eddie and took him back to the cot in our room. Just as I was turning to leave, my flashlight shone dimly on the backpack under the bed. My blood ran cold. The black fur sticking out of the pack was not beaver. I shook off the dark premonitions thinking, I'm half asleep too.

Harry woke up when I crawled back into bed. I told him about Eddie getting in the wrong bed. He chuckled.

"It's not funny. He was embarrassed!" I said softly so Eddie couldn't hear me across the room. Then I said, "Harry, I think Peter killed Tengupak. He didn't come home tonight. You know how Peter is always joking about skinning him."

Harry snorted. "Go back to sleep, Dolly. It's just your imagination."

But the next morning when Tengupak was not on the porch, Harry began to have his doubts.

"Peter, was the dog with you?" he asked.

Peter looked panicked, then answered quickly, "No, no I didn't see dog."

"I saw him go with Peter! Peter called him and he went along!" Eddie blurted out.

"Oh no, silly little boy, you didn't see. Little silly boy, come crawling in bed with me! Make me laugh! Make you cry!" Peter turned all the attention on Eddie. Eddie looked embarrassed, and about to cry again.

"Come with me, Eddie. You can help me mix the pancakes." I took his hand and led him into the kitchen.

Harry met me there. "Keep Peter distracted. I am going to follow his tracks."

I felt an uneasy chill. Now Harry had suspected the same thing I had. I just hoped we weren't right. Tengupak was more than a pet. He was a family member.

Keeping Peter distracted was easy. I just kept feeding him. Martha was still upset. I thought I knew why now.

When Harry came in the door, I immediately knew something was wrong. I took one look at his face, and sent the kids to their room.

"Get your shit together right now, Peter. You're out of here!" He demanded.

Peter turned pale and scurried for his belongings.

I noticed Harry's coat was missing. I was sure he had it on when he left this morning. Yes he had, I had helped him with the zipper when it had gotten stuck. Tears started to roll down my cheeks.

Martha got up and put her arms around me. "I'm sorry, Dolly! I wanted him to tell you."

"You don't have to go, Martha. You can stay here." I sobbed.

"No, I have to go, too. My place is with my husband. I hope we can still be friends." She said sadly.

"Henry, go heat up the airplane. Right now!" Harry ordered.

Henry jumped up and dragged the generator out to the airplane, excited about the prospect of going back to Bethel. I carried the space heater out and helped him set it up. I didn't want to see Harry harm Peter. I half wished he would. I could hear the arguing inside. Then Harry came out and motioned for me to come over.

"I finally got the truth out of him." Harry said. "At least he says that's the truth, but you know how Peter is."

"Where's Tengupak? He's dead, isn't he?" I sniffled.

"Yes." Harry said angrily. "I found him. Peter said he thought it was a bear, and shot the dog by mistake. But then that bastard skinned him! Said it was too late and there was no use wasting the pelt! I should skin that bastard!"

Harry later told me how he had covered Tengupak's carcass with his coat, and carried it to an area of deadfall, where he covered it with logs and brush. It was sad ending for a faithful companion. And it was just a preview to the problems Peter Lott would cause for us much later.

The kids were incredibly lonely without Tengupak. Eddie and Jillian stayed outside every day, calling him and looking for him tirelessly. I finally made up some story about Tengupak running off with a girl wolf to start a family.

"But we are his family! Doesn't he like us anymore?" wailed Eddie.

They were way too young for a talk about birds and bees, or to tell the truth about how their dog was killed by a family friend. So, they continued to search for Tengupak for a very long time.

## Chapter Eleven

I awoke suddenly in the middle of the night. The pale January moonlight fell softly on my bed. I sat up in bed, trying to place what had awakened me. A medley of gurgling and hissing emanated from the hot water radiators and pipes that circulated throughout the house. No, that wasn't what I had heard. I had become accustomed to those sounds.

Then it happened again. The entire house heaved and trembled. Dishes rattled and fell off the countertop with a shattering crash. The kids ran from their room and jumped into my bed.

"What is it, Mama?" Eddie asked, shaking.

"I don't know, sweetie. But it's OK, Mama's here."

Harry had gone to Bethel, taking Lisa and Henry along, a few weeks ago, intending to return the next day. But then, the temperature had plummeted to -40, and Harry did not like to fly in the extreme cold. Not only was it hard on the airplane, if anything went wrong, chances of rescue or survival were slim. So he decided to wait out the cold spell. It had stayed cold, and then got even colder. The mercury dropped to -60, and that was as low as my thermometer read. Listening to the radio, I heard reports of -80. Our large new house stayed warm with the hotsprings heating system Harry had engineered. For the very cold days, we also had a fireplace, woodstove, and a gigantic custom-made barrel woodstove.

The house still seemed warm enough, although the pipes seemed to be gurgling more than usual. Could it be the wind? The building shook sometimes in the strong wind. Maybe it was an earthquake. When Thomas Miller had been here a few years earlier, he had explained that we were on a fault line, and the gap between the earth's plates had created a fissure, from which the hotsprings had emerged. I remembered now, he did ask if I had felt any significant tremors. That's probably what it was, I thought. I snuggled back in bed between the kids, and went back to sleep.

Then next time I awoke, I was horrified to find the house cold. I could see my breath in the air. The pipes were no longer gurgling. The kids were still sound asleep, with the covers over their heads. I got dressed quickly, and feeling the radiators, found them cold to the touch. Oh no, I thought, the pipe is broken somewhere. I quickly built a fire in the woodstove and the fireplace. The mercury was still pooled in the very bottom of the thermometer.

Eddie came into the kitchen. "I'm cold, Mama."

"Come here." I said, and put on his parka and hat. "Take care of your sister. I'm going to go check the pipe. Stay inside." I started to pile on all my winter clothes.

"I wanna come along!" Jillian insisted. She had already pulled on her boots, but had them on the wrong feet.

I hesitated. Should I leave the kids in the house, or bring them along? If I had to fix anything, I would be busy and they would be in the way. They would get cold. If I left them alone in the house, they could play with their toys, but what if they decided to play with the fire, and burned our house down?

"No," I said. "You two have to stay behind. What if Tengupak comes home? You have to open the door for him. Here, play with your toys. Eddie, I want you to open the window and call Tengupak once in awhile."

I slipped out of the door quickly, feeling a bit guilty about keeping the kids' hopes up about their dog. But, I had to do what I had to do, there were no babysitters out here in the middle of the wilderness. Hearing them call out from time to time would let me know they were OK. Strapping on my snowshoes, I followed the pipeline to the hotsprings. It seemed to be fine. I did not see any of the telltale leaks that had plagued us the first year. As I arrived at the hotsprings, I was stunned to see there was no water flowing, and the narrow creek bed had completely iced over. The source of the springs had caved in and the earth had shifted to completely cover it. Several feet below, our dam was empty.

"No! Oh no!" I cried out, falling to my knees. The hotsprings that heated our home was the very lifeblood of our existence in this rugged little valley. Tears streamed down my cheeks as I clawed at the frozen jumble of rocks and soil that had suffocated the springs. Far away in the distance, I could hear the kids calling Tengupak. I sat down in the rocks and cried until I couldn't cry any more. The tears froze on my cheeks and the snot froze in my nose. What's the use, I thought. Without this hotsprings, we can't survive here. It was far too costly to fly in the stove oil we had heated the airstrip house with the first years. The trees were too sparse and far away to heat the house with wood.

Then, far away, I heard Eddie's voice again, calling out for his dog. He had not given up hope. I should not give up either. Maybe if I dug far enough down, I could get the springs flowing again, if the earth's plates hadn't completely closed during the quake.

I snowshoed back down to the house. The kids rushed to meet me at the door.

"Mama, I called and called but Tengupak never came!" Eddie said.

"You did a good job. Keep doing it. I have to go out again. I will be back soon."

I handed the kids each a frozen pilot cracker to gnaw on, put a few more logs on the fire, and went out again. This time I took a pick and some shovels with me. I went back up to the hotsprings, each breath a painful sear to my lungs. Frost had built so heavily on my eyelashes, I dared not blink or my eyelids nearly froze shut. I went to work furiously, shoveling, picking, and dragging rocks from the source of the hotsprings. After several hours of fruitless labor, I went back to the house to get a sled and pry bar. I had dug a good sized hole, but kept hitting a large rock. I had been unable to move it, so I was trying to dig around it.

Jillian met me at the door. "I fed the fire! Mama, look! It's going good now!"

I charged into the house, afraid to see what my two year old child had done. The house was still warm, and the fire burned peacefully within the stove. I let out a sigh of relief. Every bone ached, and I just wanted to sit down.

"Remember what I told you about playing with the fire?" I lectured.

Jillian looked up at me. "You said not to. But I thought you went away forever like Tengupak. I was cold."

"You did good. Just be very, very careful! Don't let the fire get out of the stove, OK?"

I dragged myself out the door, taking along a sled and the pry bar. I went back to work, shoveling the frozen clods and rocks into the sled, and then dragging it out of the hole to dump it. The hole was already at least ten feet deep. Completely engrossed in the work I was doing, I was not even aware it was getting dark. I stared at the deep pit. Not even a tiny trickle seeped out. It felt hopeless. I started snowshoeing back toward the house, crestfallen.

It was dark inside the house, and the kids had already crawled back into bed, still in their parkas and hats. The house was starting to cool rapidly. I started the fire in the huge barrel stove, and dragged a few more logs inside to dry out. They were heavily frosted and would take days to thaw out and dry off enough to burn. I clumsily peeled off my frozen clothes. Sweat had soaked through my parka and it crackled with ice as I removed it and hung it over the stove to dry. I had not felt cold while I was working because I had been generating a lot of effort, but now that I was not moving, I started to shiver uncontrollably. Finally the tea kettle started to hiss and I drank some warm water.

I turned the radio on for the seven o'clock check-in time with Harry in Bethel. I had missed this morning's check-in, but the radio signals had been weak for the past few days, so Harry probably wouldn't have heard me anyway. I sure hoped he would hear me tonight. If I couldn't get the hotsprings flowing again, we wouldn't be able to survive this cold weather. Harry had not cut enough firewood to heat the house, and the wood we had was damp and would take days to dry.

I opened a can of beef stew and put it on the stove, then went to wake the kids. They hugged me and cried. I felt terrible to leave them alone all day, but what were my options? We ate the stew, and listened to the radio squealing. I read the kids a story, and tucked them back in bed. The radio signals were weak again tonight, and I didn't hear Harry call. Thinking about it, I realized, even if he did call, he couldn't do anything to help anyway. It was too cold for him to fly. I went to bed, totally exhausted and bone-weary.

I slept poorly, getting up every few hours when the house started cooling off to add more logs to the fire. I was alarmed at how fast I was using the firewood. At this rate, I was using it faster than it could dry. I quickly made breakfast while I listened for Harry to call in the morning. Again, nothing but squelchy squeals. I fed the kids and started putting on my clothes, relieved to find that they had dried during the night.

"I'm coming along!" yelled Jillian.

"Me too!" Eddie chimed in.

"No," I said sternly. "I'm going to be very busy, and I can't take you along."

The kids whimpered and sulked, and I left hurriedly. It was still dark, so I took a flashlight along, a long rope, and another pry bar. That big rock seemed to have no end. I dug around it as far as I could, but could not feel the bottom. It was still brutally cold, and my chest hurt from breathing the cold air. But our very survival depended on this heat source, so I could not stop. Setting the flashlight down on the edge of the tunnel, I started attacking the pile of rubble. If I could get under this big rock, I might find a crack beneath to coax the hot-springs water through. Now the hole was about fifteen feet deep, and I had slanted it sufficiently to crawl in and out, pulling the sled. The deeper I dug, the more difficult it became. I would fill the sled, tie a long rope to it, and crawl out of the hole. Once I was outside, I had better footing, and I pulled the sled up by the rope. Often it would tip over and I would have to crawl back in and start over. Now I wasn't even sure which direction I needed to be digging. The huge rock seemed to have no end. My body ached, and I felt as if I was moving in slow motion.

After a few hours, I went back to check on the kids. I was aghast to find the house cold, and the kids huddled shivering in their beds. The blazing fire that I had left had smoldered and gone out. I tried several times to reignite it, but it sputtered and died. I poured a splash of snowmachine gas on the logs. It flared and went out. The wood was just too damp. We no longer had any stove oil left in the airstrip house. I felt a deep fear building inside. It hadn't occurred to me until now how much our lives were in danger.

I quickly bundled the kids in several layers of heavy clothes, until their little arms nearly stuck straight out. They began racing around the house bouncing off the walls. By now the house was nearly as cold as it was outside. I decided to take the kids along this time, for one last-ditch effort to clear the hotsprings. I didn't really have a "plan B", but perhaps Harry would call tonight and he would know what to do. Too bad Harry wasn't here, I thought, he always knows what to do.

I plodded back up to the hotsprings, the kids scampering across the top of the snow lightly, stopping often to make snow angels or bunny tracks. When I got to the big hole, the kids were curious and wanted to crawl down inside.

"What's in there?" Jillian asked.

"Is that where the dragon lives?" Eddie wanted to know.

"Go play over by the little bushes. Make Mama some bunny tracks." I started down in the hole pulling the sled.

"Give us a sled ride, Mama. We wanna see the dragon!" Eddie and Jillian both jumped into the sled.

"No!" I said. "I have work to do, or we will freeze to death. Go play!"

"But I wanna help!" Jillian howled.

"OK. You can help. Here. Take the end of this rope. When I pull on it two times, like this, I want you to pull as hard as you can, OK?"

The kids were excited about the chore. I shuffled down into the hole and went back to work. Things took twice as long with the kids here to watch. Fortunately they were good at entertaining themselves. I dug, and picked and pried a few more chunks of rock and dirt loose, and turned to pull the sled up the bank.

"Mama! Mama!" The kids were screaming. What could be wrong?! I dropped the sled and rushed out.

"What's wrong? Stop yelling if there's nothing wrong."

"Mama! Mama, I thought the dragon got you! Look!" Eddie shouted, pointing.

"Don't be silly...." I turned to look where he was pointing, and very distinctly, steam was beginning to rise from the hole! I whooped and gave the kids a bear hug. Crawling back into the hole, I found hot water beginning to seep out a small crack in the giant boulder. With the pick and pry bar, I enlarged the crack, and broke a big chunk off the rock. Water began to ooze out faster now. I began to feel hopeful. But it didn't seem to matter now how big I made the fissure, the flow of hotsprings water stayed relatively small. I started digging the bank of the tunnel down so the water would flow back into its old creek bed. Turning, I nearly bumped into Jillian.

"I told you to stay out of the hole!" I snapped. She scurried back out. I finished pulling the dirt back, and watched with delight as the hotspring water slowly began trickling down the creek bed. The kids immediately wanted to play in it. As I pulled them back, I realized my feet were wet. I only had a short time before they would freeze solid.

"Last one back to the house is a rotten egg!" I shouted, and set the pace back home. The kids, happy to be moving somewhere again, ran along, shouting and pushing each other. When we got back to the house, it was starting to get dark. My feet were beginning to tingle. I struck a match, and lighting the kerosene lantern, replaced the glass chimney. It instantly shattered. Silly me, I thought, of course it would. The house is still cold.

I turned on the flashlight and quickly found my spare set of boot liners and extra socks. After changing into the dry socks, I attempted to start the fire in the woodstove again, with the same results. We ate frozen Spam and pilot crackers, as we listened for the radio call from Harry. We could hear him very faintly, but neither Harry nor I could understand what the other was saying. I put the kids to bed dressed as they were in all their warm clothing. I heaped blankets on them and slipped out.

Walking back to the hotsprings in the moonlight felt oddly surreal. The moon shone brightly off the snow, and some spots reflected as brightly as a flashlight. Each breath I exhaled froze instantly, and the ice crystals made a rattling sound as they floated off into the frigid night air. The sounds I made snowshoeing across the snow were amplified. It was brutally cold, but I was ever so grateful the wind was calm.

Back at the source of the springs, I was thrilled to see the water creeping down into the little dam, spilling over and continuing down the creek. But the pipe was cold. On closer inspection, I found it to be frozen solid.

I went back to the house and got a hose, funnel, wrenches to disassemble the pipe sections, and the assortment of tools I might need. Throughout the night I worked feverishly trying to melt the ice in the pipes, taking them apart, thawing them, and putting them back together. A few sections were broken from the expanding ice, and these I had to replace. Rolling the heavy sections of pipe uphill was a monstrous task, but it was vital to our survival. By now my clothes were soaked again and I had to keep moving or I would freeze to death. I had tried once to start the snowmachine to help pull the pipe, but it was so cold it would not start. I was beyond tired, but I had to continue, or my children would freeze and die.

The sun came up over the mountains, but I was scarcely aware of it. I had managed to replace, thaw and repair most of the arctic pipe, and had just begun on the house radiators. At least I was near the kids now. I had missed the radio check-in time, but it scarcely seemed to matter anymore. Harry could not help me. I would have to finish soon, before I dropped from exhaustion. I sawed off the copper radiators with a hacksaw, and funneled hot water into them. The propane torch would not ignite in the cold, so rather than soldering them back together, I clamped short sections of hose over the cuts.

The kids awoke, and I fed them again, the last few frozen pilot crackers. I finally finished the bedroom radiator and decided the rest of the house could wait. We closed the door and turned the radiator valve all the way up. The room gradually became warmer. I dragged some firewood in next to the radiator, took off my soaked clothes, and crawled into bed.

When I awoke much later, the room was toasty warm, and the kids had snuggled into bed next to me. I was rewarded by the soft gurgles of the pipe, and fell soundly back to sleep, ever grateful for the miracle of the hotsprings which had saved our lives.

The next several days were busy with repairs and thawing the rest of the radiators in the house. Leaks sprung in unexpected places, and needed immediate attention before they became bigger. But at least the house was warm, and the firewood had thawed and dried enough to burn, so I was able to cook and dry my clothes. I was also able to spend more time with the kids, reading and playing games.

When Harry did finally make it home, he brought the kids a dog. She was a fluffy yellow dog, a golden retriever mix, that he had seen wandering the streets of Bethel as a stray. It was during the time the City of Bethel was strictly enforcing the leash law, due to a rabies outbreak. The police department shot all stray dogs on sight. Hot Dog was a loyal and obedient dog, and very gentle with the kids. After she arrived, the kids called for Tengupak less and less.

In early summer, we ordered 100 baby Leghorn hens. When Harry brought them up from Bethel, the kids were thrilled. Jillian could hardly set them down. They lived in a big box in the house until we finished converting one of the sheds to a chicken coop, complete with hotsprings radiator heating. During the time they were in the house, the peeping drowned out all conversations, so most of us were glad when they moved to more permanent quarters. Not the kids! They spent most of the day playing in the chicken coop.

That summer, Harold Corbin returned to survey our granted Right Of Way for our pipeline. I liked Harold. He was a quiet and mild-mannered man, and incredibly honest. Before he left, Harold approached me with a map in his hand.

"I don't know if I am supposed to let you see this or not," Harold said. "But I want you to look at this. Chalista Native Corporation filed for a site close to you. Supposed to be some sort of cemetery site."

He opened the map and pointed to the area. "It's right here. That's almost two miles from you, on the top of that mountain over there."

It was right where Harry had landed the ski plane when he first came to the hotsprings. "Why? Is there anything up there? I didn't see anything up there." I was confused.

Harold shrugged. "No, there's nothing there. And nothing Native anywhere down here either. I've done alot of surveys, and if there is a Native area, there are always signs, you know like old sod houses and rock graves, things like that."

"Then why did they put a claim up on the top of a mountain, in the middle of nowhere?" I asked.

"Probably trying to capitalize on the lodge you guys are building. That corporation has staked claims on every mine or homestead in the region. Trying to drive the white people out, that's my guess." Harold swatted a mosquito.

"Well, that's a long way from us. We aren't landing up there anymore, so it really shouldn't affect us." I tried to convince myself.

"Yeah, I know. Just proves they don't know this area well, or where the hotsprings are. Be careful,though." Harold started to pack his surveying gadgets.

"Thanks, Harold, for telling us. I don't think we will have a problem. None of our Native friends have mentioned anything." I handed the map back to him.

"You can keep that. Just thought you guys should know. You're good people, and you're doing a good thing, taking care of this hotsprings." Harold had been impressed with the story of last winter's ordeal.

Little did I know how right Harold's premonitions were, and how I would later fight to save my home from the greedy corporation.

I had little time to ponder the information Harold had given me. We were now busy dismantling the swimming pool building and pool itself, moving it to the new house, and rebuilding it there. The kids had dubbed the airstrip area "Down Below" and the new house "Up Above" due to the steep rising terrain between the places. Amongst the frenzy of building, Eddie and Jillian kept themselves entertained with makeshift teeter-totters and swings, and rocks and sticks. I was constantly on the run, fetching things for the men, and tending to the kids' bumps and scrapes. Henry, when he would come along with Harry, was a great help with the kids, but I did not trust Lisa near them.

Lisa had been acting even odder than usual. It was difficult for me to explain. When Harry was around, she was sweet and helpful, and would jump up to clear the table or help me in the kitchen. Those times, she seemed like the perfect daughter. But, during Harry's long absences, she would sometimes display violent and bizarre behavior. She would rush at me, shrieking, slapping at my face and tearing at my clothes. Sometimes she would hide under the house, steal food, and threaten to kill me or herself. I had been shocked beyond reason once to walk in on her touching Eddie inappropriately. I kept the kids away from her, and tried desperately to tell Harry that there was something wrong, and Lisa needed help. But when Harry came home, she was full of stories of how "mean" I had been to her, citing incidents that only occurred in her twisted mind. Harry would scold me, and sometimes strike me, for not taking better care of his daughter. I started to doubt my own sanity.

To add to the turmoil, in October of 1976, Harry's rental apartments and West Air office in Bethel burned to the ground. One woman died in the fire. Most of the business records and aircraft logbooks were destroyed. In the following months, Harry struggled to pick up the pieces of the business he had worked so hard to build.

*White Bear hotsprings in the winter.*

## Chapter Twelve

I opened my eyes, slowly becoming aware of my surroundings. My head throbbed. I felt warm sticky wetness on my face and in my hair. Everything looked distorted and blurry. I realized I was lying on my side on the floor. My whole body ached. I stirred, trying to sit up, but there was a weight against my chest. I reached out to touch it, and felt a small child's body against mine. My eyes slowly came into focus, and I became aware of Eddie, snuggled close to my chest, and Jillian, sitting on the floor, holding my head in her lap. When I stirred, they were suddenly there, huge brown eyes and tear-streaked, bloody little faces looking into my eyes. I tried to take in if they were OK.

"Mama! Mama, you're alive!" Cried Eddie, hugging me tightly.

"We thought you died." Jillian touched my face gently.

"We thought Daddy killed you!" Eddie whimpered.

"Where is Daddy?" I asked hoarsely.

"Gone. Daddy and Lisa went away. I heard the plane take off." Eddie shuddered. "I hope he doesn't come back. Her too."

I tried hard to remember the events preceding the attack. Yes, now it was coming back. Henry had stayed in Bethel. Lisa had been in her room writing poetry. The kids played in the corner. I had resolved to tell Harry about Lisa, about her odd behavior, about her molesting Eddie and slapping me. Not only did Harry not believe me, he became violently defensive of Lisa.

"You're full of shit, Dolly!" He had bellowed. "Take care of your own little brats!" He had shoved Eddie so forcefully, so that he fell to the floor with a moan. Jillian rushed to help Eddie up, and he kicked her, hard. She crumpled to the floor next to Eddie. I was shocked.

Eddie was handicapped. Jillian was a thin, fragile skeleton of a child. He swung his foot back to kick them again. I grabbed the heavy frying pan and charged forward, bringing it down on Harry's shoulders. He had turned, ripped it from my hands, and started hitting me. I stumbled backward and fell, striking my head against the kitchen table. As the world turned black, I was faintly aware of him shouting and kicking at my body. My last thought was of the kids.

"Run!" I thought I had whispered before I passed out.

Had they ran and hid? Had Harry beat them too? On closer inspection, I saw that most of the blood on the kids was mine. My blood darkened the floor, and nearby, a shattered glass from the table glinted in the dimming light.

"How long was I down here?" I asked.

"Two days." Jillian said.

"Don't be silly! It hasn't even been a day yet! It's not another day until it gets light again." Eddie informed Jillian.

It must have seemed an eternity to the children, thinking their mother was dead. I slowly sat up, gasping in pain. Jillian had disappeared, and now she tiptoed around the corner, carrying a glass of water very carefully, so as not to spill it.

She held it up to my lips. "Drink it." She ordered.

I felt nauseated. I didn't want to drink anything. My teeth felt loose and my mouth tasted like blood. I took the glass from her and pretended to take a little sip. Jillian disappeared again. The broken glass twinkled.

"I have to clean that up." I mumbled to Eddie. "Go bring me the broom and dustpan."

He got up clumsily, and shuffled out of the room. Jillian came back in and handed me something. "I saved it for you. For when you're sad."

I looked down at the chocolate bar in my hand. When Harry brought groceries, sometimes he would splurge and buy candy for the kids. Jillian would politely take hers, and then hide it to give me later. She had secret stashes somewhere, and whenever she thought I needed a pick-me-up, she would bring me a dusty old chocolate bar.

"Can I start the fire? Can I make dinner?" Jillian begged.

"You can make soup." I said. Jillian scampered off.

"Don't step in the glass!" I called after her. I could hear her crunching the old newspaper and setting the firewood on top of it in the woodstove. Eddie came in with the broom and dustpan. I pushed myself to my knees and crawled over to the glass. Eddie tagged along, wanting to help.

"Be careful!" I warned him. "Here. Take this dustpan and empty it into the trash bucket. Don't spill it!"

He carried it carefully away. I could hear Jillian putting the pan on the stove, and then she came over, handing me the can opener and the can of soup.

"Can you open it for me?" She asked, setting it on the floor in front of me.

I took the can opener, opened the can and handed it back. "Remember, you need to put one can of water in the pot, too."

"I know." Jillian left again. She helped me in the kitchen a lot, and I had let her make soup before.

I got to my feet gingerly, made my way to the bathroom, and washed my face. As I stood there, dabbing at the dried blood, I wondered, how had things gotten to this? Harry had always been impatient, and he had treated Henry badly from the start. Many times I had thought of leaving him in the beginning, but had always stayed for Henry's sake. And then Eddie and Jillian were born. Things had gotten better for awhile and then Harry had started to lose his temper again. Several times I had packed my bags to leave, and each time Harry would talk me out of it. He would be attentive and kind and beg for forgiveness. I would cave in and stay. I had no money, and no place to go. I loved the homestead, and when I was here and Harry was in Bethel, life was perfect. I had been able to tolerate Tara's rudeness, but Lisa's behavior was different and very disturbing. There was something so completely different about her lately, it frightened me to be in the same room as her. The kids were frightened too. Eddie had gone from being a bubbly, happy, curious boy to becoming clingy and easily upset. Jillian had gone from an energetic, giggling girl to a shy, feral creature who spent all her time outdoors.

Maybe Lisa would have an episode while she was with Harry, and he would finally see and understand, and get her some help. As far as my children, only time could heal their wounds.

"It's ready!" Shouted Jillian from the kitchen.

I walked in and reached over to help her pour the soup.

"No! I wanna do it myself! You sit down." She was far too old for her years.

Eddie sat down, and she poured his dish, and mine, and a little in hers. She ate almost nothing, and at times I couldn't understand how she survived. Food was always scarce in those years. Harry would bring food when he came, but not much. With six mouths to feed there was hardly ever enough to go around. Henry and Lisa were growing children, and always hungry. The food Harry brought would last about six days, then he and Henry would leave for Bethel again. It was usually several weeks before he would come back. Between those times, I fed the family whatever rabbits I could catch in my snares, berries I picked, and what I could grow in my garden. That was supplemented with eggs and an occasional chicken. Eddie, aged four, was learning to hunt, and had already shot a few grouse with his little .22 rifle.

I tried to keep the shelves stocked with canned food, whenever there was extra to preserve. I filled quart jars with produce from my garden, berries, or meat, and boiled them in my large canning kettle until they were preserved. I remembered my first year living here at White Bear, how I had picked blueberries, and canned them, one jar at a time, in an old one gallon paint pail on the barrel stove. Then I had gotten the canning kettle, and my prized possession, a wood cookstove with an oven. I could bake rolls and bread and pies and cakes. Looking at the rows of canned goods on the shelf was like gold to me. It made me feel warm and secure when the shelves were full. We usually had a small supply of the staples; rice, beans, flour, sugar, Spam, and canned soups. But this year, with our diminishing funds, our supplies had dwindled, and the shelves were nearly bare.

Eddie and I slurped our soup, and Jillian took what was left in the pot out and set it on the porch for Hot Dog.

"It's hot!" I heard her warning the dog. Hot Dog was smart, and would sit, waiting for the pot to cool before she drank the soup. We had run out of dog food, but Hot Dog seemed to be faring on what animals she could catch.

The next few months were filled with the daily chores of existence on the homestead. There was water to fetch, chickens to care for, the occasional pipeline or radiator leak, hotsprings care, sticks to gather for firewood, snares to check, snow to shovel. It filled up most of the day, and the kids worked hard alongside me, never complaining. After finishing their chores, they would play outside until dark. In the evenings we would play card games or read. Eddie and Jillian were already reading well on their own. The radio was silent, and we heard nothing from Harry. By now the marine band radio was starting to fade away as a household communication, being replaced in the villages with telephones. Occasionally we would hear crab fishermen far, far away, if the radio signals were just right.

Slowly the nightmares waned, and the kids ran to me less often in the night. I wondered if Harry would ever come back, and secretly hoped he wouldn't. Life was less complicated this way. But the peace was not to last.

Harry's plane roared overhead, turned sharply, and I could hear it landing. I dragged the old MotoSki snowmachine out of the shed, hitched the iron sled to it, and took off for the airport, pushing down the turmoil within. We did need groceries, I would love to read mail from friends and relatives, but I was enjoying the peace.

When I got to the airport, Harry was tying the plane down. Looking around, I was disappointed not to see Henry, but relieved not to see Lisa. Harry was acting like nothing out of the ordinary had ever happened. I started unloading the airplane. One small sack of mail, two bags of dirty clothes for me to wash, and the rest of the plane was filled with jerry cans of diesel. Where was the food? Where was Henry? Where was Lisa? I didn't know which to ask first.

Harry finished tying the wings of the plane, and now he was putting the thick quilted engine blanket over the cowling. I bent to help him fasten the straps. He hadn't really said anything until now.

"That damn Henry! The brat don't want to do any work at all! He keeps running off at the mouth, hiding out all day with his punk friends! Any time there's any work to do, he hides! I've about had it with him!" Harry ranted. "Now Lisa's running some sort of scam. She got in all sorts of trouble, and the social services sent her away to Anchorage for tests. She's pretending to be nuts so she can get money from the State. Damn kids! I've had it with them!"

That answered two questions. I hoped Henry was OK, and Lisa was getting the help she needed. I unloaded the cans of fuel and stacked them in the shed. One more look through the plane confirmed that it was empty.

"Did you bring food?" I asked carefully.

Harry exploded. "Geez, Dolly! I brought lots of food the last time! You can't have eaten that all up already!"

The last time he came, he had brought one box of groceries, and it was gone by the time he left. I wasn't about to argue with him. All I could think of right now was Henry and Lisa. I was sure that's all he could think about too. Of course he would be upset, dealing with two unruly teenagers alone. Besides, his business was taking a turn for the worse, and money was scarce.

"Sorry!" I said quickly. "We'll make do."

Harry only stayed for a few days and left again. He made no mention of the last time he was here, but we were all on edge around him. The kids were quiet as mice, but he would still find fault with them.

I was delighted when the mail came up this time, to see that I had an information packet from a homeschooling program in Juneau. I had written to them two months ago.

Eddie would be five this summer, and should be starting kindergarten in the fall. He was a bright boy, full of creative ideas. He was a dreamer, with grand schemes. Often I would hear him hammering some scraps of wood together, making something; a space shuttle, a boat, an airplane. Jillian would always test the contraptions with enthusiasm while he shouted orders from safety. That summer, Eddie built a new airplane. The previous two had not "flown" right. As I was canning the batch of blueberries we had picked, I could hear the kids outside working on it. They were making quite a racket. With shock, I realized the noises were coming from the roof of the house! I ran outside, shouting at them to get off the roof. It was too late.

"Pull the vroom-zoom bar!" Eddie instructed Jillian as he shoved the contraption off the roof.

"Weeeeeeee!" Jillian shrieked with glee. I stood horrified as my daughter plummeted to the ground in the makeshift flying craft, a lopsided combination of old boards, rusty nails, and burlap bags. Seconds later, the air filled with a thundering crash, splintering wood, and Jillian, wailing, "No! It's broken!"

Eddie scuttled down the ladder and we both ran to the wreckage. Jillian stood among the carnage, unhurt, holding the broken wing.

"It's broke! It won't fly like this now!" she wailed.

"Stupid GIRL!" Eddie shouted. "You forgot to pull the vroom-zoom bar!"

"I did! It didn't work! "Jillian shouted back, and then they were fighting.

"Knock it off, you two!" I bellowed. "No more playing on the roof! Go do your chores now! Pick up this mess!" I went back to canning berries, tremendously relieved that nobody was hurt.

Harry came home several more times that summer, but did not stay long. The lodge business was dwindling, and Harry was losing interest in it. It was too expensive to fly people up from Bethel, feed them, and have to accommodate their schedules when the weather was too bad to fly. It was typical to only get one flyable day every two weeks here in the canyon. That was not suitable for most people's schedules. They had to be back at work, or to catch a flight, and in the earlier years, Harry had taken a lot of risks to cater to their needs. And there were always the free-loaders.

Peter Lott had bragged to everyone that came into his store that we flew him up to the homestead and fed him for free. Soon every Tuluksaker wanted the same treatment. It was just too much effort and expense to take on for nothing in return. Not only did Harry have to leave behind supplies to bring people in the airplane, he also was at their mercy as far as returning. When they wanted to go home, they wanted to go NOW, and often the weather was too bad to travel. We compromised by mainly hiring Native people whenever we needed an extra hand.

Harry had again tested the swimming pool in the new site, a quarter mile from the hotsprings. The weight and heat of the pool liner had sunk it into the permafrost, where it collapsed in a lopsided pile, the contents gushing out and nearly eroding the foundation of the house. We had gotten to swim in it a little less than a month. Now we used the building for storage.

Wild game populations were declining, and I could scarcely find enough to keep my family fed. Unlike the people who lived in villages along the rivers, we did not have fish to eat. The shelves were nearly bare, and I began to get concerned. We already rationed food to one small meal a day. The garden was poor that year, and berries were scattered and hard to find.

One day, scouring the tundra for berries, I was shocked to see Jillian reach down and pick up a bug and pop it in her mouth.

"No! Ugh! Blah! Spit it out!" I ordered.

But Jillian had already swallowed it. "Why? It's good." She asked.

I hesitated. "Because we don't eat bugs."

"Why not? Rose-fly eats bugs." Rose-fly was a robin that Jillian had befriended. It lived in a little thicket of cottonwood trees near the house, and woke us up in the mornings with exuberant singing.

"Rose-fly is a bird. Birds eat bugs. People don't." I tried to reason.

"I wanna be a bird. Maybe, if I eat bugs like Rose-fly, I'll be a bird." Jillian scanned the tundra for more bugs. Even they were scarce.

"But I don't want you to be a bird. I'd miss you!"

"Oh. Well, you can be a bird, too." She slapped a mosquito and handed it to me. "Here, eat this one."

"No. I don't want it. Stop eating bugs, OK? How long have you been doing this?"

"Since I was two." Jillian made that sound old. "Sometimes I get hungry. They taste OK."

I really needed to catch something in my snares. Maybe Harry would come home and shoot a moose for us this fall. The moose would come past sometimes in the fall, and Harry shot one almost every year. But Harry was in town more than usual now. He was trying to keep the charter business going, but running out of money. He had already missed too many payments and lost several planes. So I tried not to complain when he came home without food.

*Eddie and Jillian gathering food and bugs on the tundra*

## Chapter Thirteen

"Moose! Moose!" shouted Jillian as she charged in the door. "I saw a moose!"

I jumped out of bed. The sun was barely creeping over the mountaintops that early September morning. I heard Eddie leap out of his bed and run to the gun rack. I met him there and handed him the new 30-30 rifle Harry had gotten him for his birthday. I also grabbed the old 30-06, and a few boxes of ammunition for both guns. I shut Hot Dog in the house. We followed Jillian out the door.

"Where?" I asked, wide awake now.

"It was right up there, standing by that bush." Jillian pointed.

"Which way was it going?" I asked.

"That way." She pointed down the canyon.

"I'm going to shoot a moose!" yelled Eddie. He was barely tall enough to keep the gun off the floor, but he had proved to be an excellent shot with his .22, so he was excited to shoot his first moose.

"It's gone," I said, "but we can probably find it if we walk down the trail towards Down Below. Let's go this way."

I led the way down the trail. We really needed meat, I thought. We were down to our last few meals of rice. The moose would probably stop at the beaver pond a half mile away and eat the tender new willows from around it.

Darn! In my haste, I had forgotten my glasses. Too late now to go back for them. It would most likely be a close shot anyway, and I wouldn't need them.

"Shhhh!" I reminded the kids as we neared the beaver pond. "Be very, very quiet!"

We crept along the narrow path. Suddenly Jillian was tugging at my coat.

"Mama! Look! There!" She whispered, pointing.

The moose was crossing the creek, heading up the hill into the brush. Eddie raised his gun. I lifted my gun, and through the sights I saw the blurry dark brown shape, with lighter brown antlers on the head. Good, it's a bull, I thought. Eddie and I shot at the same time, the recoil nearly knocking his five year old body over, both shots echoing into one. The moose staggered, went to its knees, lurched up, and disappeared into the brush.

"Oh no!" Eddie wailed. "I thought I hit it! I aimed real careful."

"You did hit it, son," I said. "Good job! It just went into the brush to die. We have to go find it."

"I got a moose! I got a moose! I told you I was gonna shoot a moose!" Eddie shouted.

"Shhhhhh! We don't have it yet! We have to find it." But I was just as excited as my son. Fresh meat! It would be a feast! There would be enough meat for many, many months.

I started down towards the dam, startled to see Jillian already well ahead of us, near the edge of the creek.

"Wait!" I shushed, but she was already too far ahead to hear me.

I reached the creek, Eddie at my heels. We walked upstream a short way until we found the narrowest place.

"Set your gun here," I told Eddie, setting mine against a bush. I picked him up and swung him across the creek. Then I handed him his gun, and jumped across with mine. Jillian must have already crossed somewhere. She was as swift and fleeting as a gazelle.

"Jillian!" I whispered loudly, but there was no answer. I was afraid to raise my voice in case the moose was still alive, afraid I would scare it away and we would go hungry. Walking back downstream through the brush, we found where the moose had crossed. We had definitely hit it. There was blood among the trampled grass. We followed the sign up into the thick alders. This is a bad idea, I thought , following a wounded animal into the brush with two small children. Moose could be very aggressive and every bit as dangerous as bears.

I came upon the moose suddenly in the brush. It was lying on its side, dying, eyes glazing over already as its legs kicked convulsively.

Horrified, I realized the light brown "antlers" were the huge ears, and it was a cow moose. At her belly was a tiny calf, shivering in fear, reaching out to suckle from its mother's belly as her legs scissored in death throes. It was far too small to survive the winter. It must have been born late.

"Bambi!" The brush parted and Jillian ran out, straight for the baby moose, ducking the deadly cloven hooves of the mother. She threw her arms around the calf, and it made no move to escape.

"NO! Jillian! Get away from it! Get back! NOW!" I shouted.

My voice startled the cow moose, and she lunged halfway to her feet, throwing Jillian and the calf backwards into the brush. Eddie stumbled backwards and fell. I lifted my gun quickly and shot at the moose's head. Eddie was instantly on his feet and firing toward the moose. One of the shots hit it, and it went down solidly, and stayed down.

"I got it! I got it!" shouted Eddie.

"Good job, Eddie! You shot your first moose! Stay here and watch it. If it moves again, shoot it in the ear, OK?" I crawled through the tangled alders looking for Jillian. I found her sitting in a little hollow, holding the baby moose in her thin little arms as it nestled against her like a big dog. Two pairs of big brown eyes stared up at me.

"Mama, it's Bambi! Look. He's nice. His mama's dead so we have to take care of him now."

A hundred thoughts rushed into my head all at once. The moose was young, and Jillian was excellent with animals. It would be an easy animal to raise, and keep the kids entertained. But it would grow fast, and in a few months, would be full grown. A thousand pound beast around my small children could be deadly.

"Jillian." I said quietly, so as not to spook either of them. "Go find Eddie. Let's see what he thinks we should name it."

"His name is Bambi." But she got up, kissed the moose on the forehead, whispered softly to it, and disappeared through the brush to find her brother.

Bambi. We had read that book the night before. The baby moose stood up and started walking after Jillian. Oh, this is horrible! But I have to do this, we cannot raise a moose, I thought, and it is too young to live on its own. Before I could change my mind, I raised the gun and shot it.

Jillian ran to it, screaming as if she herself had been shot. Eddie stumbled through the brush, dropped his gun, and ran to the little moose.

"Bambi!" He cried, and tears ran down his cheeks.

I realized my face was wet with tears. I turned aside and threw up. Suddenly the promise of food did not seem worth the horror of the death of the baby moose or its mama. I would have never intentionally shot a female moose. I cursed myself for not grabbing my glasses. But moose were few and far between. We may have died of starvation if we didn't shoot it.

"That's enough. We need to cut up these moose. You two need to help!" I walked off toward the cow moose, pulling the long hunting knife out of my coat pocket.

I had never killed, or butchered a moose alone before. Usually, Harry would shoot it, and we would cut it up together. Of course I knew how, it was just harder to do alone. I wrestled with the big heavy haunch, trying to hold it with my leg as I sawed at it with the dull knife. Then the weight lifted, and I looked up. Eddie had pulled on the moose leg so it was easier for me to cut.

"Thank you! Pull harder! That's good right there." I hacked off the hind quarter. Jillian crawled out of the bushes, and they started dragging it away together, arguing amongst themselves who could pull more.

"Just down to the creek, and come right back!" I started on the front quarter. I doubted the kids would make it far, but at least the task kept them busy. The meat probably weighed twice as much as the both of them. I busied myself in the task of cutting the meat. Now it was easier. It was no longer a living animal, it was meat, vital, essential sustenance to keep my family alive. I sliced open the belly, pulling the entrails out, carefully extracting the heart, kidneys, and liver. I was aware of a presence, and looked up. Eddie and Jillian watched with fascination a few feet away.

"What's that?" Eddie asked, pointing to the liver.

"It's the liver. Remember how you take it out when you clean a rabbit? Every animal has a liver. Remember last fall when Daddy got the big moose, and we had liver and onions? We can have it for breakfast tomorrow morning." I answered. "How far did you guys get?"

"Down to the creek." Eddie said proudly. "Does the little one have a liver?"

"Yes it does. Here, help me roll this over so I can get the other side." I strained to roll the moose over so I could cut off the other quarters. The kids rushed to help. With much effort we were able to flop it over.

"I wanna see the baby liver!" Eddie begged.

I hesitated. I wanted to finish cutting up this one. I didn't want to see the small moose quite yet. But, now it was meat, and it would be easier for the kids to carry. Why not satisfy their curiosity and keep them busy? I could finish cutting this one while they were carrying the little moose. I went to it, cutting it up quickly, amazed at the resilience and forgiveness of my small children. They exclaimed over the tiny liver and went right to work carting off the small quarters, racing to see who would get to the creek first. I told Jillian to go to the house and grab a hatchet and let the dog out, after she dropped her quarter off at the creek. By the time she had gotten back, Eddie and I had finished hacking the other quarters off the big moose. I wished I had asked Jillian to bring a knife sharpener, but on second thought she may have had trouble finding it.

Hot Dog was elated at the fresh meat scraps I tossed her way. She ate until she could no longer swallow, then she carried off what she could to bury. Even through her long thick coat, I could see her ribs.

I used the hatchet to separate the moose rib cage, back and neck into small enough pieces to drag. I did the same with the small moose. Then I salvaged the tongues and noses. I wrapped all the organs and loose pieces of meat in a piece of hide, and helped the kids drag the rest to the creek. Hot Dog did not want to leave the kill, although by now, there was nothing left but a few scraps of hide and the gut piles. Leaving the kids at the meat stash to make sure the dog did not carry off any, I walked back to the house and got the old Willy's Jeep. The closest place to the trail was still a hundred yards from the meat, so we shuttled it to the Jeep. It took two trips to get the meat home, and by the time we had it all hanging on our porch, it was dark.

Although I had heard it was best to age meat a few days before you ate it, we were very hungry, and there was only a few small meals of rice left, so I cut three big steaks from the baby moose haunch for dinner. It was the most delicious meat I had ever eaten. Even Jillian, who normally ate almost nothing, finished hers eagerly.

We spent many days canning the meat. Although the weather was cool in the evenings, it was still too warm to let the meat hang all winter as I had hoped to do. I would chunk up the meat, stuff it into quart jars, and boil them for three hours. It was hot, exhausting work. The kids helped by keeping the fire going in the woodstove. We were going through a lot of firewood, so I sent them out with burlap bags to look for dead branches among the brush. Hot Dog would go along, and when they returned, she would be carrying a stick of her own, tail held high. We feasted on meat, and liver, and I made my pickled heart-and tongue and jellied moose nose recipes. The jars started to fill up my empty shelves once again. There is no doubt in my mind that the moose and her calf saved our lives. We did not see another moose that winter. Small game was very scarce. Harry did not return until late October.

That fall, I began homeschooling Eddie. He was an intelligent and curious child, and most of the lessons were too easy for him. He did his homework and we mailed it off to Juneau. They corrected his tests and sent new assignments and school supplies. The program was free. Eddie embraced kindergarten whole-heartedly. Jillian, on the other hand, was feeling left out, and missing her playmate. I wrote Juneau, and asked if they could send extra homework for her to do also, so she wouldn't feel left out.

Henry came along home with Harry less and less now. The kids missed him terribly, and were always thrilled to see him. But when he did come, he did not want to stay for long. Harry told me that Lisa was still "pretending to be crazy" and the State was still trying to figure out what was wrong with her.

After a big snowstorm dumped several feet of snow, I went to check the airstrip conditions to see if Harry could make it home for Christmas. I took the big Olympic 300 snowmachine, thinking it would be more powerful, and less likely to get stuck in the deep drifts. I left Jillian and Hot Dog at home, and let Eddie sit on the front of the seat. We had barely made it up the first hill, chugging through the deep powder at full throttle. I kept it going wide open, and we made it to the airstrip without getting stuck. Thank goodness, I thought, this machine is heavy, and I doubt I could get it out myself if I get stuck. After we checked the airstrip and confirmed the drifts were too deep even for the ski plane, we started back home. I had promised to let Eddie drive on the way back, so he could follow the tracks we had just made.

Eddie was a strong boy and could handle the smaller Moto-Ski snowmachines well. This machine, however was considerably heavier and the steering was stiffer. I put my hands on the handlebars next to his.

"No, Mama! I want to steer it myself! You had your turn on the way down." He reminded me.

I took my hands away, and just that instant we hit a bump and swerved off the trail. We both flew off and landed in the deep soft snow.

"Are you OK?" I asked Eddie as I brushed him off. He nodded, disappointed and embarrassed that he had lost control of the machine.

We tugged at the skis and stomped down snow, but the beast was nearly buried. Unlike the lighter Moto-Skis, this machine was far too heavy for me to lift by myself. Still, straining and pushing, I gave it everything I had. Eddie shoved, and pulled the throttle. For over an hour we worked, digging at the snow with our mittens, packing it down, pulling at the dead weight. We finally inched it back nearly unto the trail. I gave a last mighty heave to get it over the bank, and felt something in my back pop. Gasping with pain, I sank to my knees. I couldn't straighten up.

"Come on, Mama. I'll drive you home." Eddie helped me crawl unto the snowmachine. Every bump he hit was excruciating, but he didn't dare slow down, lest we get stuck again.

I hobbled around like an old woman for weeks until my back finally healed. It was a reminder never to take one's health for granted. Although the kids were a tremendous help, it was still impossible to not lift anything and to let it heal properly.

Harry was still struggling with the flying business. The man that he was going to sell the business to had died test-flying an Aero Commander that Harry had just finished paying for. After that deal fell through, Harry started looking into the fishing industry. He bought a boat and commercial fishing license, and set out nets for herring and salmon in Bristol Bay. He hired Henry and Johnny York to pull nets for him. It seemed as if he was doing well in that line of work, and had let the charter business run itself while he was gone.

That spring, Harry brought 100 more baby chickens, 50 ducklings, and three brown Swiss calves. I was less than thrilled about the cattle. This certainly wasn't the country for them, and they would be hard to feed. In the late 60's and early 70's, Harry had planted about 30 acres of timothy and grasses on the homestead as part of the patenting process. The crop had grown poorly, and was now taken over again by tundra mosses. One pile of dirt he had dug up was overgrown, but stuck out of the tundra noticeably. Since she always left her mark there, it became known as "Hot Dog Hill".

That summer Lisa came back home to live with us. At first I was immensely relieved to have her back and know that she was safe. She had grown into a beautiful young woman, but there was just something still not right. Despite an array of tests, it did not seem that any of them were conclusive. Her bouts of delusion and paranoia had become even worse. Eddie and Jillian were terrified of her, and I had to admit I did not sleep well with Lisa back home. Often I could hear her creeping around at night and once I awoke to see her standing over me with a knife.

"Lisa! What are you doing?!" I was frightened beyond reason.

"I was going to cut your throat." She giggled.

"That's not funny!" I admonished, chills running up my spine. "Don't talk like that! They will send you back to Anchorage. Go back to bed."

Lisa wandered off, but I could not go back to sleep. The incidents were happening closer and closer together. Harry still believed Lisa was "faking it". He paid very little attention to her, and when I begged him to take her to Bethel with him, he was irate.

"Dolly, I'm too busy! I can't watch her, and I don't have a place for her to stay. She is almost eighteen, just take care of her a little longer, OK? And quit making up stupid stories! You're as bad as her!" And with that, the subject was closed.

I tried to be a good mother to Lisa, tried to make her tolerant of me, and sometimes she was sweet and kind and I thought everything was going to be alright again. Then, when I least expected it, out of the blue, she would be strange and violent and threaten to kill herself or me or the kids. I had nowhere to go for help, and no one to ask for advice. I thought often of leaving, to protect myself and my children, but I had no money or way to leave the homestead. So I did my best to weather out these troubled times.

Around this time I also became aware that Harry was not being faithful. Glancing through some photos he had sent in for developing, I noticed several pictures were missing. Holding the negatives up to the light, I could see the outlines of Harry hugging a woman. Just to be sure, I sent the negatives back to develop, and they came back confirming my suspicions. I asked Henry about it quietly in the kitchen one evening when he came home with Harry. He whispered back that he knew his dad was having an affair with a woman from one of the villages. Harry had been eavesdropping and overheard our conversation, and came storming in, threatening to kill Henry. The ensuing violence is one which I wish to forget, and strengthened my resolve to leave. But then, Harry would apologize and everything would be fine again.

In the fall, Harry brought some hunters to the lodge to get a black bear. After they shot the large bear that weekend, they wanted to go home so they could get back to work. The weather had not been great. It had rained and the airstrip was muddy. The wind was gusting from the south so Harry had to take off uphill. He told Henry to stay behind at White Bear so the load would be lighter, but Henry pouted until Harry caved in and let him get into the plane. The Cessna 207 tail sank nearly to the ground with the heavy load. I had to give it a shove to get it going and Harry roared off at full power, spraying mud and small rocks. I watched anxiously as it slowly lifted off and leveled out. It was not climbing like it should. Suddenly there was a loud pop, and the plane dropped to the tundra off the end of the airstrip, skidded, and flipped.

"Henry!!Daddy!" Screamed Eddie. I stood in horror for a second. Eddie started running toward the plane.

"No! Come here. You and Jillian need to go home and tell Lisa that Daddy crashed. Tell her to call for help on the radio. Now! Go!" I couldn't let them see their brother and father dead.

The kids started running up the trail toward the house. I ran toward the plane, relieved to see someone crawling out the window. By the time I got there, everyone had escaped the wreckage, and one of the hunters was lighting a cigarette with shaky hands. No one seemed to be hurt other than bumps and scratches. Henry limped a little but refused to let me look at his knee. The plane was totaled. Harry was in a bad mood and the men were going to be late for work. We started unloading the plane and dragging the bear meat to the the end of the airstrip.

Harry was standing at the wreckage trying to decide how to move the plane down to the airstrip when a plane flew over and landed. Lisa had called for help on the radio and Wayne heard her from his Cessna 185. He diverted and came to see if he could help. Harry was upset that Lisa had said anything on the radio because he wanted to keep the whole incident quiet. The two hunters loaded their bear into the 185 and got in. Henry and Harry stayed back to deal with the wrecked plane, much to Henry's disappointment. Henry had plans for the evening in Bethel.

Harry started the Cat and dragged the plane back on a few heavy iron sleds. He took the wings and tail off and stashed the damaged plane in the shop at the airport, building an extension to cover the tail. The whole process took a week, and when they had the plane stored for winter, Harry and Henry called J.B. on the radio and got a ride out in his plane. Harry was still upset that I had asked Lisa to call for help, as he didn't want to report the incident. The Cessna 207 was an older plane and in need of repairs before it could fly again. It stayed in the shop for many years before Harry sold it for parts, and had it flown out in a Sky Van.

## Chapter Fourteen

"Mama! Lisa drank something! She's dying! Mama! Hurry up!" Eddie stumbled in the door shouting.

By the tone of his voice I knew it was serious this time. I dropped my sewing and ran to him.

"Where is she? What did she take this time?" Last month she had swallowed a half bottle of aspirin. When I told Harry he had laughed it off, making jokes about Lisa not getting any more headaches.

"Come! She's out by the generator shed! She drank something in there." Eddie grabbed my hand and pulled me along.

I did not even stop for my boots, but ran barefoot over the sharp rocks. Lisa sat slumped on the shed porch. Her face was beet red and she was gasping for air.

"Lisa! Lisa! What did you do? Tell me what you drank! Lisa, honey, please, please tell me!" I pleaded.

Lisa broke into tears and started to sob hysterically, clinging to me. I hugged her back.

"Please, Lisa. Listen to me. Tell me what you drank so I can help you."

She shook her head stubbornly.

Eddie held up an empty can. "It was this stuff."

I looked at the can of Heet, uncomprehending. Why would she drink it? What should I do? I took the can from Eddie with shaking hands and tried to read the label, but it was too damaged. I knew it was a fuel deicer, but what were the contents? Should she vomit or would that do more harm?

"Is this what you took?"

Lisa nodded faintly.

"Why?" I thought she was getting better.

She didn't say anything, but still held me tightly.

"Lisa." I gently pulled her to her feet. "I want you to try to throw up, OK? Here." I broke off a willow twig. "Use this to make you throw up. Stick it down your throat. Please. I don't want you to die. Please.' I begged.

She took the stick. "I don't wanna die anymore." She whispered.

"Try to throw up. But if it burns bad, stop. I don't know what else to do."

She threw up a little, but said it hurt, so I decided to make her drink water. We walked slowly back toward the house. I knew some poisons were absorbed by milk. We didn't have any fresh milk. I mixed some powdered dry milk and made her drink as much as she could. Meanwhile I tried frantically to call someone on the radio. It was nearly an hour before Harry was scheduled to call and there was no one else on the air. I made Lisa lie down and tried to make her as comfortable as possible.

When Harry did finally call on the radio, the signals were bad. He couldn't understand what I was saying, but he knew it was urgent. We had a system for when the signals were bad. Usually I could hear him but he couldn't hear me. He would ask me a question, and I would say "Roger, Roger" if the answer was yes.

"Is everything OK up there?" Harry asked.

"No, no, negative! Lisa drank Heet! I don't know what to give her!"

"Slow down, Dolly. I can't understand you. Is Lisa OK?" Harry had been able to pick a few words out of the garbled transmission.

"Negative, negative! Lisa drank Heet! What should I do?"

"I just can't hear you. Is something wrong with Lisa?"

"Roger, roger, roger!"

"Is the weather OK?" Harry wanted to know.

"Roger, roger, roger!' We were fortunate that the weather was flyable that day.

"OK. Try it one more time. What's wrong with Lisa? "

"She drank Heet! She drank a bottle of Heet. You know, to deice fuel, in engines. Heet." I knew Harry wouldn't be able to hear or understand, but I was desperate and terrified that Lisa was going to die.

"You said Lisa drank something?"

"Roger, roger, roger!"

"Does she need to go to the doctor?"

"Roger, roger, roger!"

"I will call you back from the airplane radio when I take off. Do the best you can, Dolly. I'll be there as soon as I can." Harry signed off.

I was only slightly relieved. Help was on the way. But would it get here soon enough? I sent Jillian to look for another can of Heet, hoping to find one with a good label so I would know what to do to help Lisa. She brought back several cans and bottles, but none were Heet. Lisa seemed to be doing OK, although she was still crying. How long would the chemicals take to harm her? How much had she drunk? Had she really even drank any at all? Frequently in the past Lisa had threatened to harm herself, even to the extent of nicking herself with a knife once. I knew she needed help, but where were we supposed to get it? Harry brushed it off. He either didn't believe me or didn't think it was urgent. I tried hard to get Lisa to talk to me, tell me what was bothering her, but I don't think she herself knew the answer. Perhaps in time she would grow out of this.

The radio crackled. "White Bear, White Bear, this is Cessna 14Tango, just off Bethel, be at White Bear in three five minutes."

I rushed to answer . "Roger, roger, roger. The wind is calm. Good visibility." But the signals were too bad and Harry did not even hear the transmission. He repeated his message.

I bundled Lisa in a few thick blankets, and made her walk to the Jeep. I told the kids to stay home and listen to the radio. We bumped along the trail to the airport.

"Dolly, I don't wanna leave. I like it here. I like you. I don't wanna go away." Lisa sniffled.

I reached over and squeezed her hand. "Maybe you don't have to. But I want you to get better so you don't hurt yourself."

"I don't know why I did it. I don't want to go back to Anchorage."

"You can come back, you know. You're old enough now to make your own decisions. The social services can't tell you where to live." I tried to console her.

The plane flew over, circled to check the wind, and landed. Harry had brought a doctor along. The doctor, after shooing us away, did a quick examination, and concluded that the best option was to take Lisa to Bethel hospital to get her stomach pumped. I hugged her tightly and told her goodbye. They all loaded up into the plane and roared away. I drove back home, still shaking.

The next day the signals were better and Harry said Lisa was doing better, they had pumped her stomach at the hospital, and sent her in to Anchorage for psychiatric evaluation. He sounded disgusted with her and insisted that Lisa was still "faking it."

A week later, we found out that Lisa was diagnosed with paranoid schizophrenia, a mental illness that she would struggle with for the rest of her life. She spent a great deal of time in institutions. I wrote to her frequently, and occasionally she would write back. Harry would have nothing more to do with her. I had often wished that I had known earlier the extent of Lisa's illness, so that I could have been more knowledgeable and better prepared to help her and protect her.

Lisa never came back home after that incident. Henry was also gone now, having left Harry to work for the City Of Bethel. He had developed an outstanding work ethic and everyone liked working with him. He bought his own trailer and seemed to be doing well. We all missed him. Now that he was working, he rarely came to visit, for fear of getting weathered in at White Bear and missing work.

Harry had a mild case of gold fever in the late 1970's. We staked out placer gold mining claims. We spent long days clearing lines and dredging, panning and shoveling, looking for gold. We never did hit "pay dirt", but had fun exploring and discovering different types of rocks. We spent earnings from the air charter business to buy small dredges and equipment for mining. The flying business was in dying stages now. The air cargo business couldn't compete with Sea Air Motive, who had larger planes and better financial backing. Harry struggled to keep up with all the new Federal Aviation Administration regulations and requirements. Our budget was tight and we worried endlessly about the next paycheck.

## Chapter Fifteen

Harry was dying. He might even be dead by the time I could get to Anchorage, where he was in the hospital. My whole world turned upside down that day. I realized right then how much I loved my husband, and how much I needed him.

It was January 30, 1980. Harry had missed the noon check-in radio call. He had told me on the radio the day before that he was going out to Kasigluk with some men to help them pick up a plane that wasn't running right. He had planned to fly home to White Bear later that afternoon, so I was to give him the weather report on the radio before he came. He had been late calling in, so I left the radio on, waiting. I wasn't particularly concerned, as events would often occur to delay Harry's check-in time. The weather could have been bad, he could have had a flat tire on the way to the airport, the guys he was taking along could have been late, or they could have had trouble fixing the plane.

About two in the afternoon, the radio crackled, but it was not Harry's voice. I got up from helping Eddie and Jillian with their homework to answer it.

"This is White Bear, go ahead."

"Dolly, this is Pat. Harry had a bad plane accident out at Kasigluk. They medivaced him in to Anchorage."

My heart stopped a beat. "Is he OK?" I asked, but knew it was a stupid question.

"No, Dolly. He is in bad shape. He may not make it. Is there anything I can do for you?"

I didn't know what to say. I felt that my place was with my husband, but who would take care of the homestead? We had cows and chickens and a dog. The earth tremors still occurred frequently, and what if one closed the hotsprings while we were away? If the hotsprings closed again, it could disappear forever. If the pipe broke it could destroy the foundation of the house. But my husband was dying, and it seemed to be the most important thing in the world to be with him and make sure he was getting the medical care he needed.

I couldn't think. "I don't know...."

"Do you want someone to come and pick you up?" Pat asked gently.

"Can you find anyone to take care of White Bear? Could you call Henry? Does he know about his Dad?" I couldn't decide what to do.

"Yes. Henry knows. I will make some phone calls and call you right back, OK?"

It was about a half an hour later when Pat called and told me that Henry and Buzzy could come and take care of White Bear, Tim would fly them up and I should meet them at the airport in an hour. The weather was OK, but it would be cutting close to dark. I hurried and packed. I would take the kids with me. It would be too much to ask anyone to watch them while I was gone, and who knew how long that would be or where we would end up?

The plane was already on the ground by the time I got to the airport. I had scrambled around the house packing frantically, my thoughts in a jumble, and lost track of time. I gave Henry a quick hug, and loaded the kids into the airplane. As we flew to Bethel, Tim filled me in on the events. Harry and Glenn's two sons had been working on Glenn's Cessna in Kasigluk, and they had taken off from that village, Glenn flying, Harry in the co-pilot seat, and Glenn's son Jim in the back seat. The plane lifted off and started climbing out. Witnesses in the village reported hearing a loud pop and seeing dark smoke from the plane before it impacted the tundra not far from Kasigluk. Glenn was killed instantly, Harry was very badly injured, and Jim had fared the best, with a broken arm. Pat had booked me on the evening flight to Anchorage, and we would make it to Bethel in plenty of time to catch that flight.

"Don't worry, Dolly." Tim said.

How could I not worry? I hoped beyond hope that Harry would survive. I had not imagined a life without my Harry. I loved him and it seemed an urgent time to forgive his faults. I tried not to think of the possibility that I would be widowed, raising my children alone in the Alaskan wilderness. I loved my home and my husband. It would be very difficult to live at White Bear if Harry was crippled or could not fly or make a living. I wanted Eddie and Jillian to know their father as the vibrant, adventurous man that I had fallen in love with. They scarcely knew him as it were, Harry had been gone flying nearly all of their short lives.

We landed at Bethel, and I checked in on the evening flight. Although Pat had only booked one seat for me, the kindly airline agent let the kids on without extra charge. When we got to the hospital in Anchorage, Harry was still in surgery. We spent a long sleepless night in the waiting room. In wasn't until the next morning that I got word on Harry's condition. He was in intensive care, both legs shattered, his wrist, jaw and ribs broken, and unknown internal injuries. The doctors had pinned and splinted his legs and wired his jaw together. There wasn't anything else they could do. One leg may need to be amputated, they informed me.

When the doctors finally let me in the room to see Harry, I hardly recognized him. His face was swollen and black, blue, purple and greenish yellow, and tubes and wires came out of every part of his body. I took his hand, and spoke to him softly, fighting back tears. I had to be strong. Harry needed me. He did not seem aware of my presence but a nurse told me sometimes people could hear the voices of loved ones even while in a coma.

Harry was in intensive care for two weeks, clinging to life. During that time, the kids and I practically lived in the waiting room. We had no money to go anywhere else, and no place to stay until Glenn's wife generously offered to let us stay with her, so we spent the nights at her trailer. Eddie and Jillian, accustomed to the freedom of wide-open spaces at White Bear, were wreaking havoc at the hospital, fighting and tearing up and down the hallways at full speed. At the suggestion of one of the nurses, I enrolled them in school.

When Harry finally regained consciousness, he had a very difficult time communicating with me. His jaw was still wired shut, so he couldn't talk coherently. But he was desperately trying to tell me something, something of vast importance to him, and frustrated that

I couldn't understand him. Thinking it to be vital information, I got a piece of paper and a pencil, and held it for him on the hospital's clipboard, so he could scribble with his good hand. After much effort, he wrote, 'My night nurse is a nigger.' I laughed so hard tears rolled down my cheeks, but that upset Harry even more, so I gave him a quick hug and left the room while the doctor gave him more pain medication.

Harry slowly improved, and after nearly two months, against the advice of doctors, he left the hospital. He refused to do physical therapy and missed doctor appointments. He seemed to be recovering fairly well, so I did what I could to help, and tried not to nag. Harry had made some phone calls and sold two of his planes. He had just enough money left over after paying doctor bills to buy a run-down old car and put us all up in a motel. I was anxious whether we would be able to make ends meet, and if Harry would ever be able to fly an airplane again. But Harry had no memory of the airplane accident at all, despite frequent grilling by Glenn's wife and attorney, who was planning to sue the aircraft manufacturer.

During this time, our air charter business had shut down. We were strapped for cash and shocked when the hospital bills rolled in. I filled out paperwork for financial aid, but it was months before we would hear anything. As soon as he could walk with crutches, Harry made arrangements for us to go home. I was concerned for Harry because I knew it was too soon and he still needed medical treatment, but elated to be free of the depressing grind of city life and come back to our wilderness home.

After we stepped off the jet in Bethel, Joe flew us all to White Bear in a small Cessna. The kids, who had been miserable in Anchorage, barely waited for the plane to stop before they leaped out, shrieking in delight and throwing slushy snowballs at each other. The homestead was much as we had left it just a few months ago. Henry and Buzzy were anxious to get back to Bethel.

Harry stayed with us at White Bear until mid-June, and then he went to Bristol Bay to fish for salmon. I worried about him constantly while he was gone. It didn't seem as if he gave himself enough time to heal properly. But, we needed money to pay the enormous stack of bills. Unable to make payments, he had lost nearly all his airplanes. He was heartbroken as he watched the last big DC3 cargo plane rumble away, back to Anchorage for the last time. It was the end of an incredible era of early bush flying. Now larger companies took over, and the small operators had difficulty staying afloat. West Air declared bankruptcy, and Harry focused on fishing and tried his luck again at mining.

I contributed a bit to our finances with my sewing. I sewed Eskimo dresses, called qaspeqs, and sold them at tourist shops in Bethel.

While Harry was away fishing, the kids and I worked hard at the homestead, gardening, picking berries, cutting grasses for the cows, and caring for the hotsprings. The cows had turned out to be a mistake, and took more work than they were worth. I felt sorry for them as I cut down the sparse grasses to dry and store for their winter food. The previous winter they had barely survived in spite of the expensive grain we had flown in for them.

Eddie and Jillian scrambled to catch up on their homework. Fortunately, the home-schooling course in Juneau was used to our erratic schedule of mailing the homework whenever we had an opportunity, whenever a plane would land, sometimes not for several months. They were both doing very well academically, and had been able to skip a grade.

Although Harry had a fairly successful season fishing, all of the money had gone to pay bills, leaving little extra for supplies. We made do on what we could, surviving on my garden and berries and small game animals. Game was scarce again, and we had several skimpy meals of gray jays that Eddie shot. As much as I tried to pretend they were quail or Cornish hens, they just didn't taste that great. So I seasoned them heavily with the basil and oregano I had dried from my potted plants.

In the spring, Henry came home with Harry for a brief visit. I hadn't seen him in a long time. He brought a surprise, his girlfriend Freya. She was a foxy redhead, pert and saucy. Since Henry had never introduced me to a girl, this seemed to be a serious relationship for him. I was happy for him.

Henry stepped out of the plane and pulled Freya along by her hand. "Hey, Old Hag, I want you to meet someone."

I was used to Henry's joking around, and besides I had just been working in the garden, and hadn't been expecting company.

Freya jerked her hand away from Henry and punched him in the arm, hard. "Don't call your mother an old hag! That's not nice. You're supposed to respect your elders!"

I liked her instantly. Of course I didn't mind Henry's kidding around, it was just nice to have someone understand that sometimes a woman needed to feel like something other than an old hag, especially when meeting a new person. Henry and Freya seemed to be happy together. She had taught him some of the social graces that I had failed to teach him. Henry was working hard in Bethel and saving money to start his own foundation repair business. I was very proud of him, but sad that I didn't get to see him often anymore.

Harry tried his hand at trapping that winter. The snowshoe hare populations were starting to come back and with them, the lynx and red fox. He would use the Elan snowmobile to check the traps, usually taking Eddie along. Jillian, no doubt feeling left out, would snowshoe off across the mountains somewhere with her rifle, and be gone most of the day. She would often return with a type of ptarmigan I had never seen before. She showed me in a bird book, they were called rock ptarmigan, a smaller and swifter version of the willow ptarmigan which populated the lower valleys.

When Harry caught a lynx or fox, I would skin it for him. He built a few wooden stretchers to dry the pelts, and after they were partially dried, I would carefully turn them again so the fur was facing out. He took the furs to Bethel to sell them to a fur buyer. Fur prices were high in these years and he could get several hundred dollars for a lynx. He would be stuck in Bethel sometimes for weeks, and during those times, Eddie and Jillian ran his trapline on snowshoes, pulling a small plastic sled behind to carry whatever they caught. They skinned and stretched anything they caught themselves.

Harry was tired when he came home, and most often wanted to rest. It wasn't long until he turned the trapline over to the kids for good. He was still feeling the effects of the traumatic airplane accident and I tried not to nag or ask for anything. We were getting low on firewood. Usually he cut wood in the late winter when the snow was packed hard, and we dragged it back with the snowmachine. But he kept putting it off this winter, so I sent the kids out to gather what sticks they could find. Harry did not want me to try cutting wood while he was gone, in case I accidentally cut myself, there would be no way to get medical help in time.

The kids were late one day coming home from the trapline. I wasn't at all worried. They often explored a new valley or set more traps. I finished my sewing and started making dinner. I could hear them now, laughing as they stomped the snow off their boots on the porch. I had been just about to go out to the porch shelf to get a stick of margerine. As I reached for the door knob, I wondered what was so funny.

"Remember, don't tell Mama." Jillian was saying. I could hear her sweeping the snow off her boots with the broom.

I threw open the door. "Don't tell Mama WHAT?"

The kids jumped back, wide-eyed. I could smell wood smoke on their clothes. The plastic sled sat on the porch behind them, a big log roped on, and the old chainsaw tied to the top of it.

"We got wood!" Eddie said proudly.

"Shut up! She's going to be mad!" Jillian gave Eddie a little kick.

"You got wood? Where? How? You didn't use that chainsaw, did you? Your Dad is going to be really mad!" I didn't know where to start. They needed a good scolding, but we really did need firewood.

"We got more, but then the saw quit." Eddie explained, and stepped aside when Jillian tried to kick him again.

"Cuz you threw snow in the gas tank, dummy!" She said.

"YOU caught it on fire, stupid!" he shoved her.

"Stop it, you two! You know you're not supposed to be playing with the chainsaw. What am I going to tell your Dad when he gets back from town?" Harry had been gone nearly a month but I could still use him to threaten the kids.

"He doesn't have to know. I can fix the saw." Eddie told me.

"What's this about a fire? What happened to your coat?" I asked Jillian. A big hole was melted in the sleeve.

"It's nothing. I can sew it."

I gave an exasperated sigh. Eddie, excited to tell of their adventure, filled me in. They found a few dead trees and cut them up, but then Eddie had gotten cold waiting for Jillian to finish the last tree and decided to start a fire. The twigs he used were heavily frosted and the fire smoldered and nearly went out. Jillian came over with the chainsaw and tried to pour some of the gas from the tank on the fire to get it going. The flames had shot up, and started both Jillian's coat and the saw on fire. She dropped the saw in the snow and they threw snow in the tank to keep it from burning.

I gave the kids the scolding they deserved, and they nodded once in awhile as if they were listening . Eddie disassembled the entire saw, cleaned it, and put it back together. It ran perfectly afterwards. Jillian sewed a lopsided patch on her coat sleeve. I started to feel alone and left out. The kids were a team. Eddie was the brilliant instigator, Jillian was the test pilot of his ideas. At eight and nine years old, they didn't seem to need their mother anymore. A little tear rolled down my cheek as I stirred the rabbit stew. Just then Eddie needed a certain tool, and he had to ask me where it was. Feeling useful again, I found the tool, and then helped Jillian when she asked me to show her the finishing knot for the patch. I realized now, as independent as my kids were, we were all a team together.

After that, the kids and I cut wood together. I would cut up the logs, and the kids dragged them out to the trail. Then we hauled the stack in a bigger sled with the snowmachine. We never did tell Harry, and he didn't seem to notice that the woodpile stayed the same size despite our usage.

The storms were frequent, and several times a month we would get winds over 100 miles per hour. Our new house was well-built, but in these storms it would creak and groan and large sheets of tar paper would rip off the roof. It didn't seem to matter what the weather was, the kids would religiously check the traps every day. Harry would sell whatever they caught to a fur buyer in Bethel. They never saw money from their efforts, but the beaver and lynx meat became one of our staples. Eddie crafted jewelry from porcupine quills and moose antlers and sold it on consignment at the museum's shop in Bethel. Jillian sold paintings, usually of birds. Some of her work sold for $300. Although they had started contributing to family expenses at a very early age, Harry still complained frequently about "too many mouths to feed", feeling the crunch of hard times. The kids' financial cost to us was nearly nothing. They hunted and gathered their own food, schooling was free, they were never sick, and my sister sent us her children's hand-me-down clothing. Occasionally Harry would buy them boots, mostly the wrong sizes, but they would stuff them with newspaper and wear them without complaining.

## Chapter Sixteen

Tears rolled down my cheeks, and I reached up to brush them away. They were not tears of sadness. They were tears of pride and happiness. Our son was getting married. Henry looked so handsome in his white tuxedo, and Freya was stunning in her lovely dress. I just couldn't believe how fast time had flown, and that the man at the flowered arch was the same little blue-eyed boy I had met so many years ago.

It was July 15, 1982. Harry had come back early from fishing, picked the kids and I up at White Bear in the old blue Cessna 206, and flown us to Bethel for the wedding. I had spent weeks sewing dresses for myself and Jillian, and fancy shirts for Eddie and Harry. The weather had been marginal, with low fog and rain showers hanging in the mountains. Harry hesitated to take the chance, but this was an event none of us wanted to miss. When the fog lifted just enough, we piled into the plane and took off. Hot Dog, sensing the excitement and observing us dressing in "going-to-town clothes", had stayed behind at the house without having to be told.

The ceremony was absolutely wonderful. Even normally gruff Harry was touched. My favorite part was when Henry, after saying his "I-do", kissed Freya, and then turned to the crowd, holding her hand.

"Ladies and gentleman, meet my WIFE, Freya."

I sniffled happily and wiped away another tear. The reception was also well planned, and the food was delicious. I had brought salmonberry jam squares and they were a big hit. Harry gave the new couple $500, which didn't seem like a whole lot, but it was all we could afford then. They opened their gifts and then got on the evening jet, headed for their honeymoon in Hawaii. I wished the best for the new couple. They seemed so young, but happy together.

Harry came looking for me, and we gathered up the kids, said goodbye to friends, and headed straight out to the airport. I helped the kids with their seat belts and, gathering up my skirts, climbed into the plane. The weather had deteriorated even worse by the time we reached the edge of the mountains. Rain sheeted off the windshield and the plane lurched with violent turbulence. Looking back, I saw Jillian vomiting into a garbage bag. She nearly always got airsick. Turning around, I was shocked to see nothing but white.

"Keep an eye out for the ground." Harry was intent on the aircraft instruments.

Harry was an excellent pilot, but so were the thousands of other bush pilots who had been killed flying into mountains in the bad weather. I was so disoriented I could not tell if we were turning or upside down. At any moment we could impact a mountain. No one would look for us for weeks. Right now, Henry and Freya were probably changing flights in Anchorage, giggling and holding hands. At White Bear, the cow and the hens were resting peacefully in their sheds, digesting the extra rations we had left them, unaware that their existence hinged upon our survival. Hot Dog would be lying on the porch, looking mournfully toward the airport, waiting for us to return. She would probably survive awhile if she could catch enough game, if she didn't die of loneliness. It seemed vitally important that we survive, if only for the devoted yellow dog. I tried to will the clouds to part. The plane seemed to tip dizzily. I couldn't tell which way was which.

"We are going back to Bethel." Harry said grimly. "There's rocks somewhere in these here clouds."

He was focused on the instruments, so I didn't comment. I kept scanning for "rocks", but all I saw was white. Looking back, I saw Eddie, wide-eyed and scared, also staring intently out the window. Jillian was still throwing up. I reached back and squeezed Eddie's hand. He pointed out the window, excited now. The tundra appeared through the fog, tantalizingly close, willows bending in the wind. I tapped Harry on the shoulder and pointed. He looked up briefly, then turned toward the opening in the clouds, dropping even lower. We skimmed across the tundra, and then came upon a big river.

"Kuskokwim," Harry said. "We should be just above Akiak."

He dropped low and followed the bank of the river. The water, reflecting the whiteness of the clouds, was disorienting, but the trees on the shore gave some definition to the landscape. We could not see all the way across the wide river.

"DAMN!" Harry swore, turning the plane sharply.

I gasped and clung to the door strap. The tail and belly of another Cessna filled our windshield. Harry dove even lower, away from it, and turned away, out over the river. Instantly, everything was white again, and Harry started climbing. He went back to his intent gaze of the instrument panel. I thought of the other plane, somewhere out here, following the river as we had. Where was it now? I shuddered, thinking of it just ahead in the mist, unaware of us. Then we broke out of the clouds again briefly, and made our way back to the river's edge. We could only see about a half mile ahead of us. I hoped Harry knew where we were. He reached for the mic and said something to the tower on the radio. They answered back, and he didn't look pleased.

"They want us to stay in a holding pattern out here. They put that other plane in the same pattern as us." He told me.

Harry started to turn the plane in a slow circle. Suddenly I saw the flash of the other plane's wing, close. Harry swerved away from it, swearing. He stopped circling and flew straight ahead now. He picked up the mic and had another exchange with the tower, looking disgusted. By now I was ready to borrow Jillian's barf bag. We were so close, I wished we could just land.

"The hell with the tower." Harry said. "They're not out here in this. We're just gonna go in and land. Seat belts on?"

"Yes," I looked back to make sure the kids still had theirs on. "Won't we get in trouble?"

"You let me worry about that." Harry said. "There's no other planes inbound for at least five minutes, and the visibility is so bad they won't even see us land."

Just then the Bethel airport appeared out of the mist ahead, and Harry set the plane gently down on the pavement and taxied off the airport to the parking area. I could have kissed the ground. Harry's approach might have been a bit unorthodox, but he did what was the safest thing for everyone involved. He didn't always follow the rules in life. Usually the people who followed rules and didn't think for themselves died young.

"Sorry, guys. Looks like we're spending the night in Bethel. We'll try it again tomorrow, OK? Let's go get a burger." Harry started tying the plane down.

Jillian looked as if she would puke again. Eddie helped Harry with the plane, and we piled into the rusty old station wagon and rattled off to town. We stopped briefly at Harry's shack in Bethel, a dilapidated building half full of junk and extra car and plane parts. I started moving things around to make more room.

"Don't touch that, Dolly! I need to be able to find things." Harry was annoyed.

"I just want to move enough stuff to make some room for the kids to sleep." I explained.

"Every time you move stuff around, I can't find anything!" he complained.

"What's this?" I reached down and picked up a few letters, recognizing my writing on the envelopes. They had been letters I had written to my family. They were torn open.

"Don't touch those!" Harry snapped. "I spilled battery acid on them from that car battery over there."

"Oh. OK. I think we have enough room now." I looked around. Harry and I would share the bed, Eddie could put his sleeping bag in the corner next to the car transmission, Jillian could put hers in the other corner by the bent airplane prop. I wished Harry would let me clean the place up a bit.

Lying awake later that night, I thought of the cow, kicking her stall, upset at not being let out. The hens would be roosting already, murmuring to themselves sleepily. I imagined Hot Dog, lifting her shaggy head to give a long forlorn howl. I hoped the hotsprings was still trickling out of the ground. The thought of the shifting earth closing the springs made me shudder, and I quickly turned my mind to something else.

The letters. I had tried to avoid thinking about them. I had long suspected that Harry did not always mail the letters that I had written. Through the years, Harry had become jealous and possessive. He often accused me of indecencies with men who I had never met. I had little contact with the outside world, and few friends. I always made excuses for Harry's behavior, but sometimes I craved contact with family, or a conversation with another human.

My thoughts went back to the messy shack. How could Harry live like that? He should let me clean it up. But this was his "bachelor pad" when he was away from White Bear. He spent the majority of his time here. If this was how he wanted to live, it was his choice.

The next day the weather was even stormier. I paced the shack, stepping over the junk and trying not to disturb anything. Eddie and Jillian explored the junkyard outside. Harry had collected every junk car in town, it seemed, and nearly every square foot of the property had a car on it. Eddie knew the make and model of every single one. Harry had taken the station wagon and gone somewhere. He liked his solitude, and the close proximity of all of us seemed to annoy him.

Early the next morning, right at sunrise, we made another attempt to get home. This time, we made it, although the wind was still very strong. Hot Dog met us at the airport, nearly turning herself inside out with excitement. She flung herself at us, whining and licking and running from one of us to the other. I understood how she felt. It had seemed like I was gone for months, rather than just a few days. The homestead was just as we left it. The cow was delighted to get out of her shed, and the hens were hungry. Harry took off to finish up his fishing season and we went back to work at our homestead chores.

Early that September, my ten-year old son shot a grizzly bear.

Hot Dog started barking, her deep, distinctive "bear-bark". Jillian came racing in, yelling, "Bear, bear! It's after the cow!"

Eddie and I ran outside with our guns. The young cow, the last surviving one, sprinted toward us full speed, desperately dodging the small grizzly at its heels. Eddie lifted his gun and fired. The bear disappeared. The cow streaked past us for the safety of her shed. Hot Dog stopped, and standing her ground, growled at something on the ground. Eddie and I advanced cautiously. A big brown hump lay crumpled on the tundra, where it fell.

"Be careful." I whispered to Eddie. "I heard that sometimes they play dead."

We nervously tiptoed closer, guns ready. Just then Jillian stepped out of the brush and hurled a rock at the bear. We jumped back, expecting the grizzly to leap to life and charge us.

"See? It's dead." Jillian threw another rock at it, and the bear made no movement when the rock thunked solidly into its side.

"Cut it out! You coulda got us killed!" Eddie yelled at her.

Jillian snorted. "You guys have the guns."

We crept closer, and saw that Eddie had shot it in the head. It was an incredibly accurate shot for a 30-30 rifle. The bear had been moving fast and still 150 yards away. I was very proud of my son. We all worked together to skin the bear. I tacked it to the side of the house, salted, and dried the hide. Later Harry sent it away to make into a rug. The bear meat had a very strong odor. Since I had never heard of anyone eating grizzly meat, and Harry had just shot a moose, we dug a deep hole and buried the carcass.

*Eddie, age 10, shot this grizzly bear*

When Jillian turned ten, Harry gave her a 30-30 rifle of her own for Christmas. A few weeks later, she shot her first moose. She snowshoed across several valleys until she came across tracks, and then followed them even farther. After shooting the moose, she came back to get knives and the snowmachine.

"How far away is it?" I asked.

"Past the eagle's nest, maybe another mile, on the mountain to the west." There was an old abandoned golden eagle nest hanging precariously off a cliff to the north. That was nearly six miles away, but she was more excited than tired.

"We better hurry then, before it gets dark."

Harry, Eddie and I all drove Elan snowmachines with sleds attached. Jillian rode on the back of the sled. Rather than follow her winding footsteps through the brush, Jillian suggested we follow the trapline down past the eagle's nest and then cut across.

"Up there." She pointed as we neared the eagle's nest. "See that mountain top? Just down from that peak."

Harry took the lead, breaking trail up the slope. A few hundred yards from the moose, it became too steep for the snowmachines, so we butchered the large moose and slid the meat down to the sleds. It was a cow, and the meat had a thick layer of fat. It filled all of our sleds, and we finished and headed home at dusk. I drove in the middle of the snowmachine caravan, since my snowmachine's headlight didn't work.

In 1984, the fish buyer to whom Harry had given his entire season's catch went bankrupt. None of the fishermen that sold to Ocean Venture got paid for their catch that year. Harry had accrued massive debts from his new hobby, helicopters. To make the payments on his little Bell 47 helicopter, he had to sell the fishing boat. He left the fishing industry and tried a short-lived restaurant in Bethel. He started taking Eddie to town with him, thinking that his son needed more manly influences in his life. At first they were gone just a few days. Still, I missed Eddie terribly. He loved White Bear, but he also loved airplanes and cars, and didn't want to be seen as a sissy boy being raised by women. When he was gone I worried constantly, if he was getting enough to eat, was Harry treating him OK, when would he come home. It was lonely without him around. Jillian was always off on a long hike somewhere.

We spent a lot of time in the summers working on our mining claims, searching for gold, and building small bridges across creeks. We had to continuously rebuild our corner markers, as the moose and bear loved to rub against them and knock them down. Our claims spanned several valleys, so we got a lot of exercise maintaining them. In 1984, we received a letter from the Bureau of Land Management regarding one of our claims. It stated that this claim was null and void because it conflicted with the Chalista Corporation's selection of a "cemetery historic site". This was the first time we had officially heard of this selection. I had completely forgotten Harold Corbin's map from 1976. It hadn't made much sense anyway. The "site" was over two miles from White Bear hotsprings, on the top of a mountain. There was no "cemetery" there, or any indication of historical usage, other than Harry landing his ski plane there in the early 1960's. The edge of one of our mining claims overlapped one corner of Chalista's 20 acre selection slightly. So the BLM took our entire 40 acre claim away. They did not answer the many letters I wrote, or the phone calls Harry made.

"Oh well. I probably doesn't matter anyway. I don't land there anymore. Probably no gold there, so just forget it." Harry brushed it off, and I pushed back a dark foreboding that something was not right. Little did I know how right I was or that years later we would fight against Chalista, BIA, and BLM to save our home.

## Chapter Seventeen

"Is anyone on the air?" The woman's voice sounded desperate over the radio.

"This is White Bear, I hear you. Can you hear me?" I answered. Harry would be calling at any moment for the seven p.m. check-in. He usually got upset if I started any conversations with anyone on the radio. But there were very few people on this frequency nowdays, and this person sounded like she needed help.

"This is Eagle Island. I hear you loud and clear! Oh, goody! Do you have a telephone?" The woman sounded relieved.

"No, I'm sorry, no telephone here, but my husband will be calling from Bethel soon, and he has a telephone there. What do you need?"

"My son never made it home, and I wanted someone to call to see if his plane took off from Grayling."

"Sure. We can do that for you. What number should we call?"

The woman read off the telephone number, and I scribbled it down and read it back to her to double check. She introduced herself as Helmi Conatser. She and her husband and son lived at a homesite called Eagle Island, on the Yukon River between Grayling and Kaltag. It was several hundred miles from White Bear, but the radio signals were good and we had around two hundred feet of copper wire antenna stretched out for better reception. Helmi's son had taken off from Eagle Island in his airplane to fly to Grayling and back. He had never returned. We chatted for a few minutes, then Harry cut into the conversation from Bethel. I relayed the message and phone number. Harry, always concerned over the welfare of missing pilots, made the call. Helmi's son was safe in Grayling, he had been running late and decided to come home the following day.

Helmi and I became close friends. We chatted on the radio every evening at six. Harry wasn't particularly pleased but that was just too bad for him. I was delighted to have a new friend, particularly a woman near my own age, living much as I did. Over the next few years, Katy from the Anvik River, and Vanita from Blackburn also joined our radio chat group. It was a much needed comfort, as Eddie was staying in Bethel longer and longer with Harry. When he returned, he talked endlessly about cars and airplanes. Someday, I was sure, he would be a pilot just like his dad, and come home whenever he wished. But right now, I missed my growing boy.

While the men were gone, Jillian ran the trapline alone on snowshoes. She had started experimenting with tanning furs. Some turned out nicely, and these I used to sew mittens and hats for sale in Bethel. I also had more time to catch up on my reading.

It was a lovely summer day, and I relaxed a bit after working in the garden while Jillian worked in the yard. She had let the chickens out of their coop to enjoy the outdoors as she pulled up the alders encroaching on the yard. If the chickens were outside, someone had to be near them, guarding them from predators. Hot Dog would usually lie nearby, but today she basked in the sun that was spilling through the living room window.

I heard Jillian walk onto the porch, digging through the stack of tools, probably looking for an axe. Then the yard was filled with the cackling of chickens in distress. I leaped up, hearing Jillian running out, and as I looked out my bedroom window, I saw a large black bear holding a chicken under its paw. Jillian whipped off the 30-30, which was slung on her back, and ran at the bear.

"Yah! Git!" I yelled out the window.

The bear dropped the chicken and wheeled around. Jillian lifted the gun and fired at it. It kept running about a hundred feet farther before it dropped to the ground. Jillian had shot it through the heart. She searched the brush and found all of the hens, scattered and frightened but unharmed. Even the hen that the bear had caught had escaped with just a few scratches.

Jillian insisted that she didn't need any help skinning the bear, so I started supper. The bear meat would be tasty. I would have to can most of it, but it shouldn't take long, I thought as I diced a few carrots for soup. We shot a black bear about every other year, if a young one hung around the house and didn't leave. Usually we tried to scare them off a few times with a shot in the air, and we burned all our garbage so as not to attract them, but if they became pesky, we would dine on bear meat.

The soup was nearly done, and I wondered how much longer Jillian would take. I bent over the sink and washed a few dishes. Suddenly I became aware of a presence, and heard a soft ticking on the window pane. I glanced up, and shrieked when I saw a big black bear looking back at me, just inches from my face! Hot Dog, lying on the porch, tore around the corner of the house snarling.

Jillian threw off the bear hide and yelled, "Hey! It's just me!"

Hot Dog stopped growling and wagged her tail.

I laughed in relief. "Oh man! You scared me! I thought it was another bear!"

Jillian giggled. "Geez, I wasn't even trying to scare you. I thought you knew I was skinning a bear. I just wanted to show you how big it was, that I could fit inside the skin."

"It looked just like a bear! Whew! I just wasn't expecting to see that right then."

That fall, I developed a terrible toothache. My whole head throbbed with the pain in my jaw. I was pretty miserable, and could barely eat. Harry was in Bethel, and the airstrip was covered with deep snow drifts, so getting to the dentist was not an option. Jillian searched her plant books for cures and had me try various poultices. Eddie also had a helpful idea.

"My friend Bobby told me about an old miner that had a toothache. It was back in the gold rush days, and there were no dentists anywhere around. He shot a bear, and when he was skinning it out, he noticed some of the back teeth were the same size as his. So he pulled the bear tooth out, and pulled his bad tooth out. He stuck the bear tooth in, put a little spruce pitch around it, and the tooth grew right in and never gave him any problems. You wanna try it? We got lots of old bear skulls lying around. We could use one of the teeth."

I decided that I was neither as adventurous nor as desperate as that miner, and I would endure the torment until I could get to a dentist. Who knows what kinds of bacteria or diseases a person could contract from the teeth of a dead bear? It was several months before Harry was able to take me to the dentist in Bethel. I had toothaches in the past, but this was the worse. By the time I got to the dentist, my whole jaw was swollen by the abscessed tooth. Thinking back, that bear tooth may not have been such a bad idea.

    Harry applied for a parcel of land near the big lake I had walked to years ago. We staked it out and started building a small cabin there in the mid 1980s. He flew most of the lumber and building supplies in with the small Bell helicopter. In the winter, Eddie and Harry ran a trapline from the lake cabin. A few years later the villagers from Aniak and Kalskag discovered the cabin. Harry and Eddie went to the cabin only to find the supplies had been stolen and the traps had been raided. All the firewood was burnt up. It is an unspoken code of the northlands to always replace what firewood you use, so that the next people have dry wood to build fire. And stealing from traps was the equivalent of cattle rustling in the old West. Harry made several reports to the State Troopers, but nothing ever came of it. Sadly, years later, after pillaging and ransacking our cabin until nearly everything was gone, the perpetrators burnt the cabin to the ground. Once again, the troopers did nothing to find the arsonists.

    One cold winter evening Eddie came home from ptarmigan hunting with a badly frostbitten foot. He had tried to jump across a small swift creek, but came up short. He fell through the ice. The water was only a few feet deep and he got out quickly. The temperatures hovered around -20. Rather than heading straight home or stopping to build a fire, Eddie had chosen to continue pursuing the ptarmigan, as he was certain he had hit it with his last shot. By the time he had felt the first pangs of frostbite, it was too late. He limped home as fast as he could. His boot was frozen to his foot. He was trying to act like nothing was going on but a mother can tell when something is wrong. He kept stamping his foot and looked as if he were in a lot of pain, but he didn't complain. I finally got him tell me what was wrong. I soaked his foot, still frozen inside his boot, in a big pan of tepid water until we were able to pull it off. Peeling back the sock, I was shocked to see Eddie's toes were still white and frozen. I had heard a lot of different remedies for frostbite, but which was right? The old way was to rub the frozen extremity with snow until it thawed, but now the experts said that was bad. I thought the new way was to soak the foot in lukewarm water until it thawed, so that is what I did. It must have been extremely painful, as Eddie whimpered and squirmed while it was thawing. The color slowly started coming back, but he could not feel his big toe. Huge blisters developed. I worried about gangrene.

"Eddie," I said. "I think you should tell your dad tonight on the radio when we talk to him. I think he should take you to a doctor."

"No! I don't want to tell him. He'll get mad at me for not stopping to build a fire. He always preached at me to start a fire if I got wet."

I thought about it a few more minutes. Harry had left Eddie home this time and I didn't want him to go back to Bethel. He seemed to be having a good time at home, reloading bullets, hunting, playing card games and trying to catch up on his schoolwork. I didn't want him to leave. If Harry took him to Bethel, it would be another month before he would come home. But I had to think about what was best for my son. He could lose his toe to gangrene.

Seven o'clock was approaching rapidly. I had to make a decision. I turned on the radio. Eddie sat in a chair next to the stove, sipping hot chocolate, his thick quilt draped around his shoulders.

"Please don't tell him." He begged. "My foot will be alright."

I thought of his deformed feet, still slightly turned inward. He needed them. He should see a doctor, even if it was alright.

"White Bear, KYH6." Harry sounded cheerful tonight.

"This is White Bear, go ahead."

"Wow, that was quick. You must have been standing right next to the radio. Is everything OK up there?" Harry sounded concerned.

"No, Eddie froze his toe. He's OK but the toe is blistered." It just came out, and in the background I heard Eddie gasp.

"Oh man. Are you sure he's OK?"

"Yes, just his toe got frozen. I think we got it all thawed out, and it's starting to blister up pretty bad."

"I better come and get him. We can't take any chances with his feet. I'll call you tomorrow morning for the weather. How's the airstrip?" Harry was always calm and level-headed in an emergency. That was one of the things I relied on him heavily for.

"There's about eight inches of hard crusty snow, no drifts." Harry was using the Cessna 185 on skis this year.

"OK, that shouldn't be a problem. Is Eddie close by?"

Eddie shook his head that he didn't want to talk to his dad.

"He can hear you. He's by the stove but I don't want to make him move anymore than he has to."

"That's good. Sounds like you're doing everything right. Eddie, hang in there. I know frostbite hurts. We'll get you to a doctor tomorrow, OK?"

The next day, the weather in Bethel was foggy at daybreak. It was about noon before it cleared, and Harry called on the airplane radio, saying he was on the way. Jillian and I loaded Eddie into the sled, wrapped him with blankets, and carefully pulled him to the airstrip behind the Elan. Harry landed, left the engine running while we loaded Eddie into the plane, and then took off again with a roar and a cloud of snow.

The doctor looked at Eddie's foot and said we did everything right. Eddie ended up losing his toenail and much of the feeling in his big toe, but he didn't lose any extremities. The doctor didn't do much except send us a big bill. It would probably have been fine to keep him home, but I just couldn't take that chance with his poor clubbed feet.

In the early spring of 1986, I tried very unsuccessfully to make birch syrup. My sister from Wisconsin had sent me tree taps and a pan. I had read an article in a Fairbanks newspaper and decided to give it a try. The birch sap, I read, had lower sugar content than maple sap, so it would take sixty gallons of sap to make one gallon of birch syrup. The process was the same as making maple syrup. You had to drill holes in the trees and set the taps. We hung old coffee cans from the taps and collected the sap as it drained out of the tree. Then we'd to pour it in a pan and boil it until it turned to syrup.

The only problem with the whole enterprise was, the birch trees did not grow close by. The nearest stand was at least seven miles away. Jillian and I backpacked everything to the birch trees in the wet slushy spring snow. The snowmachines would have gotten stuck and besides, we were a bit short on gasoline. We set the taps, and slogged all the way home. It was a lovely sunny day, but the hot sun and slushy snow was exhausting. The next day we set out, with excitement and high spirits. I had decided, rather than lug the sap all the way back to the house to boil on the cookstove, I would build a campfire and boil it down in the woods. That would make our backpacks lighter for the trip home.

I was delighted to find the buckets nearly full of sap. Jillian scraped back the moss and started a small fire.

"Make it really hot." I reminded her.

"Yeah, OK." She took the ax and chainsaw and went to collect more firewood.

I snowshoed back to the stand of trees. The slope of a hill rose steeply out of the creek bottom, and this was where the birch grew best. Higher on the slope, the wind had blown the tundra clear, and the mosses crackled dryly as I stepped on them. I took off my snowshoes, stashed them near the snow's edge. It was easier moving around without them, especially on the steep slope. I picked my way carefully along, collecting the buckets and pouring them into the larger bucket I was carrying. The air was filled with the sweet smells of spring on the way. Somewhere, a bird sang. Down at the creek, I heard the chainsaw start, die, then start again. I stopped and listened to the saw growling and then the creaking groan of a dead spruce falling. I could hear Jillian cut it into smaller pieces and drag it through the woods as I started back with the full bucket of sap. What a lovely day, I thought, although the clouds that started to form to the south looked a bit troublesome. We should be done and home well before the storm hit.

I put the big pan on the fire and dumped the sap into it. Jillian took the bucket and went to finish gathering the last sap buckets. She had selected some excellent logs for firewood, dry and pitchy, and the fire roared. Perfect, I thought. This will boil in no time. It was so hot, in fact, that the wooden spoon I was using to stir the sap seemed too short. I needed a longer stirring spoon so I could stand farther away from the fire and my legs wouldn't get so hot. Picking up the ax, I stepped a few feet away and started chopping a small willow sapling for my new stirring stick.

I was bending over trimming the branches off the sapling when I felt the wind hit. It was a sharp gust from the east, rolling over the mountain, a precursor to the storm that was forecast for tomorrow. The valley was known for its erratic winds, especially in the springtime. I started back toward the fire and then with horror, broke into a run. The wind had blown the fire out of the pit and onto the tundra. It was racing across the dry moss toward the birch hill, where my daughter was collecting the last buckets of sap.

"Jillian! Help!" I screamed.

I tore off my coat and swatted at the flames. The wind hit the ground again and sparks flew into the stand of birch. I grabbed an empty pail and frantically tried to scoop snow and throw it at the fire. But the snow bank was too far away and it was taking too long. The fire was gaining ground rapidly. I went back to swatting it with my coat, choking on the thick smoke, my eyes stinging. I let out a sigh of relief when the fire smoldered and went out. Just ahead, another spot fire started, blown there from one of the sparks. By the time I got to it, it was too late. The bright orange flames crept greedily up the slope, lapping at the birches. Suddenly, as if deciding it loved birch bark, the monster rose with a roar. Flames shot a hundred feet into the air, and the whole hillside crackled and hissed and roared. A thick dark column of smoke boiled overhead. Jillian was still up there somewhere. My heart thundered in my chest.

"Jillian!" I screamed again, but it was hopeless. The fire had certainly cut her off. I hoped she had found a way out. It didn't seem possible. I stood there, paralyzed with terror.

"Shit! Holy shit!" Jillian gasped from behind me. She was panting hard. She had run down to the frozen creek bed just as the fire hit the hill, and then circled around under it.

"Oh man, I thought you were a goner!" I cried, hugging her.

"Come on, let's get out of here! There's nothing we can do now. Let's go home and call someone on the radio." She tossed me my snowshoes. "I probably made that fire just a bit too hot, huh?"

I strapped them on and tried to keep up with Jillian. She was moving fast, occasionally turning to make sure I was right behind her.

"I hope that wind doesn't push the fire up this valley behind us," I gasped.

"Probably won't cross the snow in the drainage bottom. I think we're safe."

I thought back to the sparks flying, starting the fire up the hill. "It could happen." I said.

"Maybe. That's why we have to get home fast and get help." She picked up the pace and I ran to catch up.

Snagging my snowshoe, I tripped and fell. Jillian stopped a few steps ahead, waiting for me. By the time I had wrestled myself out of the deep slush I was exhausted. I caught up to Jillian. She was watching something in the distance.

"Look," she said excitedly. "Plane! Maybe they will see the fire and report it."

I didn't see how they could miss it. The whole hillside was engulfed in flames, and it had spread to the next hill. The smoke rose high overhead into a giant nuclear-like mushroom. What could anyone do to stop it? Who could stop such an incredible force of nature?

The plane flew over the fire, and started circling. We stopped snowshoeing and stood watching it.

"Look! Something fell out!" Jillian pointed.

I reached for my glasses.

"It's a parachute! People are jumping out!" Jillian was excited.

"Don't be silly! People aren't going to jump out of a plane into a fire! It's got to be something else they are dropping."

As I put on my glasses, I could see two parachutes open up in the distance. We were already several miles away, but it sure did look like people under those parachutes.

"Wow! That's awesome! I wonder how they're going to put it out?" Jillian thought out loud.

"I don't know. But we should get home and call on the radio anyway."

The plane dropped below the horizon, and soon the sound faded away. We snowshoed home, not quite as fast, our thoughts on the brave men battling the blaze. When we called Harry on the radio that night, he told us the fire had already been reported, and that the parachutes were indeed dropping people. They were an elite group of wildland firefighters called smokejumpers.

Over the next few days we watched the smoke column slowly dissipate and then disappear. We got some wind with the storm and some rain, which was sure to help. I hoped the smokejumpers were warm and safe, but it didn't seem possible to find them, by now several more miles over the hills.

On the third day, a helicopter landed on our airstrip. Two men got out and pumped jet fuel from a 55 gallon barrel they had brought along into the helicopter's tank. Then they took off, thanking us for letting them use the airstrip. They told us they were going to pick up the supplies and men from the fire. The fire was out. We breathed a huge sigh of relief. I wondered how the smokejumpers had put the fire out. I had never heard of smokejumpers before. Many years later, that occupation became a familiar household word. I didn't realize at the time how much the firefighters had impressed my daughter. She would later join the ranks of the most elite wildland firefighters in the nation.

## Chapter Eighteen

"You're a grandma!" Henry surprised me with a call on Harry's radio. It was May, 1987.

"What? Oh my! Is it a boy or a girl?" This came as quite a surprise. I knew they were planning to have children eventually but I hadn't known Freya was expecting.

"It's a girl! Her name is Kayla. We just adopted her."

"Oh my. Oh that's wonderful. How old is she? Where did you find her?" I had so many questions, but our radio was hard to hear on sometimes.

"She was just born, we got her right away. It's Freya's relative's baby, she was giving her away. We got the paperwork done already." Henry sounded like a very proud father.

My heart filled with wonder. Henry was kind and patient. He would make a great dad. And Freya wanted nothing more than to be a mother. I just hoped the distance between Bethel and the homestead wouldn't keep me from being a part of my granddaughter's life. Kayla was related to the great Chief Eddie Hoffman, a longtime family friend, and now we were all related. It seemed like such a small world.

It was several months before I met my darling new granddaughter. Harry flew me to Bethel for the day. He was pretty busy then, having started Bethel Taxi company. Helmi was in Bethel for some reason also, so I got to meet her for the first time. We gabbed nonstop as Harry drove us to Henry's house. When Henry handed me Kayla, I was so surprised at how small and perfect she was. It had been years since I last held a baby. I felt big and awkward and dirty in my motley clothes. And then, Harry was in a hurry to leave again, and I handed the precious bundle back to Henry. Back home again safely, I couldn't stop thinking of the new baby, and the hopes everyone held for her. Someday, she would do grand things, I was sure. She was already bridging a cultural gap.

A few months later, we woke to Hot Dog barking fiercely. Looking out the window, I saw a strange and disturbing sight. A red fox, fur mottled and ragged, staggered drunkenly in the yard. It hit a bush and fell back, dazed.

Eddie, who had just read "Old Yeller", shouted, "It's got rabies! Don't let the dog out!"

He ran for his gun, but by the time he got back, the fox was nowhere to be seen. As he went outside hunting for it, I was terrified it would bite him. Rabies was a horrible thing. Eddie never did find the fox. For months afterward, we were all scared of getting bitten by a fox. Hot Dog, who loved chasing foxes, was kept on a leash. She had never been vaccinated in all the years we had her. The next time Harry went to town, he brought back rabies vaccines for her. It was a great relief to know Hot Dog would be protected, as she was likely to catch up to a sick fox.

The rabbit populations declined again, and predators were lean and hungry. They expanded their ranges hunting for food, and being driven out of their territories by other predators. We started seeing pine marten well above the timberline, far out of their normal range. The past winter, Eddie had caught a few of them at the lake cabin, but now we saw a few as far up as our house.

A big white Arctic wolf had taken a liking to Jillian, following her, just out of gun range as she picked berries and gathered plants. She didn't seem at all concerned.

"Be careful. Shoot it if it gets too close. It probably has rabies." I told her.

"Nah," she said. "He's just lonely. The two black ones he was with left him."

She would stand on the mountainside and sing to him in his own language, and he would answer her back from across the valley. Sometimes I wondered if Jillian ever got lonely. It didn't seem so, she spent all day outside, and evenings at her homework or tanning furs or painting birds. She didn't interact much with humans. Eddie and Jillian had been very close as children, but now Eddie was gone more than he was home, and when he was home, he didn't want a pesky girl bugging him. Harry had no use for Jillian. It was as if all the disappointments of his other daughters had manifested in his last daughter. He accused her of things she didn't do, and yelled at her if she was too loud, or too slow, or too anything. So, perhaps she had found a new friend in the big white wolf, and it seemed best to leave her to roam the mountains that gave her serenity.

Late in September, Jillian had gone up the mountain picking lowbush cranberries, while I stayed home and scrubbed a load of laundry. I scrubbed my jeans on the old washboard and rinsed and wrung them out. I was pinning the clothes on the line outside to soak up the last rays of sunshine, when I heard a shot, followed closely by another. Then silence. It was moose season. We needed meat. Maybe Jillian got a moose. Or perhaps she finally shot the wolf, now that the fur was prime. Or maybe a bear was after her? I ran back into the house and got my gun and some knives. I met Jillian walking up the trail.

"Good news, bad news." Jillian laughed. "I got a moose, but it's gonna be a hard one to pack out."

"The shots sounded like you were close to home. It can't be that bad." I reasoned.

"Oh yeah, it is. It fell in the beaver dam."

"Oh no! Why did you shoot it in the water? You should have waited for it to come out."

Jillian scowled. "I didn't shoot it there. Me and the wolf were following it for a couple miles. I waited for it to cross the creek and then shot it. But it jumped and ran before it fell, and rolled down the hill into the water."

"Well, it can't be that bad." I was soon to eat my words. Eddie and Jillian often shot moose far away, or in the thick brush, and we more often than not had a difficult time packing them out, but this moose turned out to be the toughest one we ever shot.

Jillian picked her way across the swampy tundra, flooded by the beaver pond, jumped across a few places and stopped. I saw the moose now, one antler and part of the shoulder hump sticking out of the pond.

"Oh shit. That's going to be a tough one." I groaned.

"Yeah, I know. So let's get it done, OK," Jillian said, taking the knife and wading into the muddy waist deep water.

"It's cold! You're going to get hypothermia!" I did not want to get wet but there didn't seem to be another way.

"Yeah, yeah. So what. Do you see another way to get this moose out of here?" She said, already shivering.

"Do you think we can pull it with the Jeep?"

"No, it's too far to the trail. But hey, why don't you build a bridge across the creek while I cut whatever I can get off." She wrestled with a leg. "And bring some long ropes."

"I should stay and help. My feet are already wet." I said.

"I don't want help! I can cut it up while you make a place to cross the creek."

I went back to the house and gathered as many boards as I could, some nails, hammer, ropes and loaded them on the top of the Jeep. I drove as close to the moose as I could on the trail, but it was still too far away to pull it out with the Jeep. I went to check on Jillian, kneeling now in water past her chest, cutting chunks off the moose. A big pile of meat was already on the bank.

"I hope you don't mind the way I'm cutting it up. It's too heavy to quarter and I can't see where I'm cutting so I'm just hacking off whatever I can get a hold of." She was shivering so hard now I could hardly understand her.

"You should get out of there before you freeze." I nagged.

"I'll get out when I'm done. Too hard to go back in again. Go make the bridge, OK?"

I went back to the Jeep and started dragging the heavy planks to the creek. My legs were soaked up to the knees and my teeth were chattering. The sun had gone down and ice started forming around the edges of the water. By the time I finished the bridge, it was almost dark. I went back to the Jeep and pulled out the hurricane lantern I had brought. Hot Dog climbed into the back of the jeep, wanting to go home.

"You can stay there," I patted her silky head and stretched out a piece of canvas for her to lie on in the back of the Jeep.

The mountain of meat on the bank had grown by the time I got back.

Jillian looked up. "It's about time you got back. Throw me that rope."

I dug around for the rope. I noticed Jillian had tied the knife to her arm with some string. Her hands had been too cold to hold it. I was shivering uncontrollably now.

"That's enough. You should leave the rest. It looks like you got most of it anyway. Leave it, or you will freeze to death!" I nagged again.

"Just give me the dang rope! I think we can pull it out now. It's just the rib cage and part of the back." She chattered through blue lips.

I tossed the rope and she caught it clumsily and wrapped it a couple times around something under the water and tied it with her teeth. She stumbled out of the water.

"Come on, let's pull the rest of it out onto the bank." Jillian tossed me the end of the rope. I noticed the knife, still strapped to her arm, swinging wildly, close to her body, as she gestured.

"Watch out! You're going to cut yourself! The knife!"

"Oh, come on! Let's pull this out." She looped the rope over her shoulder and threw her weight into it.

Still worried about Jillian cutting herself with the knife, I set the hurricane lantern down and pulled as hard as I could on the rope. The moose slid forward about a foot and snagged on some branches along the creek bank.

"Wait." Jillian let go of the rope and waded back into the water. "OK, you pull and I'll push."

We heaved and tugged and managed to roll most of the carcass onto the bank.

"Hold on." Jillian panted. She tugged at an antler stuck in the muck. It gave way and she sat back in the icy water with a splash. It looked so comical I had to laugh.

"It's not funny," Jillian snapped. "Let's get this thing out of the water and then we can laugh all we want."

We strained against the rope until the heavy carcass inched higher on the bank. Then Jillian cut some more meat off it, and finally untying the knife with her teeth, picked up the axe and separated the rib cage. I held the lantern up. Jillian wanted to butcher the moose herself. She was a teenager now, and more independent than ever. Given the circumstances, she was doing a fine job. After the ribs were separated, she started chopping the backbone into smaller sections. By now it was pitch black outside.

"Maybe we should go home and finish this in the morning." I suggested. We were both cold and tired, and it would be so easy to make one small mistake and hurt ourselves.

Just then, the chilly night air filled with a lonely wail of a wolf, very close in the brush. The hair stood up on the back of my neck. The hurricane lantern cast distorted shadows. Everything looked like a rabid wolf. The brush rustled. Another wolf howled from across the canyon, and another, closer yet.

Jillian looked up. "The black ones came back! We definitely need to get all this meat home, or they will eat it overnight."

We just had the one lantern, so we decided to stay together and start shuttling the meat to the Jeep. We loaded backpacks high with meat and staggered through the freezing swamp toward the trail, nearly a quarter mile away. My bridge sagged under our weight but held. The effort was actually making me warmer.

"Hey, I can feel my fingers now." Jillian said.

We dumped the meat in the jeep and headed back. Hot Dog, having heard the pack of wolves, had no desire to accompany us. She instinctively knew the age-old rift between wolves and dogs, and knew she was outnumbered. Jillian gave her a choice piece of meat to chew on, and we hurried back to the pile of meat. As we approached, two bright glowing eyes shone at us from the brush.

"Yah! Git!" I hollered. The glowing eyes disappeared, but I could feel them on my back. I shuddered. The rabid fox was still fresh in my mind.

We loaded up the meat and shuttled it back to the Jeep. We made so many trips I lost count. It was a large moose, and of course we wanted to salvage everything. The whole time, the wolves stayed close, in the brush, and occasionally we would catch a glimpse of them. Still wary of bears, who might not yet be hibernating, I carried my rifle slung across my back. It just made the whole process even more awkward, trying to balance the meat and the gun, so eventually I left the rifle at the Jeep and Jillian left hers at the moose kill. We worked late into the night. Finally there was nothing left but the head and antlers, minus the tongue. The antlers were the least valuable part of the moose, but I could use them for buttons. Neither of us wanted to extend the effort to chop the antlers off the skull.

"I'll come back and get them tomorrow." Jillian said.

We took the last load to the Jeep. The frame sagged until the fenders rested on the wheels. With a creaking groan, the old jalopy crawled up the trail and we drove home. Back at the house, we unloaded the meat onto a tarp on the porch, and decided to hang it in the morning. It was three in the morning and we were tired and wet and cold. I started a fire and we dried our wet clothes and ate a big slice of fresh moose liver before we went to bed. That moose was still to this day, the hardest we ever had to work for our winter's meat.

# Chapter Nineteen

"We'll find her body. It would be better for you to start telling the truth right now." The Alaska State trooper regarded me coldly.

I was stunned. I didn't know which hit me hardest, the fact that they were looking for a body now, or that the trooper seemed convinced that I had murdered my daughter.

Three days earlier, Jillian had vanished without a trace. When she didn't return that cold foggy day in early spring, I didn't worry much. She was often gone until after dark, exploring the mountains or watching birds. I did her evening chores, feeding the chickens and getting water from the creek, and then I made dinner. When she did not return that night, I started to get worried. The snow was melting fast and the creeks were flooding. Bears were coming out of hibernation. The mountains rumbled with avalanches. We hadn't seen the wolves since last fall, but they could be back now that the deep snow was gone from the valley. I had called out the window late that night, and stayed up all night waiting for Jillian to return. Boy, was I ever going to give her a piece of my mind! When the daylight filtered in the window, I took the 4-wheeler and drove down the trail toward the airport, stopping frequently to call out, listening to my voice echoing in the fog and then vanishing. Who knows where she was, lost, hurt, or…dead?

When Harry called on the radio, I told him Jillian hadn't come home last night.

"Did she say which way she was going when she left?" It was a question I would have to answer dozens of times in the next few days.

"No. I didn't even see her leave."

She had done the morning chores, eaten breakfast, and sometime after that had vanished. Her 30-30 rifle was gone, so she must have planned to go farther than the yard. We always carried our rifles with us in the spring and summer for defense against bears. We would shoot up in the air to scare bears away. But one never knew when you would suddenly come across a mother bear with cubs or an old boar defending a fresh kill.

The weather was so foggy, it wasn't until late that day when the planes started showing up. Harry and Eddie were the first to arrive in the Cessna 185. They unloaded gas and supplies from the plane and took off again, flying low through the passes under the fog. I went back to the house to unload the supplies and answer the radio.

"Dolly, can you hear me?" Harry's voice sounded desperate.

I rushed to the radio. Had he seen Jillian?

"Yes, you are loud and clear! Did you find her?"

"No, Dolly! I mean can you hear the plane? Go outside and tell me if you can hear the plane!"

Oh no! Now Harry was lost in the fog, in the mountains! And Eddie was with him! In the blink of an eye, I could lose my entire family! I ran outside, straining my ears for the growl of the plane engine. Nothing but silence. It seemed almost surreal. I ran back inside.

"No! I didn't hear the plane!" I told Harry.

"OK. That's alright. I climbed up above the fog. We're going to fly out a ways until it gets clearer, and then get back under it and come back home. We'll see you at the airport in fifteen minutes."

I heaved a sigh of relief. At least Harry and Eddie were temporarily out of danger. I got in the jeep and drove to the airstrip to pick them up. Harry was already on the ground, and Eddie was tying the plane down.

"We have to wait until the fog lifts. If she is lost, we're just going to confuse her anyway by circling around. If she tries to follow the plane, she will just get more lost." Harry seemed relieved to be on the ground right now.

Eddie finished tying the plane down and came over and gave me a big hug. I hadn't seen him in a few months, and he had grown a few inches. Now he towered above me.

"Mama, anything could have happened. We saw lots of bears. There were fresh rockslides and avalanches. The water is really high in all the creeks. It's so foggy, it would be easy to get turned around out there. Dad even got lost looking for her. That was pretty scary!"

I hugged Eddie back and tried to think positively. Jillian was tough and resourceful. The wilderness was her home. I was sure she was still alive, somewhere.

Soon our airstrip was overflowing with small planes, operated by family, friends and search and rescue pilots. The troopers arrived, and search dogs had been ordered from Anchorage. I was busy with feeding the searchers, driving them to the airport, and arranging sleeping places for them at night. Keeping busy helped keep my mind off whatever disaster had befallen my daughter.

I was a bit disturbed that the troopers were focusing their search close to home. If Jillian was hurt that nearby, she would have still crawled to the trail or answered my calls. Shortly after they arrived the second day, one of the troopers approached me.

"We found a place where she built a fire. Come and look at this."

Eddie and I followed him hopefully. He led us down the trail and out over the tundra toward one of our mining claims. He pointed to a small stack of sticks and an old charred fire pit. It was nearly overgrown in weeds.

Eddie snorted. "That's over a year old! That's where Jillian and I were panning for gold long time ago. Our hands got cold so we built that fire to warm up. Look! There is grass growing in it. It is old and hasn't been used for a long time."

"It's too close to home. Jillian would never have gotten lost that close to home. My kids know this country like the back of their hands. She has to be farther away." I stated, wondering if the trooper knew what he was doing.

The trooper looked thoughtful. "Does your daughter have a boyfriend?" He asked.

Eddie and I looked at each other and laughed. The thought was almost preposterous. Jillian was still a young girl. She had no interest in boys at all. Where would she meet a boy, anyway? She hated going to town, so she hadn't been around other people in years.

The trooper looked at us defensively. "My daughter is the same age. She has been dating for over a year. She would run away for her boyfriend, if she was told she couldn't see him. It's just something I had to ask."

It started to make sense now. The troopers didn't know Jillian. They were looking in ordinary places for an ordinary little girl. Jillian was no ordinary girl. She was practically feral, spending all her time outdoors and avoiding humans. But something the trooper said formed a shred of doubt in my mind. What if she had run away? We would never find her if she didn't want to be found. She knew these mountains too well.

"No." I said with certainty. "Jillian didn't run away. Why would she run away? She doesn't like people. Where would she go? She's not into boys yet, either."

"Just had to ask, that's all. Did you have an argument with her or anything?"

"No, no, we get along fine. I don't think she ran away."

"Well, the search dogs are on the way. They can find a body under the ground, you know, if it's buried by, say, a bear or an avalanche." He was looking at me strangely.

I opened my mouth to say something, but right then another plane flew over, and I rushed to the airstrip to greet it, and find a parking spot for it. Henry stepped out of the Cessna 180 and gave me a big hug.

"There's more people coming to help search." Henry had a lot of friends in Bethel and often helped out with search and rescue missions.

It was wonderful to see Henry again. I hadn't seen him in a long time. He filled me in on current events in his life. Kayla, nearly a year old now, was starting to walk. Talking to Henry was a much-needed diversion from the current happenings. He always had a way of making me feel better in times of distress.

By the evening, the house was crowded, and the planes droned overhead continuously. Sometime during the second night, just as I finally drifted off to sleep, I awoke suddenly with a start, the shock of some unknown horror rapidly fading from my mind.

"She can't be dead!" I whispered. But I knew now Jillian was either dead, or very close to it.

"Shhhhhh. It's going to be OK. Go back to sleep." Harry mumbled.

The third day, the two police dogs arrived from Anchorage. I gave the handlers some of Jillian's clothes from the laundry pile and they set out on the search for scent, now several days old and diluted by the rain. Once again, they focused their search close around the buildings and within a half mile radius.

"We have to start somewhere," explained one of the dog handlers.

It appeared to be hard work, and the dogs had to stop often for rest. Hot Dog, unaccustomed to other dogs, growled at the newcomers, so we tied her on the porch out of their way.

Harry did not come in for dinner, and I went to look for him. I found him sitting on an old jeep tire behind the shop, crying. I had never seen Harry cry before. I sat next to him and put my arms around him.

"It's my fault. She ran away. I yell at these kids too much. I don't mean too, I'm just not good with kids."

"I don't think she ran away. It's not your fault if she did. It doesn't have to be anybody's fault. Things happen, you know." I tried to soothe him, but the twinge of doom still lingered from the previous night.

I had a difficult time sleeping that night. Our house was filled with people, in every bed, on the couch, in sleeping bags on the floor, and it was difficult to walk without stepping on someone. I finally drifted off into a restless sleep. I was awakened sometime in the night by Henry's voice.

"Get up everybody! She's back!" Henry whooped.

I sat up in bed, wondering if I just dreamed that. The room was pitch black. It was three in the morning. But then I saw the flashlights, and heard everyone talking at once. I ran out of my room, nearly bumping into people rising in the confusion. Jillian stood in the middle of the room, looking awkward and uncomfortable with all the attention.

Then Henry was hugging her, asking, "Where the hell have you been?"

Everybody was talking at once so she didn't have to answer. They were all talking about the thick fog and how they almost got lost themselves flying in it. It would be pretty easy for a young girl to get lost, wouldn't it, especially if she really liked to explore. Jillian nodded and told the troopers, yes, she did get really lost, but somehow we all knew that wasn't the truth. Everybody was just so happy she was back, they didn't want to spoil it.

After it got light, everyone left, and life pretty much went back to normal. Harry was a little more patient with the kids. Jillian still spent all her time outside, but now she told me where and when she was going.

Years later, Jillian told me about her adventure. She had thought that nobody really liked her and life would be easier for everyone if she left. Packing a few meager supplies in a backpack, she slipped away, headed east for Canada. She had eaten plants and fresh ptarmigan eggs along the way, travelling nearly forty miles through the mountains and across raging streams. She had reached the Aniak River, and sometime very late the second night, had tried to ford the mighty expanse. But the powerful current of the flooding river had dragged her under, her backpack filling with water like an anchor on her back. She had nearly drowned before slipping out of the pack and being swept up against a tree that had fallen into the river. Pulling herself out, she was disappointed to find herself on the same side of the river, with no matches or supplies. Temperatures hovered around freezing that night, so she had to keep moving to keep warm. Turning around, she walked back home. She had decided to keep walking through the night. She passed sleeping grizzlies in the thick brush. She navigated rockslides. Entering the yard, she saw the two police dogs, and patted them on their heads before she went in the house. She wasn't really sure what she was going to say, but nobody really asked, so she didn't have to say anything.

A few weeks after Jillian's return, Harry wrecked the Bell 47 helicopter. He had decided to shuttle us all, one at a time, to the lake cabin for a few days. Jillian was to go with him first, as she was the lightest and the fuel tanks were full. Eddie and I watched as the helicopter lifted off from the yard, hovered a second and then started toward the cabin. Suddenly it lost power and descended rapidly, spinning as the tail rotor struck the creek bank. Eddie and I rushed to the helicopter. Jillian and Harry got out, unhurt, but the fragile tail boom of the helicopter was damaged. We pulled it back into the yard with the Jeep. We didn't get to go to the lake cabin that spring.

In June of 1988, a helicopter flew over and landed at the hotsprings. Since it is a violation of federal regulations to use motorized vehicles within one quarter mile of a natural hotsprings, we rushed to see who the perpetrators were. We were surprised when Peter Lott stepped out, puffed up with importance, followed by two other men, and a pilot. The kids hadn't seen Peter since they were very small, and ran up to greet him.

"What's going on here?" I asked the pilot, who introduced himself as Lucky Wilson.

"It's some sort of elder Native interview on hotsprings usage. We are going around to all the old hotsprings and recording what the elders say. This man knew where some hotsprings were, so they brought him here, because they couldn't find the other old hotsprings by Tuluksak."

"What about the one by Bogus Creek, or Bear Creek?" I asked, still puzzled that they had to break the regulations by landing the helicopter next to the hotsprings.

"We looked all over the place, but couldn't find any of those springs, so they wanted to come here."

In the background I heard Peter talking loudly about his days as a reindeer herder.

"All up in these mountains, and cook 'em in the hotwater spring," he was saying. The two men were hanging on his every word, coaxing him along with suggestions.

"Peter! Hey, whatcha doing?" I asked him loudly.

He turned toward me. "Who is that woman?"

"It's me. Dolly. You stayed with us here, don't you remember?"

"Oh, Dolly. I stay in their house. I steam there in their house, and down there in their old house. And over here, they had little bathhouse, I steam there too. All this here, all these mountains, I used to herd reindeer, and the other hotsprings, we used to cook. Hot! Hotter than a boiling kettle. That's how we used to say it." Peter had always rambled in broken English, but now he almost sounded demented.

"Where's Martha?" Jillian asked hopefully.

"Who is this? Too-big girl. Bigger than me. Too big."

Jillian looked away, embarrassed. She had grown tall, and towered over the shorter man.

"Remember me, Peter? I'm Eddie." Eddie stuck out his hand.

Peter brushed it away and laughed. "Oh, little boy big too. Go-go, snowgo. Go-go! Go-go! Sometime in the night come crawl in bed with me! Cry! Like little girl, this boy!" He laughed harder.

Eddie looked embarrassed now, too. What was Peter up to? Why was he acting so odd?

Peter turned back to the men and started rambling about reindeer.

"What is this about?" I asked one of the men.

"We are documenting important Native events." The man said. He seemed uneasy and shifted his weight uncomfortably.

I snorted. "Reindeer herding was not a Native thing. It was a government project forced on the people. They didn't even want it. Look, they just let it go a few years later. You should be doing this where it actually occurred."

"We couldn't find the other place." The man seemed even more ill at ease.

Over the years we had several geologists, hydrologists, archaeologist, and BLM officials do studies on the hotsprings, so what difference did it make, if they wanted to stand there, in the swarms of mosquitos, and make up stories? I told the kids to keep an eye on them, and went down to the house to make coffee and snacks for our guests.

Shortly afterward, Jillian came down too, to help me. The two men, she said had been rude and kept trying to chase her away. She still remembered enough of Martha Lott's Yupik to pick up a conversation between Peter and the interpreter.

"He said, 'don't let them know what we are doing. Say it all in Yup'ik when those people are around.' Mama, Peter's different. How come Martha didn't come? Those guys are creepy, but the pilot is nice." She helped me set the table, and then went back to tell the group that there was fresh coffee and food at the house.

I fed the guests, and they left later in the afternoon. As we watched the helicopter take off and fly to the south over the hills, Eddie said,

"Peter said they were going to the other old hotsprings. The one they used to cook in, long time ago. Do you think he was acting weird? He kept mixing stuff up. Those guys told him what to say and then he said whatever they told him. What do you think is going on?"

"Watch where they go," Jillian interrupted,"I wanna find the old place he was talking about."

The helicopter disappeared over the hills, and the sound faded away.

"It's a long ways away. Too far to walk from here, he says." Eddie swatted a mosquito. "Mama, why do you think Peter was being mean like that?"

"I don't know, son," I pondered. "Sometimes people say mean things to make themselves feel better. It's strange. When people are mean, lots of times they are hiding something, and they feel bad about themselves for it, so they try to make people around them feel bad too. I don't know why they brought him, and why Martha didn't come too. It sure is strange."

We turned to go back inside the house. It wasn't until many years later that we would discover what Peter Lott and the two men were up to, and the shocking extent of meanness involved.

# Chapter Twenty

"Beaver ball soup! I smell beaver balls! Yummm!" Eddie exclaimed with delight as he stomped the snow off his boots. "When is it ready?"

"Another fifteen minutes." I stirred the soup.

"Beaver balls, beaver balls, yummy yum yum." Eddie sang, and the kids laughed.

It was one of our favorite recipes although sometimes I think the kids liked it so much because of the name. Despite being called 'beaver ball soup', there were no actual beaver testicles included in the tasty concoction. The 'balls' were simply chunks of ground meat much like a meatball. Beaver was a big staple in our diets, and to add variety to the classic roast beaver, we cut the meat off the bones and ran it through a hand-operated grinder. The finished product was just like ground beef, and we substituted it for beef in recipes. The kids coined fun names for the recipes, for example, beaver meat pizza became beazza.

"Hey, can you write that recipe down in my cookbook?" Jillian asked.

"Oh sure. That's a good idea." I had made a cookbook of favorite family recipes for Jillian, so she could make our favorite dishes without having to ask me what amounts and ingredients every time.

I picked up a pen and started writing it in while I waited for the soup to finish cooking.

*Beaver Ball Soup*

*1 pound ground beaver meat*

*1 egg*

*2 tablespoons white rice*

*1 tablespoon Worcestershire sauce*
*1/2 teaspoon garlic powder*
*1/2 teaspoon oregano*
*1/2 teaspoon pepper*

*Combine above ingredients and shape into 1 inch balls. Drop the meatballs into saucepan of boiling water. Cook for 10-15 minutes. Then add soup ingredients:*

*1 onion*
*½ cup celery*
*2 carrots*
*2 potatoes*
*2 tablespoons rice*
*1 can tomato sauce*
*1 teaspoon oregano*
*1 teaspoon chili powder*

*Add more water, about 5-6 cups. Bring to a boil and simmer for 25 minutes.*

More often than not, I would have to substitute ingredients. I cooked with what I had. There was no running to the next door neighbor's for a cup of sugar. Harry bought the staples when they were on sale, and we had very few frills. Worcestershire sauce, for example, was not always something I had in stock. Most often I would substitute it for vinegar or ketchup. And then a new recipe would be born. I thumbed through the cookbook, smiling at some of our inventions, like curried lynx, and salmonberry jam squares.

Then the soup was done and I ladled it into our bowls. Harry was in Bethel, so that made cooking easier for me. Although he loved hunting, he didn't care for wild game meat, and I would have to cook something different for him. It was tiring having to cook two meals. Harry would scoff and make fun of the kids while they ate their favorite dishes. I tolerated his behavior because he usually brought the food he wanted to eat along for me to cook, and rarely stayed more than a few days.

Harry was busy in Bethel with the cab business. He also sold sand from his lot, hauling it with a dump truck to people's yards. It was a lucrative business, as the fine glacial delta silt eroded yearly, and houses sank into the permafrost. Every year, people needed more sand on their lots to keep their houses from sinking and shifting. Henry had started a business leveling the foundations of houses and was doing quite well. But Harry did not have Henry's business sense, and he constantly overextended his financial resources. He borrowed money with high interest rates, and bounced checks. None of the equipment he was using was paid for, and he missed payments frequently. He had big dreams and aspirations, but not the money to make it happen. Harry had disassembled the little Bell helicopter for rebuilding, and was in the process of purchasing a bigger Fairchild helicopter. I worried constantly about our family budget, as the rabbit population was low, and there was little food remaining in our stockpiles. The kids had to snowshoe over ten miles now to their beaver traps.

Harry had left Eddie home most of this winter, as he was "too busy" to be a father to him. Eddie had grown into a fine, handsome young man, towering over six feet tall. But he was a teenager now, doing things teenagers do, racing up and down the road at night in his old car, smoking pot, partying with shiftless friends, and pilfering to pay for it all. He had quit doing his schoolwork, and only occasionally helped his dad. It was just a phase that every teenager goes through, but Harry was pretty impatient with him.

I was glad to have my son home and hoped he would have some time to think and decide what his priorities were now. As a child, he had lived and breathed airplanes, and I was sure that he wanted to fly. Harry had arranged for Eddie to get some flying lessons in Bethel, but after a few lessons, Eddie stopped going. Eddie still had difficulty with his feet, and it was a challenge for him to operate the brake and rudder pedals in an aircraft. Still, he could tell you anything you wanted to know about any airplane in existence. Now, he loved cars too, and could tell you anything about them also. Maybe he would be a truck driver instead of a pilot.

Eddie loved White Bear, and trapping beaver was one of his favorite things. Always competitive, he had to catch more animals or pick more berries, or be the best at whatever it was that we were doing. During his childhood, Jillian and I played along, letting him beat us at nearly everything. Eddie had so many obstacles in his life to overcome, being born handicapped, and torn away from home at an early age, that we were happy to indulge a few whims to help his self esteem.

As we relished our dinner, I thought ahead to moose season. Moose had been scarce this year, and we hadn't got one in the fall. Perhaps Eddie would shoot one next month when the winter season opened. We had a few more meals of beaver, and Eddie had just shot a ptarmigan. I still had a few boxes of potatoes left from my garden, and berries we had canned over the summer. We would get by like we always did.

Our food supply the next month was scanty, at best. The trapline yielded very little. One day, Eddie and Jillian came home, excited that they had caught a weasel. Jillian cleaned it, stretched the hide, and threw the carcass in the frying pan. We didn't have much for seasoning, so she opened up some Lipton tea bags emptied them over the meat. After it cooked, there wasn't a whole lot to it, but we ate it anyway. Hungry as I was, it was possible one of the worst things I had tasted. Needless to say, that recipe never made the family cookbook.

Moose season opened, and the kids spent days hunting. They had no luck, and found no tracks. Then, they came home one day, very upset and scared.

"What's wrong? What happened?" I asked Eddie.

"Damn drunken bastards shot our moose! Right out from under us! And then they shot at us!" He snarled.

"What?! Oh no! How far away? Oh no!" I had never thought of other hunters taking our moose.

"We found tracks about ten miles away, down way past the eagle's nest. We tracked it another couple miles, and then it doubled back. Jillian kept it moving, and I went back to a little clearing and waited for it to cross." Eddie stopped for breath.

"Oh, you were quite a ways away. Nearly to the tundra's edge, then?" I asked.

"Yeah. Way past Tootsie's cabin. Then we heard snowmachines, big, expensive new ones, and these two assholes raced up into the clearing, and the moose was running all-out right ahead of them. The one guy shot it point-blank after it fell down." He stopped again, steaming mad now.

"When did they shoot at you?" I asked.

"I'm getting to that. They shut their snowgos off and started drinking from a bottle and talking. Then they noticed me standing at the edge of the clearing, and the one asshole started cussing me out in Yup'ik, calling me names, and then he just pointed his gun over at me and shot! Right at me!" Eddie was still trembling with indignation.

"What did you do? Did you shoot back at them?"

"No, they had me dead in their sights. They would have killed me. Jillian was back in the brush, and shot up in the air, to let them know there was someone else there. Then we both ran like hell, and met up back past the eagle's nest."

"Oh man! We should tell the troopers. They might be able to check snowmachine tracks or something." I was aghast that anyone could do such a thing to my children.

Eddie snorted derisively. "The troopers won't do shit. Because it's Natives. It's not fair at all. They have big expensive snowmachines, and food stamps, and live on a river where there's lots of fish to eat! They spent hundreds of dollars in gas to drive that far, and shoot the moose we were after. They saw us, and saw our tracks. They didn't need the meat like we do! Same thing with our trapline getting raided down by the lake. The troopers aren't going to do shit, because it's natives and natives can do whatever they want."

"We'll have your dad make a report anyway. Did you get a good look at the men?"

"Yeah, I'd recognize them anywhere. I wish Jillian had put a hole in their snowgo or something instead of shooting up in the air."

Jillian said, "Yeah right. They were too far away and I'm not as good a shot as you are. I might have accidently hit one of them."

"It would have served them right, shooting at me! The law isn't going to do anything to them. It's not fair. I was born here. I'm more of a Native than those two assholes are, with their great big snowmachines!" Eddie was pretty upset, and rightfully so.

That night, we told Harry on the radio, and he echoed Eddie's sentiments about lack of justice, and that the troopers would do nothing.

"Just make the report anyway, and if the guys get caught for something else, maybe we will know who they are." I begged.

"Ok, OK, Dolly! I'm damn busy down here, and don't have time for this. But, we'll see what I can do. Put Eddie on the radio. Have him describe the men the best he can." Harry said.

Eddie picked up the mic and proceeded to give a full description of the shooters.

"OK. Stay close to home, and keep your guns with you. If they come onto our property, shoot 'em. Ask questions later." That was Harry's advice.

I shuddered. It was a problem I had not foreseen. We lived so far from any of the villages, so far off the river, off the beaten path. In all my years, I had never seen another human that we did not bring here ourselves. No one travelled this far up into the mountains from their village. But then, the kids had been a long way from home. Perhaps Harry was right, and they should stay closer to home. I wondered if they would listen to that advice. I needn't have worried. The kids, especially Jillian, were so terrified they barely left the house for the next month. And when they went anywhere, they were armed to the teeth.

## Chapter Twenty-One

"Dolly, the kids are in jail over in Aniak." Harry said on the radio.

"What?!" I didn't understand. It couldn't be. It was some sort of mistake. Eddie and Jillian had taken the Elan to the edge of the tundra, with the last five gallon jug of gas, to look for caribou. It was rumored that the caribou had changed their migration patterns and were near the big lake.

"Eddie and Jillian are in Aniak. In jail!" Harry insisted. He didn't sound at all pleased.

"Oh damn, oh no! What did they do?" I envisioned an armed confrontation with the people who shot at them.

"They broke into the store for food. They had guns with them, you know. That doesn't look too good. The troopers called me up and told me to come up and get them, but hell, I'm just going to let them sit there awhile. Damn kids are nothing but trouble. How the hell am I going to get that Elan home? Shit." Harry didn't seem to want to say any more on the radio.

I was shocked. What the hell were the kids doing in Aniak? It was 45 miles away. We couldn't afford the gas. Eddie had said they were going looking for caribou, and when they didn't return that night, I thought maybe they had shot one, and decided to camp overnight because it was dark.

I paced the floor. What should I do? Harry should go and pick up the kids. Instead he was worried about the stupid old rundown junk snowmachine. I worried and fretted about it all night. The next morning I pleaded with Harry.

"Go pick up the kids! Just take your plane over and pick them up, before they get into any more trouble."

"Nah. I'll just leave them there. Besides, now the State is involved, and they're going to fly the kids here to Bethel tomorrow. Maybe they'll learn a lesson. They'll have to go to court." Harry sounded strangely resigned.

I had no idea what they had done, or what the charges were against them. I was furious at Jillian! She had no right to get Eddie into trouble with the law. Why had she jeopardized her brother's future?! Without her, Eddie was merely a dreamer. Jillian was the doer.

I needn't have wasted my time fuming about it. At the court hearing the next day, Harry informed me that Jillian had confessed to everything, and denied Eddie's involvement. All charges against Eddie were dropped, and Jillian was sent off to juvenile detention in another town far away.

Harry brought Eddie home a week later, and I got an abbreviated story from him. They hadn't seen any caribou, or any sign near the lake, but cut across a fairly fresh snowmachine track. Eddie had decided to follow it and see if it was one of the men that shot at him. A few hours later, they reached the river, and decided to go to Aniak instead. Eddie had about $200 cash from last year's trapping. They planned to buy groceries and come home. But it was late and the store was closed when they got there. Eddie had told Jillian to break in, get the food, and leave the money by the cash register. Then he left to go look at the airplanes at the airport. A plain-clothed police officer had seen Jillian prying open the door and gave chase. Jillian, cornered and terrified, had pulled a gun on him, and then the whole place was swarming with troopers. Eddie, driving back from the airport, had been caught in the middle of it, and had given up peaceably. Jillian had been arrested also, although not so peaceably, and had accrued a number of assault charges.

Over the next several months, Eddie and I took turns staying at White Bear. I went to Bethel with Harry, for the first time in years, and he put me to work driving one of the taxi cabs. He insisted we needed to make more money to get a better lawyer for Jillian. But every time we did get a financial break, he used the funds to purchase another junk vehicle. I got my cab driver's license and drove one of the cabs, giving all the money I made to Harry. I assumed he would be driving also, in the second cab, but frequently, I would look in the rear view mirror and see his old pickup truck following me. He had always been suspicious of me, but this seemed pointless. He used up more gas following me than if he just drove the cab himself, and let me stay at home. The uselessness of it all wore at me, and our tempers were short.

Meanwhile, Eddie stayed at White Bear, caring for the animals and the homestead. It was a safe place to leave him, and kept him out of trouble while we were working. But it was hard on Eddie. As much as he loved the homestead, he was a social person, and did not like being alone. He missed his friends and his carefree life of partying. I relished the solitude, but to Eddie, a teenager, it was nearly overwhelming. Harry would bring me home, and then Eddie and I would exchange places, and everything was better for awhile. Then Eddie would start drinking and partying again and Harry would bring him back to White Bear. I would have to go back to the useless grind of driving cab, for money that Harry practically threw away, living in Harry's filthy hovel, enduring his jealous accusations. This was not how I wanted to live!

During the summer, Hot Dog died. She was an old dog, and the strain of her family's long absences took its toll on her. She was very devoted to me, and often wouldn't eat when I was gone. Eddie hadn't noticed that she was sick until one morning he found her, cold and stiff, lying by the kitchen door. The homestead was lonely without a dog, I found, when I returned the next week. I had taken Hot Dog's quiet gentle companionship for granted.

A few weeks later, Harry and I kept noticing a pack of stray dogs, most of them puppies, roaming the streets of Bethel. They were lean and ragged, and would surely be shot by the city animal control officer soon.

"You ought to grab one of those. They're just going to get shot anyway." Harry pointed to a small brownish puppy. "Take that one."

Harry pulled off the side of the road, and I knelt down, offering a piece of chicken to the dogs. They crowded around, sniffing warily, and I reached out and grabbed one by the scruff. We were stopped just off the road, and creating a bit of a traffic jam, so I tossed the puppy in the truck and got in quickly. She whimpered a bit, looking out the window at her pack, and then settled in to finishing the remains of our lunch. The vet happened to be in town, so I took the puppy to get her shots and much needed worming medicine. She rode in the front seat of my taxi cab with me on all my routes. Soon Harry began calling her "Taxi Dog", the name that stuck with her for the rest of her years.

In the fall, Eddie shot a big bull moose, dropping it neatly just at the edge of the yard. He told us about it on the radio that evening and started butchering it himself.

"Get your stuff," Harry told me. "Meet me at the airport. We have to go help Eddie butcher that moose."

I gave a shriek of delight. It was as if a thousand pound weight had been lifted from my shoulders. Taxi romped playfully at the end of her leash, sensing the excitement. Even Harry was more cheerful as he loaded the plane. We left a small space between the cargo for the dog, and tied her leash to the seat back. She whined a bit, scratched at the backs of our seats, then quivered in terror as the plane sped down the airstrip and hurled itself into the air. When we got to White Bear, Harry flew low over the house, making the tight turn in the box canyon and dropping down a few feet off the ground to buzz Eddie. I saw Eddie stand up from the moose kill, and wave his knife. We landed, and Eddie roared down the trail in the old jeep, glad to see us.

"Hi! Boy am I glad to see you guys! Actually, I got a pretty good start on butchering my moose. I'm just glad you're here to help me can the meat!" Eddie was so excited he almost didn't notice the puppy.

I gave Eddie a big hug, and then started unloading the supplies. I untied the leash and the dog shot out, racing in circles, barking and rolling in the grass. I felt like doing the same thing myself.

"Oh, good. We need a dog. There's so much meat scraps from butchering, it would seem like a waste not to have a dog to eat it." Eddie patted Taxi on the head.

Harry had just bought a freezer in Bethel, so he suggested, rather than canning the meat, we wrap it and store it in the Bethel freezer. We spent the next few days slicing all the meat up, and then Harry took the load to town. Eddie and I and the new dog stayed home, and life seemed perfect. There was much to do. The garden was in shambles and wood needed to be split. We caught up on the chores and played card games. Eddie was glad to have company, and I was glad to be home again. If only things could just stay this way. But soon Harry was back to pick up Eddie. Harry had odd delusions, and couldn't stand the idea of me being alone with another man, even if it was our own son. It was both insulting and degrading. I watched them fly away, and then went back to digging up the last of the potatoes before the ground froze.

The days flew by at the homestead. The puppy grew into a beautiful German Shepherd mix, fast and athletic, but with a mind of her own. She would spend hours worrying at some hapless animal, racing in circles and barking until the animal died of terror or exhaustion. Taxi didn't seem to comprehend any verbal commands, so I was forced to keep her inside much of the time. She retaliated by destroying whatever was within reach. Still, I adored her. I had a German Shepherd when I was younger, and it made me frisky, too.

Later that winter, we got word that Jillian had served her sentence and was being released on probation. Harry was quick to drop her off and leave again. For him now, everything was back the way it should be. He didn't want to leave me alone at the homestead. He didn't want Eddie to stay with me. Harry couldn't stay with me himself, because he had to work. He didn't understand that I had no problem with being alone, that I cherished the solitude and freedom. Who knew what Jillian would be like now, she had been away from home for the first time and under these difficult circumstances.

Jillian pretty much went back to her old routine, roaming the mountains and keeping to herself. The probation officer that flew up to check on her was full of mothering advice. I nodded once in awhile, and then asked her how many children she had. None. No wonder she knew it all. Jillian and I got along fine, although I knew she sensed my distrust of her. She had developed quite a dislike for Taxi, and I took it personally.

"Mama, it doesn't have anything to do with you. I just don't like her. She barks all the time, chases off game, pisses all over the floor. You're always yelling at her. She never listens. I don't think she is a very smart dog."

I was slow to realize that Jillian was indeed right. It took about three years to house-train that dog, and to her dying day, she never understood a single verbal command. She had a strong herding instinct, and anything that moved had to be bitten and worried until it stopped moving. That included the 4-wheeler tires, although she had been run over several times already, and porcupines. Taxi would come home covered in quills, and Jillian and I would pull out hundreds of the sharp barbs while Taxi whimpered in pain. Released once again, she would go right back out, often the same day, and return covered in quills. After about two weeks straight of pulling quills, I finally agreed to keep Taxi on a leash for awhile.

"That poor porcupine is probably just about bald by now." Jillian laughed. "But look at all the quills we have! We can make a lot of earrings from those."

I sewed and made jewelry, and Eddie would take my crafts to Bethel when he came home with Harry. I was finally able to save up a little bit of spending money for the rare times Harry took me to town. Jillian was tanning the furs she trapped and giving them to me to sew with rather than giving them to her dad to sell. She would be gone all day on the trapline, and return tired and covered in frost and wood smoke. She would skin her catch and work on the furs she was tanning, and by then it was late at night. She was far behind now in her schoolwork, but I hesitated to nag. The trapline made her happy, and we needed the meat and fur.

"I want to come along on the trapline." I told Jillian one morning.

"Oh." She looked surprised. "OK. Just don't make me wait on you. I'm putting out another set today and want to get it in before dark."

But she did wait on me, not so patiently, as I searched for a pair of gloves and adjusted my snowshoe bindings. Taxi turned herself inside out with delight at the adventure, and her shrill yapping echoed through the clear winter air. When we finally started out, Jillian breaking trail through the fresh deep snow, Taxi turned her attack on Jillian's snowshoes. Jillian tripped and fell. It looked funny and I couldn't help but laugh.

"It's not funny. You should leave the stupid thing at home, if it's not going to listen." Jillian snarled.

"She's not stupid! She's just having fun!" I defended Taxi instantly.

Jillian stormed off up the hill and I struggled to follow. Taxi took off after a jay, and I stopped often to call for her. At the top of the hill, Jillian stopped and waited for me, and when I caught up, panting hard, she took off again, breaking trail effortlessly through the deep snow. Suddenly she stopped and raised her gun. Looking where she was aiming, I saw a ptarmigan, sitting very still at the edge of the willows. Just then, Taxi burst out of the brush, barking, racing straight for the bird. Startled, it rose and flew away before Jillian could shoot.

"Well, there goes our dinner." She stomped off again.

I struggled to catch up, Taxi now worrying over my snowshoe bindings. Jillian stopped again to wait for me, and the dog raced ahead. By the time we got to the first lynx set, we found Taxi howling, with her foot in the trap. She bit Jillian a few times while she was releasing the dog. My voice was hoarse from calling the dog. By the time we got to the beaver traps, it was too late, and Jillian decided not to put in the new set she had planned to do that day. We walked home, Jillian in stormy silence, myself still shouting for the dog to come, and Taxi, still barking intently at something along the way. My trapline excursion had been a disaster. Jillian barely said anything to me the rest of the evening.

The next morning, I was shocked when Jillian asked, "Are you coming along, or what?"

"I thought you didn't want me along." I said.

"I don't care if you come along or not. Just not that damn dog. She can stay home. You want her to get caught in a trap again? Next time maybe she'll break her foot. You want to ruin the whole day screaming at her? Or would you rather to go along on the trapline and have fun?"

I tied the dog out of reach of anything, and put on my snowshoes. Taxi wailed forlornly and nearly strangled herself trying to slip her collar.

Up ahead, Jillian dropped into a crouch, and then lifted her rifle. She shot once, and a fat ptarmigan fluttered, dying, in the brush. She went over and picked it up. Good, I thought, dinner! Maybe it was good we didn't bring the dog after all.

When we got to the beaver pond, Jillian started a small fire and hung her coat on a branch.

"Won't you get cold?" I wondered.

"Nope. Not while I'm chopping ice. But later, I will be cold, when my gloves get wet, and that's what the fire is for. Will you keep it going?"

Jillian attacked the ice with the big metal bar. Ice chips flew. She stopped a few times, scooping the ice out of the hole. I was getting restless standing there waiting. Jillian tossed me the ice pick.

"Want to give it a shot?"

She went over to warm up by the fire and I started chopping. It was surprisingly more work than I had anticipated. The hole was already several feet deep, but still no sign of water. Jillian came back over, and we traded places.

"How thick is this ice?" I asked.

"About here." She gestured on the ice pick, at about the four foot level. Then she started chopping again.

We took turns until the water started to show in the bottom of the hole. Jillian finished the hole fast, trying to avoid getting wet by the splashing water.

"Now we set the traps?" I asked hopefully.

"Maybe. Maybe not. We have to check first if the hole we chopped is over the channel the beavers use." The beavers used the same path every day to swim from their house to their stockpile of food under the ice. Their continuous usage eroded away a deep channel.

Jillian knelt on the ice, pressing her forehead against the rim of the hole, straining to see into the water.

"Nope," She says. "Too shallow. We have to make another hole. Maybe over here?"

She picked up the ice pick and started chopping again. I sighed with disappointment. Jillian looked up.

"Hey, you don't have to hang around if you got somewhere else to be. This might take awhile."

"No, that's OK. Here, give me that bar. It's my turn."

I picked at the ice until my hands stung and my arms ached. Jillian stoked the fire, gathered more wood, and came back again to take over. The second hole turned out to be just as futile as the first. Jillian looked into it, and then pointed to the ice a few feet over.

"Right there. I bet that would be the channel."

The last hole turned out to be right over the main beaver thoroughfare. I looked under the ice where Jillian showed me, and could see the deep trench, littered with shiny peeled twigs. She compressed the heavy beaver trap under her knee and carefully lowered it into the water. It dangled from a wire, and this she attached to a log on the top of the ice. Next to the trap, she dropped a few snares.

"Ready to check the other set?" She asked, stomping out the fire and putting her coat back on.

"Uh, yeah, I guess. How far is it?" It was starting to get dark.

"Half mile. Where we turned around yesterday. That's my last set."

The ice was thinner in the next hole, due to the daily chopping. The traps were snapped but there was no beaver in them. Jillian reset the traps.

"They get smart after awhile and learn how to snap the traps without getting caught. This is where I caught the last beaver."

We snowshoed home. Taxi was just fine. I shouldn't have worried so much. After that, I accompanied Jillian on the trapline nearly every day. I left the dog at home. I had never realized how much work went into trapping, and now I had a whole new appreciation for the tender young beaver we feasted on the next day.

*Beaver Jillian caught*

## Chapter Twenty-Two

Henry's plane buzzed low overhead. I ran outside, wondering what was up. I hoped everything was OK! Jillian and I jumped in the Jeep and roared off for the airstrip.

When we got there, Henry was swatting mosquitos by his plane.

"Hi! Harry didn't tell me you were coming home! Is everything OK?" I asked, handing him a can of mosquito spray.

"Yep!" He grinned. "I got a little surprise for you! Somebody has been bugging me all week to see her Grandma!"

"Hi Grandma!" Kayla shouted, jumping out of the plane. She ran into my arms.

"Oh, Kayla!" My heart melted with grandmotherly love as I scooped her up and held her in my arms. What a wonderful surprise! She had grown so much since the last time I had seen her. Occasionally, when he got off work on the weekends, Henry would bring Kayla to see me for a few hours, but it didn't seem often enough!

"Tell Grandma what you wanted to tell her now, honey." Henry prompted her.

Kayla looked at me with absolute delight. "I'm staying with you!"

"Just overnight!" Henry said quickly. "She's been bugging me about it every day. Is that OK with you?"

"Of course!" I answered with happiness. What a great honor that my son trusted his beloved daughter with me! "She can stay longer if she wants to."

"She probably won't want to. She's still a little girl yet, she'll miss her mommy by tomorrow." Harry unloaded a duffle bag and a large box of food.

After hugging me and fussing over Kayla a bit, Henry left. I watched him tip the wings before he disappeared out of sight. Kayla and Jillian were giggling about something as Jillian loaded the bag into the Jeep. It was good to have the happy little girl around. For such a young girl, Kayla was very outgoing and adventurous. Most children would still be clinging to their mommy and daddy, not spending the night in the wilderness with their grandma.

We baked cookies and had a goofy little tea party. Kayla brought a hen in from the coop and put a little scarf around it. It was one of the fancy breed chickens I had ordered the year before, speckled black and white with a comical little tuft of feathers on the top of its head. It looked so silly, sitting in the chair pecking at a cookie. We all laughed until tears ran down our cheeks. The noise startled the hen, and she cackled, which made us laugh harder. Then she had a little "accident" on her chair. Kayla stopped laughing and looked at me wide-eyed.

"That's OK." I gasped. "She just got excited and pooped her pants! Do you know what that white stuff the chicken left is?" I asked.

"Nooooo." she answered, puzzled.

"That's chicken shit, too!" I grinned.

Then we laughed so hard our sides ached. The hen nonchalantly started pecking on another cookie.

Kayla came to visit me more often in the following years. We had so much fun when she was around. I saw the world again through the wondrous eyes of a child. Eddie and Jillian loved having Kayla around, and even Harry was not nearly so grumpy.

Over the summer, Harry had borrowed money, using Eddie's name, and purchased a Cessna 172. The idea was that Eddie would have his own plane to learn to fly with, and Eddie would pay the bill. But Eddie was hugely disappointed.

"Mama, it's not the kind of plane I want. I don't want to pay this big bill for a plane I don't want. I wish Dad hadn't done that! I want to buy my own plane, the kind I want." He grumbled.

"Your Dad means the best for you. Why don't you just use it to learn to fly, and then sell it and buy what you want?" I asked.

"Because I want to learn in a different kind of plane. I don't want this one." Eddie insisted.

I shrugged. I didn't know enough about airplanes. Eddie knew what he wanted. I knew Harry was just trying to give Eddie a little shove in the right direction, to give him goals and put him on a better path, but to start his young life out paying for something he didn't want seemed like a frustrating conflict to Eddie.

Shortly after that, Eddie moved out of Harry's Bethel house. Henry gave him a small shed, which he put on the back of a big flatbed pickup truck, and slept where he parked. Henry offered him a job, and over the next several years, Eddie worked for Henry sporadically. Eddie didn't come home as often, and I missed him so much. But he seemed to be doing a bit better now that he was forced to be more independent. Although he lacked motivation, Eddie was an intelligent young man. In April 1991, Eddie obtained his G.E.D. with the highest score ever recorded in Alaska. That record is still standing today.

Meanwhile, Harry also had trouble with his chosen aircraft. His Fairchild Hiller 1100 helicopter had engine troubles on the trip to Alaska and made an emergency landing just outside of Yakutat. Since it had been immersed in sea water, the entire craft had to be disassembled and rebuilt. After more than a year rebuilding the helicopter, J.B. and Harry brought it up to White Bear with supplies. J.B. was to fly our Cessna 185 back to Bethel, and Harry was to fly the Hiller.

J.B. had engine trouble on the way to Bethel and had to make an emergency landing in a very small clearing between trees off the Kuskokwim River near Tuluksak. The plane was damaged but J.B. wasn't hurt. What saved him was his calmness and vast experience as a bush pilot.

What made that day very memorable was that on Harry's landing at Bethel with the Hiller, the landing skid collapsed, tipping over the helicopter, shearing off the rotors which came through the bubble just inches from Harry's head. The first flight after the previous year's repairs, and the Hiller was a total loss. Two aircraft wrecked in the same hour of the same day!

Harry was now struggling with the cab business, but making enough money with hauling sand to rebuild his old blue Cessna 206. But he still had payments to make on the completely useless helicopter.

Jillian and I gardened and picked berries in the summer and trapped in the winter. The fur prices had dropped dramatically, so there was no point in selling furs. I helped Jillian tan the pelts and used them to sew with. Tanning was a lot of work, and very time consuming, but a useful way to spend the long dark winter evenings. We sat around the dim kerosene lantern and worked the pelts while we played Scrabble or read books. At daybreak, we would snowshoe the trapline. Jillian had extended it to a ten mile loop. It was good exercise, and we would go every day, no matter what the weather was doing. Sometimes, the wind would shriek and the house would rattle and I could barely see out the window through the driving snow. Jillian would put on her parka and go out anyway.

"It always looks worse than it is. Once you're outside in it, it's not that bad. You just have to be prepared for anything, dress for the weather." Jillian stated.

Harry had taught the kids from an early age never to leave the house without their hats and mittens, and to carry matches and string and a knife in their pockets.

We didn't have very much gasoline back then, so using the snowmachine on the trapline was not an option. What gasoline we did have, Harry had siphoned out of the wing tanks of his airplane when he had extra. Since Harry was short on money, he did not leave any gas behind for several years. We rationed it carefully to be sure there would be enough to use the snowmachine or the Jeep to pick Harry up from the airport when he came. Normally, we would have had enough gas to use the snowmachine to drag the year's firewood supply home. But not this year. The timber grew about two miles from the house, so it would be quite a haul to carry it home on snowshoes. And that's exactly what we did.

Then, Jillian spotted a nice stand of well-cured dead spruce along the creek at her last beaver set, five miles away. She cut and stacked the wood along our trail, and on the way home from the trapline, we would each pull a toboggan piled with firewood. It was a difficult and exhausting toil, but the reward was great as we watched our woodpile grow larger every day. Jillian, energetic and tireless, would often make two trips a day. It turned out to be a good thing she did, as soon the trail conditions became even more difficult as the heavy wet snow began to melt.

One lovely spring day Jillian put on her backpack and started out the door.

"Wait!" I called after her. "Where are you going? Maybe I want to come along!"

"Up in the mountains, just to go for a hike. If you're coming, you better hurry up."

"Do I need to bring anything? Do we need snowshoes, or did the snow freeze hard enough last night?" I asked.

"I'm taking mine along for a little ways. If we hurry up, we won't need them, because we will be back before it starts melting."

I grabbed the snowshoes, tucked them under my arm, and took off after Jillian, excited to see what kind of adventure she was off on. I had always wondered about the places she went by herself all these years. She followed the trail a ways, then turned back to look at me.

"I'm leaving my snowshoes here by the trail. It doesn't look as if we are going to need them." She stuck the snowshoes up in the snow and I set mine next to hers.

Then she took off up the side of the mountain, stopping occasionally to wait for me.

"Go on, just go ahead, you don't need to wait for me," I panted.

"OK. See the top of that mountain there? That's where I'm headed. Go through that patch of brush right there, and then it's clear all the way to the top, no more brush."

She took off again, and by the time I had beaten my way through the thick brush, I could see her far ahead, zigzagging across the slope above me. I continued on, marveling at the intricate tundra mosses on the slope. I picked my way carefully across fields of loose shale, and started angling upward. It appeared as if the top of the mountain was just ahead, but as I crested the rise, another terrace rose ahead. I continued onward, wondering how I would find Jillian up here, and what direction she had taken. Finally, I summited the last slope, and saw Jillian ahead, sitting in a boulder field on the flat top of the mountain.

"Oh hi," she said, patting the rock next to her. "Pull up a boulder and take a break. Nice up here, isn't it?"

I looked around. It was an incredible view, a majestic panorama of mountains rising up in every direction. The sky was clear and blue, and the distant mountain ranges reflected its hue. Looking behind us, I could faintly make out the house, a tiny dot nestled in the bottom of the canyon. I felt small and insignificant amongst all the grandeur of the wild Alaskan landscape. I said something of the sort to Jillian.

"Really?!" She said, sounding surprised. "It's the opposite for me. I feel big and powerful like the mountains when I'm up here. It's like, I'm a mighty giant, and this is all my territory. There's no other people as far as you can see in any direction. That's total freedom, right there. Think of all the people in the cities, trapped there, hating their neighbors but stuck living next to them. And all the wars and crime and hatred in the world. Up here, there's no people to fight and steal your food and shoot at you. You know what? Elbow room is the greatest wealth in the world. You and I, we are the richest people in the world."

I looked back out over the mountains again, this time as if through Jillian's eyes, and now I saw what she meant. I felt so free.

"I wonder if things were better for people in the old days." I pondered.

"Definitely not!" Jillian snorted. "In the old days, people fought even more. The Eskimos and Indians, for example. All down there along the Kuskokwim, they fought and killed each other over nothing. Just hated each other because they were different, that's all. The early settlers too, killing the natives, and the Holocaust, and witchcraft trials. I think this is the best era to be alive."

Jillian stopped suddenly and looked around at something in the sky. I looked up, and then I heard it too, a sharp cry of a hawk, and the whistle of wind through its wings as it dove at us. It sped past on folded wings, then rose sharply, calling out shrilly.

"Gyrfalcon," Jillian said. "She probably has a nest somewhere around here. She hunts the rock ptarmigan up here, I see her here pretty often."

I looked down in the canyon, and far away, I could see my own nest. I felt warm inside, and thinking back to all the hardships and toils we had endured over the years, I realized how much my home meant to me.

"Hey," Jillian broke into my reflections," see those mountains over there? There's a neat place on the other side of those, some big towers of rock. You want to go check it out? It's only a few hours hike."

"Yeah. Let's go!" I said, catching Jillian's enthusiasm.

"We can angle around from here and catch the next ridgeline. That will be the easiest."

Jillian started off, slower this time, waiting for me. The slope was slick, and in a few places, we had to circumnavigate the dangerous slides. We descended until we reached a gentle slope and then started climbing again. The snow was still packed hard. The weather was absolutely beautiful, although a bit hot with the bright sun reflecting off the snow. We stopped and took off our coats, and Jillian put them in her backpack. After a few hours hiking, we stopped and drank from an ice cold mountain stream. The snow was starting to melt by the time we got to the rocky ridge. We marveled at the odd formations, and then decided to start back before the snow became too soft to support our weight. The sun was hot against my skin, and my eyes began to water with the brightness. The snow now took on a pinkish tint. I stumbled once, disoriented, just as Jillian looked back at me.

"Hey! Where's your sunglasses?! You could go snowblind out here in this sun." She lectured.

"I forgot them." A pang of fear shot through me. Snowblind! It was already starting to happen. That's why the snow looked pink and distorted.

Jillian came back and handed me her sunglasses. "Here, use mine for awhile."

"No. That's OK. I don't need them. You keep them." I felt foolish for forgetting my own sunglasses, especially at this time of the year, when the reflection of the sun off the snow was so bright.

"Why don't we take turns wearing them? You wear them for an hour, then I'll take them back." Jillian compromised.

We hiked along, trading the sunglasses every hour. It helped immensely, for without those sunglasses we would probably both been snowblind. The walking became increasingly difficult, as now the afternoon sun had softened the snow, and we sank in nearly every step. We took turns breaking trail, and the second person had an easier time following the leader's footsteps. In some places, the snow was nearly hip deep. We got to the last mountain behind the house, and Jillian decided to take a shortcut.

"We can pick up our snowshoes from the trail tomorrow. Just sit on your butt and slide down this last slope. See, there's brush right there to stop us at the bottom." Without further ado, she plopped down and went careening down the slope.

I hesitated. It looked awful steep and slippery. But when Jillian stood up at the edge of the brush and waved, and I looked past her at the house, I suddenly wanted to get home and sit down to rest my weary legs. I sat down carefully, but before I was ready, I began to slide out of control down the slope. I whizzed down the icy field and the next thing I knew, I was sitting in the brush at the bottom.

"Wasn't that fun? Want to go back up and slide down again?" Jillian asked.

"No! I'm ready to go home."

The house was close, and soon we were shaking the snow out of our boots on the porch. My eyes were red and scratchy for days, and my legs ached, but our spirits were light and free.

## Chapter Twenty-Three

"Mama, do you think you would be OK here alone all summer?" Jillian asked me one day.

"Of course! This is my home. Why, where do you want to go, what are you going to do?" I queried.

"I don't know. I thought maybe I could go to town and get a job for the summer. Dad's always complaining about how much money it costs to feed us, I figured I could pitch in a little."

"What would you do?" I asked.

"Maybe I'll be a wildlife biologist. Or work on a crab boat a few months. I heard they make pretty good money." Jillian pondered for awhile.

"Yeah, I think that would be good for you, to get out and see the world a bit." I thought back to myself at Jillian's age, wanting to get out and explore.

Jillian looked uncertain. "It's just, well, not that I worry about you alone or anything, it's well, you know, you and Dad fighting, I worry about him hurting you." Jillian was the family peacekeeper, and at any sign of violence, she would try to defuse the situation.

"I can handle your Dad just fine." I retorted. Harry hadn't struck me in a few years, his eruptions less intense, reverting more to verbal abuse.

"Great. And while you're at it, can you tell him I want a ride to Bethel with him next time he goes? Please?"

"You should ask him yourself."

Jillian sighed, and grumbled a bit, then went outside to feed the chickens. Yes, I thought, she should go away for awhile, to see the world and try new things, and meet people. She hadn't been to town since the Aniak debacle. And now that she was done with her schooling, she might be able to find a job. She had never had her own spending money. It would be good for her to learn some life skills other than how to survive in the Alaska wilderness.

It was a few months before Jillian found the courage to ask her dad to take her to town. Harry had come up to drop off supplies and stayed the weekend. After breakfast one morning, he announced that he would be going to town the next day.

"Um, hey, do you think I could get a ride to town with you?" Jillian asked shyly.

Jillian and I both held our breath. Harry sat in silence for a moment and then snorted derisively.

"What the hell do you want to go to town for? Want to go and whore around like your bitch sisters?"

"I want to get a job." Jillian said quietly.

"Yeah, sure. You want to go whore around like all the others did. You're just a worthless slut like your mother."

He continued to derail her and Jillian got up and left the house. It wasn't anything particularly out of the ordinary for Harry, and Jillian was resigned to it. She came back inside a few hours later, after Harry had cooled off and was taking his nap.

"I guess that meant no. I'd rather stay here anyway. It's just that I thought I could make some money and help out more." Jillian cast off her disappointment easily.

But the next morning, as we were getting ready to take Harry to the airport, he turned to Jillian and said, "Get your shit ready if you're going."

It didn't take long for Jillian to get ready. She had very few possessions, so she just grabbed an extra change of clothes hurriedly before Harry could change his mind. She gave me a hug at the airport.

"I'll talk to you on the radio every night. If you have any problems, let me know right away, and I'll find a way to get home."

Then she crawled into the plane and they took off. I watched the plane disappear over the ridge, and the sound slowly faded away. Now I was completely alone. The idea didn't bother me a bit. I had some new books Eddie had brought me a few months ago, and soon

I would be gardening and picking berries. I just hoped Jillian would be OK in town.

The next day, Jillian called me on the radio, disappointed that she didn't already have a job.

"I filled out lots of applications, and talked to the Fish and Wildlife guys. But they said I need a college degree to be a wildlife biologist, and I don't have money to go to school. I called some people about the crab boat job, but they said they wouldn't hire me because I'm a woman. Women are supposed to be bad luck on a boat, or something."

"Well, hang in there. It's only been a day, you know. Where are you staying?" I asked.

"Dad let me stay in the little shed. I got to go, I'm going to go check out the fish plant."

I didn't hear from Jillian for a few weeks after that. Harry didn't know where she was, but continued to make nasty comments about her. Finally, Eddie, who was between jobs at the time, stopped by Harry's house to talk to me on the radio.

"Jillian's working at the fish plant. The pay is low, but food is included, and she's staying over there in one of the equipment rooms. She wanted me to tell you to put the radio on at six instead of seven, because that's when they have their shift change, and she can come over and talk to you once in awhile."

"Oh, that's good news. Yes, six. I'll put the radio on at six. What are you up to?" I asked him.

"Not much, just broke and trying to get by. Jillian's trying to get me a job at the fish place too, maybe I'll take it." Eddie sounded hopeful.

"You should. How's your truck running?" I didn't know what truck Eddie was driving now, but that was his favorite subject, so I listened to him talk awhile, and then he had to leave.

Harry came back on the radio and told me he was coming up the following weekend. I tried to suppress my disappointment. I was enjoying my solitude and peace. I was busy planting the garden, and didn't want to stop what I was doing to wait on Harry. He insisted on having his meals on an exact schedule, even if I was in the middle of doing something else. Harry didn't do anything to help out with any of the chores of daily living at the homestead, and when he was around, my workload doubled.

That summer, Harry, perhaps feeling guilty about me staying alone so much, spent more time at the homestead. It was a difficult adaption for me at first. I made adjustments and sacrificed my personal time and tried not to say anything to antagonize Harry. He continuously complained about the kids. I just kept my mouth shut, because nothing I could say to him would change his mind anyway. I spent a lot of time out in the garden, or in the chicken coop. Their little shed was warm, since it was also heated by hot water radiators. My assortment of rare breed hens were gentle and tame, and would often ride around on my shoulders as I cleaned their coop. They had all become pets, and I had long since ceased to cull the flock. I usually had around twenty hens. A few would die each year, and when the numbers dwindled and the hens got several years old, I ordered more chicks from a hatchery in Missouri. They arrived, cheeping loudly, at the post office in Bethel, and Harry would fly them home. The little chicks lived in a big box in Jillian's room until they were old enough to integrate into the old flock. Harry ordered fifty pound sacks of chicken feed for them from Anchorage, and I supplemented their diet with kitchen scraps and leftovers from my garden. When I was working outside in the yard, I'd open their coop door and let them peck and forage for a few hours. I was careful never to let them out when Taxi was loose, as she could not be trusted around the hens.

One summer day, while I was out in the chicken coop gathering eggs, I heard Taxi barking more intently than usual. Peeking out the door, careful not to let any hens escape, I saw the dog streaking past, with a small black bear on her heels. Taxi made a beeline for the back porch door that I had left open. Both her and the bear disappeared onto the porch. I hollered as loud as I could, cursing myself for not bringing my gun with me as I usually did. Harry was inside the house, taking his nap, and I hoped the noise would awaken him, that he would shoot the bear. I didn't want to go into the enclosed porch area, where the angry bear would be trapped inside. It was a small bear, just a few years old, but it was still a bear. After contemplating a few moments, I knew I would have to go in, to save my cowardly dog. I picked up the shovel I used to clean the henhouse with, and stepped toward the open porch door.

Right then, I heard Harry shouting and a black blur flew past me out the door and disappeared into the brush. I ran in, expecting to find the gory mauled carcass of the dog. Instead I met Harry, out of breath and holding his rifle.

"Dolly, are you OK? There was a bear on the porch! Are you OK? Did you see it?"

"Yes, I'm fine. I saw it run into the brush. Where's Taxi? Did you see the dog? The bear was chasing her."

Right then, Taxi crawled out from under the porch boards, and started barking again. I scolded her for bringing back a bear. It wasn't the first time her misguided herding instincts got her into trouble, nor would it be the last.

Harry was still a bit excited. "I was just waking up from my nap, and I heard something scratching at the door. I thought it was the dog so I got up to let her in. I opened the door, and the bear was right there! Right in my face! I hollered and ran for the gun. I guess the bear was more surprised than I was!"

Harry was right about the bear being surprised, as it did not come back around the house again that summer. Often I would see bears while I was out berry picking, and I would steer wide around them. Only occasionally, bears would become pesky around the house in the spring, and become part of our dinner.

Eddie went to work at the fish processing plant with Jillian that summer. They were both trying to work as much overtime as possible, so it was rare to get a radio call from them. Then, I was even more grateful for my friendship with Helmi. Her cheerful voice and our long conversations broke up the silence. In addition to the marine band radio, we had an AM/FM radio with a very long wire antenna stretched out, and we could receive radio broadcasts from stations as far away as Dillingham and Nome. When the air waves were just right, we could hear Russian radio stations. While I was in my room sewing on my old treadle sewing machine, I often put the radio on and listened to the news. The only drawback was that the radio took "D" batteries, an expensive commodity. I was very sparing with my usage of the radio, and did not leave it on for very long.

Fishing season ended, but the kids stayed on at the fish plant helping put things away for the winter. They had a little more free time, and I would get to talk to them nearly every day. I was excited to hear that Henry was planning to have our annual White Bear picnic on Labor Day. In the last few years he came up during the summer, bringing hot dogs and marshmallows and sodas, and we would sit around a campfire and tell stories and eat until everyone was stuffed. But this year, he had postponed the picnic because Eddie and Jillian were both working, and he himself was busier than usual.

Harry brought Eddie and Jillian up in the Cessna 206, and shortly afterward, Henry buzzed low overhead in his plane, with Freya and Kayla on board. We had a happy reunion, and Jillian and Kayla went outside to start the campfire in the yard. Everyone was sitting around the kitchen table talking and laughing. Eddie was telling of fun times working at the fish plant, of impromptu fish gut fights with the crew, and the new parts he had bought for his truck. Henry was filling me in on all the latest gossip from Bethel.

He looked around to see if Jillian was still outside, and then said, "Hey, you'll never guess where I saw Jillian yesterday."

"Where?" I asked, dicing the potatoes into the potato salad.

"She was out at the airport, with that new flight instructor guy. Hey Dad, what's that new flight instructor guy's name?"

Harry looked disgusted. "She's probably whoring around with that guy. None of my girls have any sense. Flight instructors don't make that much money. If she thinks she's gonna get rich off him, she's stupider than I thought."

"I don't think she's dating him. I saw her getting out of the airplane. The pilot's side. I think she's taking flying lessons." Henry said.

Harry guffawed loudly, and Eddie looked shocked. Just then Jillian and Kayla walked back in.

"Hey sis, what were you doing out at the airport with that flight instructor guy?" Henry asked bluntly.

Jillian took a step back and looked as if she wanted to disappear.

"Flying," she said softly, and looked at the floor.

Everything was quiet for a few minutes. I heard Eddie gasp, surprised. Flying was supposed to be his thing, his dream, and now his sister was going to do it before he did. I could see the hurt in his eyes. Eddie needed to have something to strive for, believe in, to be better at than his sister. It wasn't fair to him that she should take that away from him. She should let him get his pilot's license first. I had no idea that Jillian was even interested in flying. She, who always threw up at the very sight of an airplane.

Then, it dawned on me. Eddie had many years that he could have learned to fly. He was given every opportunity, but he did not follow up on it. Perhaps it was not his dream after all. Or maybe Jillian's motivation would spur him onward. Now I knew why Jillian had tried to keep it a secret. She didn't want to hurt her brother.

Henry, who hadn't realized the repercussions of spilling Jillian's secret, beamed with delight and pride in his sister.

"How many flight hours have you logged?" he asked.

"Only four and a half." Jillian mumbled. "I just went up a few times."

"You ain't smart enough to be a pilot. You should just try to find yourself a rich husband." Jeered Harry.

Jillian looked right at him, and said brashly, "Yeah, well that's not the only thing you're going to be pissed off about. I bought Mama a ticket to Wisconsin for her birthday to see her family. But here, you can have the rest of the money I made this summer." She tossed an envelope on the table in front of him.

I dropped a bowl in shock. Did I just hear my daughter right? She bought me a ticket to see my family?! Oh no, Harry was not going to like this!

I was right about that. Thankfully, Freya and Kayla were present, and Harry did not explode like I thought he was going to. He was upset at the chain of events beyond his control, but managed to keep his cool. The fat envelope of money in front of him didn't hurt either.

The conversation went to other things as the picnic progressed, but everyone was lost in their own thoughts. Everyone left later that afternoon, except for Jillian. Since fishing season was over and she had given all of her money to her dad, she had no desire to go back to Bethel. Eddie wanted to go back, because he was in the middle of fixing a truck. I could see he was still having a difficult time absorbing the news of Jillian's endeavors. But now, perhaps, he would drive himself harder to accomplish his goals?

I couldn't believe Jillian had bought me a ticket, with her hard-earned money. Although I had rare visits from family members over the years, it had been many years since I had been out of Alaska. I looked forward to seeing my family, but dreaded leaving my home. What if the weather was bad, or it snowed too much and I couldn't get back? Jillian had told me she would stay home and take care of the homestead, so why did I worry so much? It was just that the trip was such a long ways away.

Jillian, as if reading my mind, said, "It will be good for you to get out and see the world." She laughed, seeming relieved that the drama was over. "Did I sound like your mother?"

"Thanks for the ticket, but you didn't have to spend all your money on me!" I said.

Jillian shrugged. "I didn't. I took a few flying lessons and gave most of the money to Dad. Oh yeah, I ordered a bunch of supplies from Anchorage, chicken feed, rice, flour, stuff like that. Dad is gonna be upset when he has to pick it all up from the post office!"

"I didn't know you wanted to fly. How come you never told me?" I asked.

Jillian shrugged. "I figured it would be easier to fly myself than have to beg for a ride. Besides, it's kind of fun."

Harry took me to Bethel the following month to catch the flight to Wisconsin. I was so nervous about leaving, but the weather was beautiful. In fact, everything went smoothly, and all of my flights were on time. I had a wonderful visit with my family, although it seemed that no one could understand my desire to live alone in the Alaskan wilderness. After a week, the hustle and bustle of the small community seemed overwhelmingly chaotic, and I looked forward to the trapline and gathering firewood. Then, the vacation was over, and I hugged my family goodbye, with tears in our eyes, and boarded the jet, heading home. I wondered how many years would pass before I would see them again. Perhaps they would come to visit me. Things had changed since I had last been outside of Alaska. The ten days I was gone had seemed too long, I thought as I changed flights in Seattle. There was the excitement of travel, the wonderful reunion with beloved family, the reflections of old days, but in the end, my heart belonged to my wilderness homestead.

Harry met my jet in Bethel, but told me we would have to stay overnight before going home. Jillian had called on the radio and told him the weather was bad. She would call again in the morning. The next day while we waited for the morning fog to lift, I went to Swanson's store in Bethel. Shopping through the aisles, I encountered Peter Lott. I approached him and held out my hand.

"Oh, Peter. I'm so sorry to hear about Martha." Martha had passed away earlier.

"Dolly! Hi Dolly, camai! Martha was a good woman, my wife, he was right too! He told me, he says not to go, it was a bad thing I was doing, that it's your home. But I wanted a helicopter ride, to go for a ride. That's why he didn't come, he knew it was wrong, he didn't come along, even if my Martha wants to say hello, camai to you, her good friend. He says, that Dolly he is a good woman, Dolly, he says don't do this to her!" Peter gushed out. Tears tickled down his leathery old cheeks.

I had no idea what he was talking about. Most of the time I could piece together Peter's rambling broken English, and I knew the Yup'ik language did not differentiate between male and female, but today my mind was on other things. Still, Peter's remorse touched me deeply, and I wiped away a few tears and gave him a hug. I had no idea what he was talking about. Perhaps it was about Tengupak. But that seemed so long ago, I had nearly forgotten the troubles of the past.

"It's Ok, Peter." I said.

"No, no, it's not right. My wife he was right, my Martha, he was a good woman, he knew what was right. We are all one people, the same people, with the same god. God doesn't want us to hurt each other, that's what my Martha says to me. We are all the same, the one people under god. He was good, good woman. He was so angry at me. He says I did a bad, bad thing." Peter was genuinely hurting and I had no idea why.

"Peter, it's OK. I don't think you did anything wrong." I patted him on the shoulder consolingly.

"No, no, I did a bad thing to you, my good friend. They tell me, no Peter, you don't tell them up there what we are doing, you just say it how we tell you and you get a helicopter ride, get to see the country. I say what they tell me, but my wife, he knows. He say it was very bad, to try to take your home away, that's Dolly's home, my wife say."

I tried to make sense of Peter's ramblings, but the only thing I could think of was his visit a few years ago, with the men in the helicopter. I didn't think he had meant any harm from it, or that it affected us at all, but it did confuse me that they had been doing a reindeer herding documentary at the wrong site. No, as strange as it had seemed, that encounter hadn't threatened our home at all.

Before I had time to talk to Peter any more, Harry came into the store looking for me. I quickly said goodbye to Peter, hugging him and once again giving him my condolences about the loss of his wife, and my dear friend Martha. Then I rushed off to the airport with Harry.

On the flight home, I pondered Peter's odd ramblings again, and then dismissed the incident. I wasn't until years later that I would understand what he was trying to tell me, and the full horror of what Peter Lott had done would hit me.

## Chapter Twenty-Four

"I'm going to walk to Bethel," Jillian said, out of the blue one day in March.

"What? Why?" I asked.

"I want to go to work again, and then get my pilot's license." She answered.

"Why don't you just ask your dad for a ride?"

Jillian snorted. "Remember what happened last time? Nah, I want to walk. The days are longer now and all the rivers are froze over good. Shouldn't take more than a week or so."

I mulled it over. It was an incredibly long distance, over a hundred miles, but Jillian was fit, accustomed to hard labor and could snowshoe effortlessly for miles. It wasn't for me to say whether she did go or not. She would just go anyway, slipping away without telling anyone, so it was best that this time I knew where she was headed. Harry was in Bethel. Was she going to tell him before she went, or just go, and tell him later?

"Are you going to tell your dad?" I asked.

"Nope. You are. After I leave. Give me three days, and then you can tell him on the radio."

I sighed, not sure I wanted to be stuck with that task.

"In three days, I should be to Tuluksak. I can leave a message on the hotlines."

Hotlines were public radio announcements that were aired twice daily after the news, when people could call up the radio station and send messages or birthday greetings to others.

"I'm going tomorrow." She said.

I watched Jillian pack her sleeping bag, a tarp and a few meager supplies in a small plastic sled she would pull behind her. I made suggestions on what to take, but Jillian took very little. She said she wanted to travel light and fast, and get to the Kuskokwim river before the snow conditions worsened. Right now, the snow was hard packed, but one still needed snowshoes to stay on top of it.

She left the next morning, just as it was starting to get light. It was a lovely day, light just filtering through the windows as I watched her striding out over the snow covered mountains, pulling the sled along behind. I felt a momentary longing, a fleeting desire to accompany her on this great adventure. But then the reality of it sunk in. It was a very long distance, and I would have slowed Jillian down. I loved going on day hikes, but didn't care to get too far from the homestead. Besides, someone always needed to be here, to care for the animals, and the hotsprings, which still occasionally choked itself off with debris during the earth tremors. I loved being here, in my mountain nest, surrounded by the magnificent beauty and freedom of the wilderness. I knew Eddie and Jillian loved it too, but they were young and restless, and needed adventure. I wondered what Eddie was doing right now, and if he would come to visit me more often if Jillian got her pilot's license.

I went about my day, thinking occasionally about the long journey ahead of my daughter. How would she know where to go? She had no compass or map. What if she got lost? She knew the mountains close to home, but once she got out of her territory, she might become disoriented, particularly if a storm hit. She told me she was planning to take a shortcut through some steep mountains, and then head out across the open tundra until she reached the river. What if she slipped and fell down the mountains, or broke a leg? Nobody would look for her for at least a week, and by that time...

I shook off the thought. I finished eating dinner, did the dishes, and put on the kerosene lantern. I picked up a book, but couldn't really concentrate on it. Around midnight, just as I was about to blow out the lamp and go to bed, I heard a clattering on the porch. Jillian was back!

I opened the door and asked, "What happened, how far did you get, did you forget something, are you alright?", all in one breath.

Jillian unbuckled her snowshoes. I noticed her clothes were covered in ice.

"I fell through the ice. Figured I'd lose a whole day drying out my clothes, and I didn't want to be late getting to Tuluksak, didn't want you to start worrying, so I just turned around. I'll dry out my stuff and start out again in a day or so when everything's dry."

"Oh man. Of all the things I was worrying about, falling through the ice wasn't one of them! Are you OK? Did you get cold? You're all covered with ice!" I fretted.

"Yeah I'm fine. I didn't get cold as long as I stayed moving. That's why I came back. It was easier to come back than try to start a fire out on the tundra to dry my stuff out." She started peeling off a few layers and shaking the ice off.

I started the fire up again, and put on a can of soup, while Jillian tended to her things. After she had changed her clothes and hung everything on the clothes rack to dry, she came over by the stove.

"Mama, remember Peter Lott telling us about the old hotsprings at the edge of the tundra, where they had the reindeer corral? I think it's near where I was. I kept getting whiffs of sulfur and the river ice was really thin. I think maybe that place closed up from the quakes, but maybe the hot water still seeps underground into the river, and that's why the ice was so thin."

"Well, that makes sense. How far were you?" I asked, pouring the soup into bowls.

Jillian sat down. "I don't know. It was clear on the other side of these mountains back here, I'd say, maybe eight or nine miles? It would make sense, too, the reindeer corral being over there, out on the windswept tundra where they could feed, and Bogus creek is plenty deep, so people could boat up the river a ways and haul reindeer meat down. Too bad nobody took care of that old hotsprings. Too much work, I guess, and nobody used it like we do this one."

We ate our soup and then went to bed. I was relieved that Jillian was home and safe, but a few days later she was on her way again. This time, to avoid having to cross the river with thin ice, she decided to loop all the way around it behind the mountains. The detour would add at least an extra 30 miles to her journey, but it was safer. She took off again, and I went back to pacing the floor, imagining the worse.

Of course, worrying was pointless. It didn't make Jillian's journey any safer.

The second day after Jillian left, Harry flew over in his plane. I pulled the snowmachine out from its storage place on the porch, hitched up the sled, and went to meet him.

"Where's Jillian?" Harry asked as he was tying down the plane.

"She's walking to Bethel. She'll be there in a few days." I said bravely.

"What?! Walking to Bethel! That's the stupidest thing I've ever heard! Why didn't you stop her?" Harry roared.

That was the stupidest thing I'D ever heard! Jillian was a force of nature. Stopping Jillian was like stopping an earthquake, or a cyclone.

"She wanted a good adventurous long hike." I said.

We unloaded the scanty supplies, and Harry's dirty laundry, and took the snowmachine to the house, Harry driving and myself riding on the back of the sled.

The next day, the KYUK radio announcer read off a message from Jillian that she had reached Tuluksak. I was surprised at how fast she had gotten there, since she made a big detour. Now that she was on the Kuskowkim river, it wasn't as likely that she would get lost, but I still worried about her falling through the ice again. It turned out that my concern was needless, as two days later Jillian herself called me on Harry's scratchy old radio and told me she was in Bethel.

"I saw Dad's plane was gone, so I figured he was up there. Eddie showed me where Dad left the key for him so I thought I'd let you know I got here OK. Is everything OK up there?" Jillian said.

"Roger, roger, everything is fine here! You made in down there fast! How was the trip?"

"It was great! The snow conditions were perfect. I even jogged a little once I got to the Kusko ice."

Jillian talked to me nearly every day on the radio, and sometimes Eddie would come down and talk to me too. Jillian told me that she rolled her sleeping bag out in the rafters of an abandoned building, and since she didn't have money, ate out of dumpsters.

"Just like living in the wilderness! Follow the ravens when you get hungry!" she laughed.

Then she got a job at the store, and another as ground crew for the airlines, and was too busy to talk to me on the radio. Eddie was working on and off for Henry driving dump trucks, so he didn't check in on the radio much either. After a few weeks, Harry went back to Bethel, and I was alone again. It was like a vacation for me. I read my books, and sewed, and took naps, and cooked whenever I felt like it, or not at all if I didn't feel like it.

Harry kept me informed about the kids, more or less, as his comments were often disparaging and not always accurate. When fishing season opened, both Eddie and Jillian went back to work at the fish plant. The flight instructor had left town, so Jillian was not able to take any more lessons. Eddie had convinced her to take over payments on the Cessna 172. He had stopped paying on the bill years ago, and now a hefty interest had accrued, and he was in danger of losing the whole investment. Jillian hesitantly agreed and handed over every paycheck to pay for the mortgage. Toward the end of the summer, she had paid the plane off entirely. The next day, Harry informed me that she had nearly wrecked it, and was in trouble with the FAA for flying without a license. Henry went with her to talk to them, and had helped her straighten the mess out. The Feds agreed that the whole matter would be forgotten if Jillian got her pilot's license. Since there were no flight instructors in Bethel, she travelled in to Anchorage and went to a flight school there. It was more expensive than she had anticipated. Soon she ran out of money. Henry, who had whole-heartedly supported his little sister's desire to fly, loaned her enough money to finish. In January, 1994, Jillian got her private pilot's license.

Eddie was still a bit jealous and feeling left out of the excitement. Harry was not at all supportive of his daughter's achievement and sternly told her that she was not allowed to land the Cessna 172 on our homestead airstrip. I was angry at Harry and felt he was being cruel and controlling.

"Dolly, I don't want Jillian to fly up here right away. It's too dangerous. The strip is short, the weather is bad, and the approaches are tricky. She needs to get some experience first, flying somewhere safer. Flight schools just give you a license. Truly learning to fly comes later, with experience." Harry explained.

I was not a pilot but I could see the wisdom in his words. Even good pilots had crashed on our airstrip. It was tricky, and Jillian did not have much flight time.

I spent much of the winter alone. I set rabbit snares, but did not run the trapline. Sometimes I would sit on the living room couch and watch the northern lights dance across the sky on the long cold winter nights. I marveled at the splendor of the glittering array of stars and the sheets of reds and yellows and greens that cavorted overhead.

There was plenty of food now. Jillian would send boxes of food up with Harry, filled with an assortment of treats that we had always considered commodities, like yogurt and candy. One particular box she sent puzzled me a bit. The lettuce leaves were shriveled and strewn throughout the box, and the tomatoes were badly bruised.

"Did this box fall out of your truck?" I asked Harry.

"No, maybe Jillian dropped it. She came out and put it in my plane before I left." Harry said.

Since there wasn't much other fresh produce, I rinsed the lettuce and cut the bad spots out of the tomatoes and salvaged enough to make a salad. That night, Jillian called on the radio, and I asked her about the box.

"The stuff in that box you sent was pretty smashed. I was able to get a salad out of it, but just wondered, did you drop it, or run over it or something?"

"You made a salad out of it?!" Jillian was laughing.

"Yeah, that's what you sent it up here for, isn't it?" I asked.

"No. I got that stuff out of the dumpster for the chickens. Didn't you see what I wrote on the box?" Jillian was still snickering.

Later, I looked at the box and saw scribbling on the flap: "For your chickens. Do Not Eat."

It was a good idea, and the hens loved it. From then on, Harry gathered produce scraps and stale bread from the store when he was coming home, as the plane would usually be nearly empty anyway. The hens gobbled up the fresh greenery ravenously, and I was able to save a lot on the chicken feed bill.

During the winter, the snow got deep on the airstrip, and Harry put his Cessna 206 on skis. It was a heavy cumbersome airplane in the deep snow, and our airstrip was narrow. Every time he landed, I had to wade out onto the airstrip and help him turn around to park. I pushed on the tail with all my strength while Harry ran the engine at full power. The resulting prop blast took my breath away, and often my hat and glasses. It had been so much easier with the Cessna 185 that Harry used to own, and both of the kids helping to push. Later, the powerful wind swept the field clear of snow, and Harry removed the skis.

I wondered how Jillian was doing on her flying. She wasn't working now. Henry had let her stay in a little room above his shop. Harry told me she was dating some "no-account low-life", but I wasn't sure if that was true. She was flying a lot, and Harry was sure that her boyfriend was running drugs. The plane would disappear in the worst weather, and often return with extra dents and scratches. At first, Harry had been concerned, and called every airport in the state looking for her when the weather was bad and she did not return. Often he would call on the radio in a panic, asking if Jillian had landed here at the homestead. Then he gave up and decided not to get involved. I didn't know which of Harry's stories to believe, so I stayed neutral. Well, hopefully she was getting some flying experience and would make it home someday!

Only a month after Jillian got her pilot's license, she made her first landing at the homestead. I heard the plane circling high overhead and raced down to the airfield on the old Elan. I held my breath as I turned the last corner, looking for an airplane, not knowing who had flown over. I saw the tail in the tiedown, and then the whole plane came into view. Eddie was helping Jillian tie the wings down. Eddie! I gave a shout of glee and leaped off the snowmachine to give him a hug. I hadn't seen my son in nearly a year! He was tall and thin and looked very happy to be home.

"Whooo-eeee, did you see that! Did you see us land?!" Eddie cackled.

"No," I said, "I just got here."

Jillian came over and gave me a hug. She was still quivering with excitement.

"Good!" She snickered. "I'm glad you didn't see it."

"Awww, it wasn't that bad! We just got a little bit low, that's all." Eddie said.

Jillian went over and sniffed the prop. "Hey, look, we hit the top of that spruce. Check it out, it's all green on this side and smells like pitch."

Eddie walked over, and they examined the prop together.

"Well, looks like you're a real 'bush' pilot now!"

The kids howled with laughter, but I was horrified. If the prop had been in the bushes, the landing gear would have been even lower! They could have snagged a wheel and crashed. Harry was right, Jillian had no business landing here until she got more flight time.

"The airport is on a slope. It creates a visual illusion, makes it look like you're too high when you land uphill. It's easy to get too low." Eddie explained.

"Next time I'll know better, stay a little higher." Jillian said.

We started unloading the plane. It was jammed full of boxes of groceries, the mail, treats for the chickens and the dog. I drove the snowmachine home, Eddie rode the sled, and Jillian jogged up the trail. It was just like old times, I thought as I started making dinner and listened to Eddie's tales of driving dump trucks on the Kuskokwim river ice between villages.

"How long will you stay?" I asked, hoping it would be awhile.

"I have to go back in a couple days. Mike wants to go to Tuluksak this weekend." Jillian said.

"Who's Mike?" I asked.

"Her worthless bootlegger boyfriend." Eddie taunted.

"Shut up! He's fun and he pays for gas. Your Billy-Bob friends are way more worthless! Where do you think they get their money?" Jillian retorted.

"Now, now, don't fight, you two! Jillian, why don't you make some cookies? Eddie, tell me about your truck. Is it running good now?" I interrupted.

The kids stayed a few days and then left for Bethel. I watched with nervous anticipation as the little Cessna taxied out for takeoff, flexing its wing feathers like a giant prehistoric fledging, then with a growl, hurled itself into the sky and flew away with my children. Over the next few months Eddie and Jillian dropped in frequently. Jillian was getting better each time at landing on our challenging strip. Then Eddie went back to work at the fishery, and Jillian was off for a new adventure, joining a wildland firefighting crew in Fairbanks. I sighed. I didn't mind being alone at all, I just missed my children. But this was the time of their lives they needed to spread their wings and explore their world.

## Chapter Twenty-Five

The sound of a plane woke me from my deep slumber. Jumping out of bed, I grabbed my pants and ran outside. It was late summer, and the sun was just starting to come up over the mountains. Jillian! I thought sleepily. She had called Harry and told him she was back from a big fire in Washington and that the crew was laid off for the season. The plane dipped a wing. I jumped up and down excitedly and waved my pants at it. It circled, and I ran back inside and got dressed.

Roaring down the trail in the old jeep, I turned the corner to the airport, and saw the plane, right where I anticipated it, in the tiedown area. But Jillian was nowhere in sight. Instead, a man stood by the plane. Who was he? Where was Jillian? I looked around, expecting her to jump out of the bushes. As I got closer, I saw that the man was Chris Murphy, and the plane was not Jillian's.

"Hi, Dolly, is everything OK?" Chris greeted me looking concerned.

"Yes. Yes, everything is just fine. I was expecting Jillian to fly over. I thought you were her! She's coming down from Fairbanks." I gushed, embarrassed.

Chris started laughing. "I thought I'd land and check on you. I was just flying over, and it isn't every day someone flags me down with their pants!"

I laughed too, still a bit embarrassed. I barely knew the man. It was good of him to check if I was OK. He took off, still laughing, and I went back home to make breakfast.

Jillian breezed through a few days later, on her way to Bethel to reunite with her boyfriend. She had bought a trailer in Bethel, so I didn't expect to see her much, but over the next few weeks, Eddie and her stopped in frequently. In early September, she landed on her way to McGrath. Harry told me on the radio that she was headed up, so I was waiting at the airport when she came in. It was a beautiful day and not much wind, so I didn't worry much when the plane appeared around the corner of the mountains. But as I watched it descend for landing, I noticed it swerving and heard a few quick bursts of the throttle before it sank onto the strip, bounced a few times, and sped past, brakes squealing. I ran out, heart beating fast, but saw the plane slow down by the time it reached the end of the strip, slow enough to make the turnaround to taxi back. Well, I thought, these mountains have some strange air currents, so it was probably a bit of turbulence that accounted for the less than perfect landing.

Eddie stepped out of the plane, grinning, and gave me a big hug.

"Did you see that? I worked the throttle! I helped land the plane! Did you see?" He was pretty excited and proud of himself.

"Yes, yes, I saw. It looked okay." I evaded. It was nice of Jillian to let Eddie practice with the throttle, but not here, on this short strip.

"We're on the way up to McGrath. I'm done working for the summer. Hey look, I brought you a bunch of silver salmon! I had them in Dad's freezer. I hope I didn't bring too many for you to can?"

"No, no, that's wonderful! Thank you so much! I haven't had fish in a few years, you know. Your dad hasn't brought any for awhile." I said. Our small creeks didn't have any salmon, so I relied on Harry to bring fish from Bethel.

I started unloading the airplane. Jillian was on the other side of the plane, and when she stepped around and I saw her, I gasped. Her entire face was black and blue and purple, one eye swollen shut, and her arm dangled uselessly at her side.

"Oh no, oh man. Did Mike…." I started.

Eddie snorted. "Hell, Mike's a big wuss. She's more likely to beat HIM up!"

Jillian glared at him through her one good eye. "It doesn't have to be that way, you know. Nobody has to beat anybody up. Mike's a nice guy. Nope, I wrecked his dirt bike out at the pit."

Eddie laughed. "Yeah, Bill was telling me all about it. Jillian took a big jump and landed wrong. Mike's motorcycle is trashed."

"You should go to a hospital, get that looked at." I fussed.

Eddie made a show of walking around Jillian staring at her arm. Jillian giggled.

"Yep." He said. "I looked at it now. That's broke, and probably that too, so don't move it for a month or so, OK?"

"I'm serious. What if it doesn't heal straight?" I insisted.

Jillian scowled. "You know I can't afford to go to the hospital. I wish I had been born Native! How come you had to marry a white guy, anyway? Being white sucks! Nah, I'll just take Eddie's professional opinion. It'll probably go back together eventually."

"How on earth did you fly like that?" I asked.

"I worked the throttle for her! Did you see? Jillian, did I do a good job? Did I?" Eddie beamed.

"Yeah, you did fantastic! Good job. But maybe, next time, a little less throttle right at the end, OK?" Jillian suggested.

After the plane was unloaded, they got in again and took off. I still didn't like the idea of Jillian flying while she was so badly hurt. I busied myself in canning the fish. I had just gotten my new pressure cooker in the mail, and was elated to discover that it only took 90 minutes rather than three hours to can fish, as the old canner kettle did. I canned several batches of salmon, and stacked my jars on the shelf. My shelves were overflowing now, and I needed to build some new ones.

That fall, my dear friend Helmi died at her Eagle Island cabin, and I missed our conversations immensely. Harry was having a lot of health problems, and spent more time at home, where I could fuss over him. He frequently had severe attacks of gout, and would be laid up for weeks. He had just been diagnosed with diabetes, and his energy was sapped. Fortunately, Harry was now old enough to draw Social Security, so he had a check coming in every month. He had quit driving taxi cabs, and shut down the business.

Right after Christmas, Harry and Eddie went back to Bethel, and Jillian decided to stay an extra week to trap. A big storm hit, and over two feet of fresh snow dumped on the airport. Jillian, whose Cessna was not rigged for skis, was stuck, but didn't seem to mind as she went full swing into trapping. It was just like old times, I thought, as

I snowshoed along after her. The temperatures plummeted to minus forty.

"Glad I'm here! My trailer gets really cold and my car won't start in Bethel." Jillian said as she added another log on the fireplace.

Harry told us on the radio at night he heard that the caribou herd was migrating past the big lake. Jillian and I decided to take the snowmachine out to look for them, as she had just siphoned ten gallons of fuel out of her wing tanks for us to use at White Bear. The next morning we hitched up the sled and packed up a few knives. Jillian was still trying to figure out which gun to take.

"I should try out this new gun I got from Eddie's Billy-Bob buddies. They said it's supposed to be a great long range caribou gun. I haven't sighted it in yet though. Maybe I should just take my 30-30." She mulled it over, and then ended up taking the new gun.

We set out down the trail, and then veered off over the mountains, trying to avoid the deep snow in the timber. Jillian pointed out that we could go out through the mountains and then circle around back to the big lake. That way we wouldn't get the snowgo stuck. I carefully maneuvered across the steep slopes while Jillian hung on to the back of the sled. Crossing the ridge, the snowmachine dropped suddenly out from under me as a cornice broke away. I was so startled, I let out a yell and then I landed right back on the seat, grabbed the throttle and kept going. I looked back and Jillian was still clinging to the sled. After about an hour, we broke out of the mountains and started across the open tundra. Scanning ahead as I drove, I saw a small group of dots in the distance. I stopped.

"Caribou!" I pointed.

"Yeah, I saw them. They're pretty skittish. See, they are running already! Look, I bet if we hustle, zip out there behind that little knoll where they are headed, I bet they will run right past us."

I jumped back on the snowmachine and we zoomed at top speed across the tundra to get to the knoll. Several times I was suspended from the handlebars, and have no idea how Jillian managed to hang on. We reached the knoll and shut off the snowgo. Jillian and I crawled to the rim and waited for the caribou. They appeared, getting closer, flowing gracefully, stopping occasionally to graze, unaware of our presence. The steam from their breath hung in a little cloud above their tawny bodies. Jillian had taken her scarf and hood down, and was watching them through the scope. I wiggled my toes inside my bulky bunny boots to keep warm and wondered if we had created a cloud of steam. I was almost afraid to breathe, for fear of spooking the herd. They were close now, and the big bull in front lifted his majestic head and sniffed the air. Jillian's rifle flicked past him without hesitation and settled on a small bull lagging toward the back of the herd. Good, I thought, that one looks tender. My mouth watered at the thought of fresh caribou steaks. Caribou had never come this close before, so we only tasted the meat when Henry would bring some from his hunting around Bethel.

The caribou were very close now, and I marveled at the striking patterns of their coats as they filed past. Any time now, Jillian would shoot and they would scatter. I anticipated the sharp retort of the rifle, and the herd galloping away across the tundra, hopefully leaving behind the slow young bull. I wondered what was taking so long. Glancing over at Jillian, I saw that she had already ejected a few bullets, and had her pocketknife out, fooling with the gun. She raised the gun again, and then lowered it in disgust. Reaching in her pocket, she pulled out some matches, struck one, and held it inside the chamber of the gun.

"Be careful!" I whispered.

She aimed again, but the gun wouldn't fire. I handed her another box of bullets, but they didn't work either, and neither did the matches, scraping at the chamber, or even hitting the firing pin with the back of the knife. The caribou were slowly drifting away, almost out of range now. I regretted now that I hadn't brought a gun along as well. Now the caribou were out of range. Jillian stood up, and threw the useless gun to the ground and started jumping up and down on it.

"Oh you stupid little gun," She screamed. But that's not really what she said. The blue cloud of vulgarity that coiled out of her lips would have made a sailor blush.

"Oh be careful, that gun might go off!" I warned.

Jillian stopped jumping up and down on the gun and gave it a mighty kick that sent it whirling through the air, the blue steel barrel glinting in the cold winter sun as it cartwheeled and fell. Then she looked after the herd forlornly.

"Looks like we aren't going to have caribou steaks after all. Stupid gun! I should have brought my 30-30!"

"Come on," I said. "Let's go home before it gets dark. You left a lot of gas, so maybe we can go back out again tomorrow."

"They'll be gone by then." Jillian said.

She went over and picked up the gun and threw it in the sled. We followed our tracks back the way we had come. When we got to the mountains, we had considerable difficulty getting over the passes. After hours of shoving and hoisting and grunting, we managed to pull the machine through the deep drifts, which had stacked up on the lee side. Driving down had been a breeze, with gravity on our side, but going back up was a whole different story. When we finally got home, it was dark and we were exhausted.

The next morning, we decided to pursue our quest for caribou again, before they migrated on. We both took our 30-30s this time. We followed our same tracks as the day before, and after passing the big lake, we saw a band of caribou. I came across them suddenly, and shut the snowmachine off. They were already scattering. I looked back to where Jillian was tracking a small bull with her rifle, waiting for a clean shot as he moved away from the herd. The rifle cracked loudly in the crisp air, and the sound echoed across the tundra and through the far away mountains. The little bull stumbled, and went to its knees. The rest of the herd bolted, and then stopped a few hundred yards away and began to graze unconcernedly.

Jillian grabbed a few knives out of the sled and we walked up to the caribou. It lay on the tundra, its soft brown coat blending into its surroundings, legs twitching as it expired. Jillian set down her rifle and unsheathed a very large knife. She crouched over the caribou, grinning like a rabid she-wolf, white teeth bright against her wind-burned face.

"I just got this knife. It's advertised to be super sharp, they say you can stab it through a car door and it will still be sharp." She said, pulling the caribou's head over her knee and raising the knife to drive it into the throat and bleed it out.

"You didn't get it from the same guy that sold you that gun, did you?" I joked.

Jillian shot me a dirty look right at the same time she was stabbing the knife downward. She yelped, jumping back, the caribou pinned to her leg by the big knife. The caribou struggled feebly, Jillian's leg jerking as it moved, and then the caribou took its last breath. Jillian grasped the knife with both hands and tugged at it, but it was driven in deep. Finally she pried it free, and spread the cut fabric of her snowpants to look at the wound. I could see the shiny white bone, and then blood began gushing out.

"Man, that was dumb!" Jillian exclaimed, laughing.

"You should do something about that, stop the bleeding!" I panicked.

Here we were, in the middle of nowhere, and my daughter was bleeding to death! I have no idea which way to go to get to the closest village, and going home would be a tremendous effort. Jillian might not make it!

"Nah, I'll let it bleed for awhile, to clean out the wound." Jillian seemed unconcerned and began to butcher the caribou.

"It's bleeding too much! You'll bleed to death!" I fussed.

"Nope, probably not. I wouldn't bleed to death unless I hit an artery. If I hit an artery, blood would be spurting, like all the way to the snowgo over there." She waved the knife in the direction of the snowgo, a hundred yards away. The snow was red with her blood now.

The blood wasn't exactly spurting, I decided, it was more like pouring out. I tried to sort out in my frightened mind what to do. We should leave the caribou here, and take Jillian back home. Harry could come and pick her up with the ski plane. I said something of the effect to Jillian and she scoffed.

"It's just a little cut. See, most of this is caribou blood." She drew a line in the snow with the knife. "There. My blood, caribou blood. Way more caribou blood, now isn't there. Why don't you go get the snowgo and quit fussing? You're starting to get annoying."

"Just stop the bleeding, OK?" I begged.

Jillian scooped a few handfuls of snow onto the wound. It turned red and froze into bloody icicles. Then she tore off the end of her T-shirt and tied it around her leg.

"There. Happy now? This load is going to be too heavy to get back over the mountains. I think we should cut across and go up through the timber and get on the trapline trail. What do you think?"

"I think that's best, too. I don't think you should be pushing the sled with your hurt leg."

I walked back and brought the snowgo over. Together we loaded the meat and hide onto the sled. Jillian quietly thanked the caribou spirit, and we took off, the snowmachine straining hard with the additional load. I could feel the load lighten as Jillian jumped off the sled and ran along behind, pushing. We made it to the edge of the timber, and then started through the trees. Instantly, the snowgo became mired. We strained and tugged and got it out. I noticed Jillian's wound had broken open again.

"We should unload the caribou, and I should take you home instead." I suggested.

"Wolves would get it. I think you can make it if you keep going fast. I'll take the snowshoes and catch up to you when you hit a hard packed trail." Jillian argued.

I didn't like the idea at all but there weren't any other options that didn't involve throwing Jillian bodily onto the sled and tying her there. As she was tougher than I was, that wasn't even an option. Jillian gave the sled a shove and I took off, wallowing through the drifts, the heavy iron sled dragging along behind. I swerved often to avoid trees, but after turning a sharp corner, the sled snagged a tree, and the snowmachine ground to a halt. Stepping off the machine, I sank up to my waist. I unhitched the sled and struggled to pull it and the snowmachine onto firmer snow. As I toiled, I worried constantly about Jillian. Had she laid down in the snow and died? What should I do? Then she was there, panting from the jog through the deep snow, shoving the sled out of the hole.

I got stuck several more times before I hit the harder packed trail. Jillian, who had to be one of the toughest people I'd ever known, jogged on snowshoes about fifteen miles through the deep snow with an injured leg. By the time we finally got home late that evening, even she was exhausted.

# Chapter Twenty-Six

I paced the trail at the airport, nervous and worried, waiting for my children to arrive from Bethel. There was a big storm moving in. I had heard the blizzard warning on the public radio this morning when I had anxiously listened to the weather. It was Christmas eve, 1995.

Harry had arrived in the old blue Cessna 206 about two hours earlier, and said that Jillian should be right behind, bringing Eddie in her 172. He had waited at the airport with me for a short time, then became very tired and took the snowmachine up to the house. The weather hadn't been too bad when Harry landed, wind only about

*Approach to White Bear Airfield*

five miles an hour from the north and good visibility. That morning I had given the weather conditions to Harry over the marine band radio, and he said he would pass it on to Jillian. Maybe the forecast storm will be late, I thought, perhaps it won't get here until tomorrow. Right now the weather was perfect. The crisp air smelled of spruce needles, and off across the creek somewhere I could hear a ptarmigan's gurgling call. Soon Eddie would be home, and he would go ptarmigan hunting.

I reflected back over the summer as I waited. I had been busy as usual at the homestead. In addition to my regular daily tasks, I had been battling the beavers, who decided to add another tier to their dam of the end of the airstrip. The resulting flooding had washed out a good portion of our already short airstrip. Every day I would tear down part of their dam, and every night they built it back up, until the water froze solid. Although physically demanding, it hadn't been an altogether unpleasant task, even though the mosquitos were vicious near the water. I enjoyed some company from a family of mink, which we rarely saw around our shallow streams. Harry had used the D8 Cat to try to salvage the damaged portion of the airstrip, but it was still bumpy and soggy. It should be froze good enough now, with a thin layer of snow, I thought, as I paced another lap, ears straining for the sound of a plane.

Jillian had spent the summer firefighting, this time in southern California. It seemed like a perfect job for her because she loved it. Eddie had worked at the fish plant again, and saved me some salmon from one of the discard totes. After fishing season, he had gotten in a bit of trouble drinking and driving. He left the state with a friend, driving the AlCan highway to California, ending up not far from where Jillian was working before he ran out of money. Jillian bought him a ticket back home and loaned him most of her summer's wages to help him get back on his feet. Eddie had difficulty accepting the loss of his driver's license. He got around Bethel on a bicycle, and missed driving his beloved truck a great deal. I hope life turns around for Eddie pretty soon, I sighed to myself. He sure had a rough go of things in life. We all did our best to help him out, especially Henry, but sometimes it seemed as if the odds were stacked against my son.

I was jerked from my thoughts as a sharp gust of wind hit the side of my face. It was coming from the south. Looking back towards the house, I could see puffs of snow starting to wisp off the tops of the mountains. Some of the taller peaks had disappeared in the billowing white clouds. Hurry up, come on, kids, get here soon before the wind hits the ground, I fretted. What could have gone wrong? Did they crash along the way? Maybe the weather in Bethel had closed in and Jillian couldn't get a clearance to depart the airport. Maybe the plane wouldn't start. Jillian's car could have broken down on the way to the airport. Maybe Mike had talked Jillian into staying in Bethel. He was such a smooth talker. I couldn't decide whether I liked him or not. It didn't matter, as long as he was good to Jillian. She could have picked a better companion, I thought, but then perhaps people said the same about me.

Looking back over the mountains, I was shocked to see them disappearing rapidly as the clouds boiled over the ridgeline. The canyon seemed oddly quiet and surreal, and then I could hear it, the wind howling through the passes. I shivered, but not from the cold. Please, please hurry, I begged. It was late, and would be getting dark soon. The sky took on a soft white hue, the same coloring as the snow. Even walking was disorienting in the whiteout. Soft, fluffy, friendly snowflakes began to drift downward lazily, and then, as the wind hit the valley, became driven with urgency to race each other to the ground. The wind stopped, and suddenly hit me in the face from the north. Then it switched back again to the south.

"Backwash," Eddie had called it. "It's as if the wind has to suck in a deep breath to start blowing again. It's dangerous when you're landing, because it can blow you right on past the touchdown point. It's tricky to set up for."

Eddie could explain anything you wanted to know about flying. He would make a good flight instructor or teacher, I thought, if he just gets his act together and stops partying so much and gets away from his shiftless friends. But who was I to say, I had few friends now that Helmi had passed away. Eddie had a lot of problems in the past year. There had been the DUI, he had gotten a bad case of chicken pox, and after that he had cut open his hand helping someone fix a truck. He was always broke, and could never hold down a job after fishing season. In the winters, he worked sporadically for Henry, quitting whenever he felt like it. Henry had a lot of patience for him, but sometimes that would wear thin and he would berate Eddie with no more disrespect than any big brother would show. Eddie, however, was a sensitive person, and sometimes took things to heart. I just wished Eddie would come back home for awhile to get his life back together. He seemed so happy here, hunting ptarmigan and reloading bullets.

With a sickening feeling, I realized the weather had rapidly deteriorated and now I could barely see the end of the airport through the pelting snow. The wind shrieked and howled, bending the brush over and stinging my face with the sharp snow. I wished I had some way to know where my children were. Did they even take off, or were they lost in the blizzard somewhere along the way, flying blindly through the clouds until they crashed into a mountain. I shuddered at the thought and tried to wipe the image of a crumpled aircraft fuselage out of my mind. Jillian didn't have much flight time, but she had already flown in some pretty challenging conditions. I would wait another fifteen minutes, and then it would be too dark to land anyway. I would take the spare snowgo out of the shed and drive up to the house and listen to the marine radio, hoping for the kids to call and let me know they were OK. There was no way to contact anyone else now that the radio frequency we were using had become obsolete.

I walked toward the shed, deciding that the weather was indeed far too bad to land here now. The wind was gusting to thirty miles an hour now and frequently shifting to the opposite direction. The clouds had dropped to nearly tree level, and the south end of the airstrip was obscured. Just then, as the wind backwashed, it carried a growling hum with it. I could briefly hear the plane circling in the fog down the canyon. I raced to the edge of the strip, scanning the clouds intently, hoping they would part and spit out the little Cessna. The wind shifted back to the south with full intensity and the sound was blown away with it. Oh no, what if they can't find the airport? What if they are lost? What if Jillian is still expecting the wind to be from the north, and she flies up into the canyon to land to the north, and gets into the clouds and hits the mountain? I had no way to tell her the wind had switched direction. My heart fluttered wildly in my chest like a panicked bird.

All at once I saw it, the little brown Cessna right above the trees, landing light blinking brightly on its wing and it floundered in the turbulent air, being thrown about as carelessly as a feather in a hurricane. I didn't want to watch, couldn't bear to see it dashed against the ground in a tangled heap, but somehow I couldn't tear my eyes away from it. The plane sank out fast and appeared just about to touch down, when the powerful backwash hit hard. I watched as the plane sailed past where I stood by the tiedowns about mid-field. Then it was on the ground, brakes squealing, loose gravel flying, fishtailing wildly as it tried to slow down before the end. At the end, barely discernible through the fog, it made a fast turn, skidding into a controlled slow taxi back to the tiedowns.

"Yeah! How about that?! Looks like we got here just in time. Sorry to make you wait, Mama." Eddie apologized as he disembarked the plane.

"Oh gosh, I was so worried! Your Dad said you would be right behind him! That was hours ago!" I gave Eddie a big hug.

"Yeah, I know. We couldn't heat both planes up at the same time. First we heated Dad's, and then put the heater on this one for an hour. But we had some problems with the heater and had to go all the way down town to borrow a different one. We made it though, didn't we?" Eddie smiled.

"I heard you circling about a mile out. Did you get lost?" I asked.

"Nope, we just had a little bit better weather there, and Jillian was trying to decide whether she could make it in, or turn around and go back to Bethel. I told her she was a big sissy if she didn't try it."

"I was trying to figure out the wind." Jillian explained. "I couldn't see the other end of the strip. If I shot an approach and had to go around, I don't think I would have been able to see where I was going."

"Yeah, I know! I wish I could have somehow told you which way the wind was coming from." I lamented.

"Do you see that big gust hit us from the north?" Eddie asked. "We landed long and almost didn't get stopped in time. Pretty good flying there, huh? Got stopped with only one brake working!"

"What!? How come you didn't fix the brake? You know your dad always tells you not to take off with things not working right!" I scolded.

"We didn't notice until the preflight. It was already late, and if we had to drive all the way back downtown again to get the stuff to fix the brake, it would have gotten dark before we got here. I told Jillian a real pilot doesn't need brakes anyway." Eddie informed me.

"That's right." Jillian grinned as she started unloading the plane. It was packed full with presents from Henry and lots of food. Ever since Jillian had started flying, my shelves overflowed with food.

I looked at my children, tall and lean and enough alike that everyone thought they were twins. Having them here, safe, was the best Christmas present I could have asked for.

"Hey! Mama, why don't you take this little handheld radio? You can use it to tell me which way the wind is next time. But it only works close, maybe three to five miles away in these mountains." She handed me a boxy blue radio.

"Oh, I don't know if I can figure out how to use that. Don't you need it in your plane?" I asked.

"No, I got my panel mounted radio working now, so I don't need it. You should keep it. Eddie can show you how to work it. It's not very complicated."

Ever since that Christmas Eve, I became White Bear's "air traffic advisor". At the first sound of Harry's or Jillian's plane flying into the valley, I would turn the radio on the Common Traffic Advisory Frequency and give the wind and airfield conditions.

Over the winter, Jillian made many trips home. Sometimes she brought Eddie, and sometimes he would be too busy to come. How I cherished those memories of the three of us, sitting around the kerosene lantern playing cards and drinking cocoa!

In early May, before she took off for firefighting again, Jillian made one last trip home, bringing Eddie.

"Mama," she said when Eddie was out of earshot, "Eddie is acting a little odd. I'm worried about him. Can you talk to him and make sure he's OK?"

"What do you mean? Eddie is fine. Don't worry about him so much. He has to learn to live his own life." I lectured.

I couldn't see anything too wrong with Eddie. He was probably at a turning point in his life, trying to figure things out. He had just joined a church, a strange denomination where it was a sin to drink hot cocoa. It seemed to make him happy, so we drank herbal tea instead.

Right then Eddie walked back in the kitchen, "What are you guys talking about?" He asked.

"About you. About that weird-ass creepy cult you joined. What's up with that, anyhow?" Jillian teased.

Eddie looked defensive. "I like it! I love my Lord. I know I'm a better person because I go to church. You should try it, you heathen!"

"Shut up, fool! If I burn in hell cuz I drank hot cocoa, I don't think much of THAT religion." Jillian ribbed.

"Knock it off you two! Eddie, you can believe in whatever you want. I used to go to church a long time ago with my folks. It took me a while to figure it out that I have a better religion watching the sun set over my mountains. Have you tried other churches?" I interjected.

"No. I go to that church because I have friends there. I like it. Mama, would you still love me if I was a fool?" Eddie looked dejected.

"Of course, sunshine! I'd love you always and forever no matter what you were!" I walked over and hugged Eddie, and sang him the song I used to sing when he was a little boy.

"You are my sunshine, my only sunshine, you make me happy when skies are gray…"

Eddie stayed home for three days, spending a lot of time with his nose stuck in his new bible. The morning they left, he arose cheerfully and said, "It's such a beautiful day to be alive!"

And indeed he was right, it was a lovely May day, the fresh smells of spring and the twittering of newly arriving birds filling the air. Eddie seemed sad to leave, but he wanted to get back to town so he wouldn't miss church, and Jillian had to catch a jet for California. I stood at the airport long after the plane disappeared from sight, listening to the sound fade away. It was the last time I would see my son alive.

## Chapter Twenty-Seven

"Eddie shot himself." Henry's eyes were swollen and red. He stood next to Tom's plane at our airstrip.

My heart completely stopped.

"What, what do you mean? Is he dead?" I stammered. I couldn't grasp the concept. I had seen Eddie just a few weeks earlier.

"Yes," Henry broke into tears, and we held each other and sobbed.

"Why? Why? Oh why Eddie?" I bawled into Henry's shoulder.

"I don't know. He just got depressed, I guess." Henry said.

"I guess we should go tell your dad." My mind reeled and my legs felt weak, but I knew I needed to take action, to do something before the sorrow and grief consumed me entirely.

It was May 29, 1996. Harry was up at the house, recovering from the latest attack of gout. The snow was still melting and the trail was very muddy. I hadn't gotten the jeep battery put in yet. I had just stopped using the snowgo. When I saw the plane fly over, I had jogged down to the airport.

We started walking up the trail together. I felt oddly surreal. Sharp pangs of agony hit me occasionally, and I made no effort to stop my tears.

"Are they sure Eddie shot himself?" I asked. I just couldn't believe Eddie would do such a thing. Not Eddie, who just weeks ago, had said it was such a beautiful day to be alive.

"Yes." Henry said. "But they took him in to Anchorage anyway. They are sending him back out tomorrow."

"Did he leave a note? Did he say why?" I wasn't sure I wanted to know.

"No. Nobody found anything."

"Did anybody tell Jillian yet?" I asked.

"No. I couldn't find the number for where she's working." Henry said.

Henry filled me in as much as he could. He had noticed Eddie was behaving differently. Eddie was not showing up for work in the mornings and often, he would have to go to Jillian's trailer, where Eddie had been staying this spring, and nearly physically drag him to work. Henry had a long talk with Eddie that evening, and had been concerned to leave him alone. But Freya was expecting Henry home for dinner, and he was late, and eventually had to leave, deciding there wasn't much else he could do, and Eddie would have to get over it himself. Later, Eddie had left and visited some friends, and then went back to the trailer around three in the morning. He shot himself in the head with Jillian's handgun.

It seemed so terrible and pointless, the violent end to a precious young life with so much potential. Harry was devastated. I had no words to describe my anguish. Only another mother who has lost her child to suicide could know how I felt, and the agony I endure to this day. For one's child to die before oneself was against nature itself. Constantly, every waking moment, I fretted over it, blaming myself, blaming everyone else, wishing I had one more chance, to reach back in time and change something, to soothe the troubles in Eddie's mind, to physically reach out and stop the bullet that killed him. My grief consumed me. People often said, "It will pass. It will get better," but I could not envision a life without Eddie, could not imagine how this emptiness in my heart would ever pass. My very heart and soul felt completely crushed.

Harry left his plane at White Bear and flew back to Bethel with Henry and Tom. It was not a time for a grieving father to operate an airplane. I spent the long sleepless night alone, pacing the floors, wishing this horrible drama was not real, that I could just awaken from this terrible nightmare and see my son sitting at our kitchen table, wishing I could give him one last hug, that I could say something to him to make him realize that suicide was not the answer.

Late the next afternoon, Henry's friend LJ flew up with Jillian and they walked up to the house.

"Oh Mama," sobbed Jillian, "This is all my fault. I should have given that stupid gun back to Mike."

"No, no, Eddie would have just found some other way to do it." I sniffled.

"I don't know. Why, Mama? Didn't he know how much everyone loves him? I knew something was different, but I never thought he would kill himself! Oh, man, Mike gave me that gun for Valentine's day, then he asked me for it back. I should have given it back to him." Jillian lamented.

"It's too late to change anything now, honey. We have to be strong and go on with our lives." It was something to say, but it was not advice I took myself.

We left extra food and water for the animals and walked back down to the airstrip. Jillian and I flew back to Bethel with LJ.

Eddie's funeral was the following day. It was held at the Moravian church, not Eddie's church, merely for the convenience of its central location in town. Eddie had touched many lives in his short life, and the building overflowed. The many hugs and comforting words were much appreciated, but nothing could replace the tremendous loss I had endured. Seeing my son in his coffin was a vision I have tried to erase from my mind. It was as if seeing Eddie lying there, dressed by the funeral home in clothes that were not his, wearing a tie, made his death real and unchangeable. I tried to hold back my emotions amongst the large crowd, knowing if I let the grief take over, I may not be able to sit through the service.

The service was not worth sitting through. In fact it was the most heartless and cruelest thing a grieving family should have had to endure.

The pompous preacher started out the sermon, "Eddie is a sinner and he will go to hell. His soul has been lost forever. He committed the ultimate sin for which there is no redemption. Eddie was a very bad person for this, and that is why you, the family and friends of this young man, should turn your hearts to Jesus Christ and be saved."

My mouth fell open, not believing what I was hearing. This was a time for consoling a grieving family who had suffered an unfathomable loss, not a time to tout one's personal religious beliefs. Besides me in the front pew, I felt Jillian bristling with rage. She snatched up a bible. I put my hand out and stopped her before she could spring to her feet and hurl the heavy tome at the pompous bastard. Thinking back, I probably should have let her give that man a well-deserved thump on the noggin. I probably should have stood up and said something, and stopped his blathering nonsense. The preacher went on with his spiel, and several people, including Jillian, got up and left. I turned my mind off and sat through it without listening. After it was finally over, Martha and Walter stood up and emotionally sang a beautiful song. The tears started flowing again, and I went outside. Kayla and Jillian stood in the parking lot. Kayla had written in huge letters in the sand, 'I LOVE YOU EDDIE'.

"It's so Uncle Eddie can see it from where he is." She explained.

I gave them both a big hug.

"I had to get out of there, Mama. I'm sorry. I just couldn't listen to that hypocritical bastard any more. The Christian Jesus committed suicide in a way, too! Who the hell is he to say what he said! What an asshole!" Jillian seethed.

We chartered a Cessna Caravan to fly Eddie home to White Bear. Many pilots and friends flew up, and together we dug the grave on the side of the little hill overlooking the house. It was rocky and the ground was still partially frozen, but Henry had brought along a jackhammer and there were at least a dozen strong men to wield the picks and shovels. Harry got the Jeep going, and Jillian shoveled the last few snow drifts, so we could get it down the muddy, slippery mountain trail to pick up Eddie's coffin.

My son is buried on the hill where as a child he would hunt ptarmigan and trap mountain squirrels. Often I visit him and sing to him, "you are my sunshine, my only sunshine, you make me happy when skies are gray…please don't ever take my sunshine away…" It seemed as though all the sunshine in my life had disappeared that fateful Memorial Day. It was a long, long time before those dark and gloomy clouds would finally start to lift. Even now, many years later, my heart aches with the loss that can never be replaced.

I am forever grateful to the many, many people who were there for me at the worst time of my life and in my time of need.

*Eddie's mountainside burial*

## Chapter Twenty-Eight

I awoke in a hospital bed, disoriented and confused. Where was I? What was happening to me?

"It's OK, Mama. I'm right here. You're going to be OK now." Jillian was holding my hand tightly.

"Do you want some more water, Dolly?" asked Harry.

I nodded, and then noticed at least a dozen little paper cups on the stand next to the bed. Harry walked off, no doubt relieved to have a task.

"You gonna be OK, or do I have to start digging you a hole?" kidded Henry.

"I think so. I'm just coming back into myself now. Where am I?" I asked.

"You're in the hospital in Bethel. You were acting odd this morning so I flew you to town. I don't know what's wrong." Jillian told me. Later I learned that she had already told me the same thing dozens of times.

"I'm fine. You should take me home. I want to go home now." I insisted. Apparently I had said that dozens of times too.

I must have faded away again, because the next time I became aware, I was in a plane. Jillian informed me that we were in a Medevac Lear Jet, headed for Anchorage. I faded away again, and awoke fully alert, in the hospital in Anchorage.

"Are you OK now, Mama?" Jillian asked me.

"Yes, I feel fine." I answered.

Jillian looked doubtful, having heard that answer a few too many times already. A nurse walked in.

"Good morning, Dolly. How are you feeling today?" She asked cheerily.

"I'm fine. I think it was just an emotional overload. My son committed suicide last year. I think my brain just shut off for awhile." I answered.

She nodded. "That can happen. Do you know what day it is?"

"It's sometime in April. I don't know exactly what day, I usually don't keep track."

"That's fine. Do you know what year it is?"

"It's 1997. Did they find anything wrong with me?" I wanted to know.

"No, all of your tests came back fine. We have you scheduled for an MRI, just to be sure. Do you remember anything before you got here?" She queried.

"I remember a little bit of being in the hospital in Bethel, but don't remember how I got there. I remember I was in a Lear Jet. I feel fine, I just can't remember anything that just happened. But now I feel as if I'm stepping back into my body."

My thoughts were still fuzzy and confused. What was wrong with me? Did I have a brain tumor? Was I going to die?

"What about White Bear? Did we leave food for the animals when we left?" I asked in a panic.

Jillian patted my hand reassuringly. "Dad said he was going to fly up today. Everything will be fine. Let's just get you better. Dad will take care of White Bear."

Over the next few days, I endured a battery of tests, all of which came back fine. The doctors were puzzled, and for lack of a better term, called my episode a transient ischemic attack, although I was otherwise healthy and had none of the symptoms associated with that affliction. I was functioning normally, but merely had no short term memory, and to this day, have no memory of events preceding my hospital visit. The incident shook me to my core. It was as if I had completely lost a day of my life. What if it happened again? What if my mind blanked out completely and I became lost in it forever? The doctors assured me that I could live a completely normal life and would possibly never have another incident.

After hearing that diagnosis, we headed home. The weather was fine when we got to Bethel, so we got in Jillian's airplane and headed to White Bear. The one lesson I brought back from my scare was that I needed to get a grip on my grief, and let it go, and begin living again, before I let it consume me both physically and mentally. There was no getting Eddie back, no changing what had already been done. I did my best to become more aware of the things going on around me, the beautiful splendor of the wilderness. I cried when I felt sad, and didn't try to hold it back. One of the friends who helped me tremendously was Joyce Freeman. I met her last summer when she and her companion Ken landed in a Civil Air Patrol plane, looking for the source of a malfunctioning emergency locator transmitter. We had become close friends, and they frequently dropped in, using Ken's 172.

A few weeks went by, and I had no more memory lapses or physical problems. I started gaining back confidence. I was able to talk more openly about Eddie's suicide, which had seemed like a taboo subject back then. But what helped me through my hard times the most was the little bundle Jillian brought home from one of her hikes.

It was a cold and rainy day in the first part of May. I was surprised when I saw Jillian come back from her hike carrying her coat in her arms. She came through the door with a huge smile, the first time I had seen her smile in nearly a year.

"Look, Mama." She gently unwrapped the coat.

At first I wasn't sure what I was looking at. The pale, dough-like blob laid lifelessly on the coat. Then it unfolded and, with much effort, lifted an enormous gaping beak.

"A raven?!" I asked.

"Yes. Isn't he adorable?" Jillian held him as tenderly as a mother holds a newborn infant.

Adorable wasn't exactly the word I would have used, but the little creature did have the unique charm of a helpless young creature.

"Where did you get it?" I asked.

"There was a nest in the willows back past the rock ledge. He was on the ground and I thought he was dead. I put him in the nest, and he got pushed out again, but I was standing right under the nest, so I reached out and caught him. It was a pretty big fall for a little guy too! Too many in the nest. There were seven and they usually have five. He's too young to survive on the ground. Look. He doesn't have any feathers and his eyes are still closed. Must be only a few days old. I'm going to raise him and then let him go when he can fly."

"Won't he peck your eyes out when he gets big?" I asked doubtfully.

"Nope. Not any more than a dog would. Besides he will be grown up in a month or so. I bet he's hungry. What do we have that I can give him?" She asked.

I went out on the porch shelf and got some leftover moose meatballs and some bread. Jillian sat down and put the bird in her lap. It was very hungry, and greedily swallowed everything she put into its cavernous maw. She made up a little box with soft dried grasses, and put it in her room next to her bed. Every few hours she fed it, and within a few days, it regained strength considerably. We named him Mitaka, the Siberian Eskimo word for raven or trickster.

The first time I fed Mitaka, I was nervous about hurting him. I gently placed the food in his bill.

*Mitaka graces our life*

"No," Jillian said. "You have to push it farther down so he can swallow it, so he doesn't choke." She demonstrated with the expertise of an experienced mother bird.

I fed him, not so daintily now, and he ate hungrily. Then, as if the effort exhausted him, Mitaka laid his head gently in my hand. I felt a warmth rushing back into my empty heart. Suddenly I felt necessary and needed. He buzzed contentedly in his sleep, and Jillian answered him back. We giggled.

Mitaka did not stay small and helpless for long. Little black pinfeathers began to push out, and soon erupted into marvelous iridescent black plumage with hints of green and blue. His eyes were wide open now, and he took in everything with curious enthusiasm. He hopped along behind us or sat on our shoulders wherever we went. Jillian would talk to him in his own language, and one day I heard myself cawing just like them.

Jillian was planning to go to work a bit later this spring. She had accepted a job offer from the smokejumpers, a very coveted and difficult position to obtain. Their rookie training started in the first week of June, and she spent most of her time working out and getting ready for the intensive month of 'boot camp'. We had built a pullup bar on our porch, and since there weren't any good places to run around the homestead, Jillian would fly over to Aniak a few times a week to run on the roads there. She usually invited me to ride along with her, to spend an hour or so in town and fly back. But leaving the homestead made me nervous.

"What if we get stuck over there?" I asked.

"We won't. It's a nice day. If clouds start coming in, we will zip over and get home before they do. It's only a twenty minute flight."

"What if we break down?"

"Then we fix it. Or find someone else to take you home."

"What if your dad finds out?" I asked.

"He won't unless you tell him. You wouldn't tell him, would you?"

"No! What if the wing falls off and we crash?"

Jillian snorted. "It's not going to fall off. That's why I do a preflight. If we crash, we will walk home."

"What if we're too badly hurt to walk?"

"Then we turn on the ELT and wait for someone to pick us up."

"What if we die in the crash?"

"If we die, then we're dead, and nothing is going to matter then anyway." Jillian explained patiently.

Somehow there was logic in that, and having exhausted all possible what-ifs, I reluctantly crawled into the plane. Jillian squirmed with delight. Right after takeoff, she looked over at me.

"Still scared?"

"No." I smiled convincingly.

"Then let go of the 'OH-SHIT' strap." She grinned back.

I realized I was still clinging to the strap on the door post. I gingerly loosened my fingers, and realized that the plane was not going to fall out from under me. Jillian started pointing out things, an eagle flying near us, a cow moose with twin calves in the bushes. She didn't seem to be paying any attention at all to keeping the plane in the air.

"Hey!" I said, alarmed. "Fly the plane!"

Jillian laughed. "I don't have to. It flies itself. I just steer it once in awhile. What did you want me to do, flap my arms to help it fly?"

She let go of the control stick and flapped her arms. The plane stayed on exactly the same path. The smell of old sweat filled the small cabin.

"Pew! You stink. You're not going to the store like that, are you?" I laughed.

"Nope. I brought an extra t-shirt in my backpack. After I run, I'll change. Then we can meet up at the store."

I had flown with Jillian on a few previous occasions, but was still used to Harry's serious and attentive flying. Jillian flew differently, easily and naturally as a bird. I remembered once asking Eddie why he always flew up with Jillian instead of Harry.

"Jillian's more fun! Besides, she lets me fly sometimes." He had answered.

Jillian touched down in Aniak smoothly, so smoothly in fact, that I couldn't even feel the wheels hit the ground. We rolled into the parking area and stopped.

"See you later, bye." Jillian took off running.

I wandered around the small town, bought pretty stamps at the post office, found some free books at the library, and made some phone calls from the store while I waited for Jillian. She came in, face flushed from the wind and exercise, and we bought a few groceries and walked back toward the plane.

"Did you have a good run?" I asked.

"Yeah. I hope you didn't mind that I was late. I ran an extra loop, so around fifteen miles I think."

We took off and banked toward the mountains. Looking toward the distant peaks, I saw the clouds starting to swirl. The plane bucked with turbulence as we crossed the last ridge and set up for approach to our short mountain airstrip. Jillian reached down to pull her seatbelt tighter, and accidently hit the buckle. It clattered to the floor. She was on final approach now, and didn't want to release the controls to pick the seat belt off the floor. I had a fleeting thought of reaching down for it, but then I would be in Jillian's way, and distract her during the crucial time of landing. Soon we would be on the ground anyway, and Jillian's landings were normally very smooth.

We sunk out over the trees, and flared for landing. Just then, a powerful tailwind hit us, and we floated most of the way down the airstrip, past the safe touchdown point. Jillian added full power, trying to wrestle the plane back into the air to make another approach. The engine sputtered and coughed. Ahead, the mountainside filled the windscreen. With sudden shock, I realized we were going to crash. We didn't have the power to clear the mountain. Then Jillian was shutting everything down, totally calm, and I had a feeling that this wasn't this first time she had an emergency in an airplane.

The next thing I knew, I was hanging from my seat belt with a very close-up view of tundra in the windshield.

"You OK?" Jillian asked.

"Yeah." I wasn't sure yet if I was.

"Here, undo your seat belt. Hold on here, or you'll fall. Now, I'll open the door for you, and you get out. Be careful, it's a long ways to the ground. I'll hold your arms." She was completely calm, as if she crashed an airplane every day. She helped me get out, then swung out and dropped to the ground.

The plane had hit the tundra right off the end of the airstrip and stood on its nose in the soft tundra mattress. The damage appeared fairly minimal. My foot ached from where it had jammed abruptly into the rudder pedals. Just bruised, I thought. I looked over at Jillian. She hunched over and threw up.

"I'm alright." She insisted. "Probably just ran too hard." She dabbed at a bloody lip. "Just bit my lip, that's all. Man, I'm sorry! I didn't mean to dump you on your head like that. You sure you're not hurt?"

"No." I said. I could put weight on the foot, so it probably wasn't broken.

We used the Jeep to pull the plane back into its tiedown. Jillian was devastated. It was less than a week before she had to report for smokejumper training, and now her plane was broken and she would miss her jet. There was no way to walk out, as the rivers were running high and much of the lower tundra was flooded.

"Why don't you ask your dad for a ride?" I suggested.

That night on the radio, she did, and Harry seemed pleased to be asked. He would be up the next day to pick her up. The next morning, my foot was much better, but Jillian was hobbling around like an old woman.

"Maybe you shouldn't go to smokejumper training like that. You'll hurt yourself worse." I suggested.

"No, No! I'm fine. I have to go. I might never get another chance, and besides it's too late for them to hire someone else to replace me." Jillian insisted.

She winced as she put on her shoes and started jogging down the rough trail. I followed her in the Jeep, Mitaka sitting on the seat beside me. Jillian was far slower than usual, and appeared to be having a difficult time. When we got to the airstrip, she was gasping and retching.

"I'm totally fine," she said, wiping bloody foam from her lips with her sleeve. "Just got to push myself a little harder, I guess I'm out of shape."

She went over and picked up Mitaka and started fussing over him. He chortled happily and snuggled against her. Then Harry landed, and it was time for her to go.

She gave me a big hug and said, "If you need anything let me know. I can come back, you know, if you have any problems."

"I'll be fine. I have Mitaka! For a little longer anyway. You be careful and have a good summer." I said.

And then they were gone, and I was alone. Well, not really alone, because the hungry little raven and Taxi and my hens kept me entertained.

A week later, Harry told me that Jillian had called him, and told him that she had washed out of smokejumper training. She hadn't been able to pass the first physical test the first day. I was shocked, knowing she had trained hard for it, and that smokejumping was a very important goal for her. I realized then Jillian had been hurt a bit worse than she let on. Harry said she found a job on another fire crew in Oregon, and planned to work the rest of the summer anyway. I worried frequently over her health, but it was a slow year for fires, so Jillian had time to heal up.

Harry spent more time home again over the summer. We were busy with his latest scheme, installing a telephone at White Bear. It was a complicated and expensive endeavor. We used the tracked Nodwell to haul supplies to the top of the nearest mountain. There, we set up a repeater station that relayed telephone signals from the village of Chuathbuluk, 50 miles away. The antenna and unit needed power and heat, so we set up a small wind generator to power 12 volt batteries, which ran a small diesel heater and the relay unit. Then we strung over a mile of telephone line down to the house, where, for the first time ever, we had a regular telephone at White Bear. The system, however, was wrought with problems, and the majority of our time was spent working out the kinks.

My new friend Joyce visited me often that summer. She was an avid animal lover, and just enthralled by Mitaka.

"I see ravens all the time in Bethel, but never this close up! My, my! What a personality this guy has!" She gushed as Mitaka sat on her arm and regaled her with his extensive vocabulary of raven gibberish.

Mitaka had turned into a beautiful bird, and flew along after us wherever we went. Harry was mildly tolerant of him, understanding that he was Jillian's pet. The bird had his mistress's curious, mischievous personality and loved to explore everything new. He would land on my head, chortling with delight and telling me all of his little raven adventures. He stole shiny things and loved to make me chase him. He stashed extra food in little cracks he found around the house. Since he was getting a bit big and rambunctious for the house, I made him his own bachelor pad in one of the sheds, sawing the top half of the door off so he could come and go as he wished. He loved it, but still occasionally followed me into the house.

One day, I noticed a large hawk sitting in the trees above his shed. Mitaka stayed in his shed until I chased it away. Then he took off, teased Taxi with a dive bomb, and disappeared on one of his excursions. I never saw him again. I missed him terribly and spent hours calling and looking for him. I couldn't imagine him leaving on his own, he was still young, and very bonded to me. I saw the big hawk several times, circling overhead or perched in nearby trees, and now I knew without a doubt that it had killed Mitaka. Although I was very sad, I was honored to have known such a fine feathered friend, and to this day, I answer every raven that caws as it flies overhead.

In December of 1997, we got a notice from the BLM that they had decided to take away our 40 acre hotsprings lease. Over the years we had applied for and held various leases for the property around the hotsprings. I was puzzled, and read the letter over and over, trying to understand it. It stated that they had denied it because they thought it was redundant. Since we already had State of Alaska water permits for usage of the hotsprings, and a granted right-of-way to transport the water in the pipeline across the quarter mile to our house, they said that we "didn't need the lease". I was quite concerned and wrote several letters on the matter, none of which I would ever get a response to. Our new telephone system, as luck would have it, was on the fritz. When I finally did get in touch with someone at the BLM, they were unable to find any record or reference number to the supposed decision not to honor our lease. Harry went to Bethel saying he would "take care of it", and I thought nothing of the matter until years later.

## Chapter Twenty-Nine

"Dolly! Hey, Dolly, get your coat and come with me. I have something to show you." Harry was excited. He had just driven back from the airstrip.

I wanted to finish the dishes and my cup of coffee, but the urgency in Harry's voice made me stop what I was doing and get ready. What could possibly have intrigued Harry so? He wasn't a man to be easily impressed by trivial details.

"Hey, do you still have any of that bread left?" He asked. He had bought a huge garbage bag of stale bread from the bakery for my hens.

"Yes, there's still lots! I started drying some so it won't mold." I answered.

"Bring some along." Harry said.

I grabbed a few loaves off the shelves and wondered what he wanted to do with it. For an instant, I dared to hope he had seen Mitaka, but that possibility could not exist. It had been a year since the raven's disappearance, and the hawk's presence had signified Mitaka's untimely fate. Maybe he had found some other animal in need of assistance? It hardly seemed like Harry. He was an avid hunter, and seemed to have no remorse for shooting anything. But over the years he had softened, and now he no longer shot at jays or anything he wasn't going to eat. I was glad, because I had a rule at my home: you don't kill anything you are not going to eat or somehow use. Killing for the fun of it is a needless waste, and something I could not fathom, but perhaps it was one of those mysterious male traits.

We bumped along the trail out to where we had been working one of the mining claims. Harry was as excited as if he had found gold, but what did that have to do with bread? As we pulled up to the gravel pit he was making to resurface the airstrip, I noticed he had moved the D8 Cat. He had made one pass and pushed a load of gravel to the south end of the airstrip, and then he had stopped. We parked near the Cat and sat in the truck waiting.

"What is it? What am I supposed to see?" I asked. My coffee was getting cold at home. I should have brought it along.

"Shhhhh. Just wait. They will come out again."

Who were 'they'? And why did 'they' need bread? Just then the brush parted, and two little husky puppies bounced out, and then three more, tumbling over each other on their way to the truck, squeaking and cavorting as they bounded toward us.

"Oh! Oh, where did they come from?" I whispered.

Harry, careful not to make sudden movements, nodded toward the brush. A lanky grey wolf stood there nervously, whining and anxiously trying to call her pups away from us. And just behind her was a darker wolf, perhaps the dad. So they were wolf pups, not huskies! They looked so small and cuddly.

Harry beamed. "I think they live in that bank over there. I'm not going to move any more gravel, I don't want to ruin their den. Here, give me the bread."

He eased out of the truck and walked slowly to the front. The fearless little puppies bounded over, and stopped just a few yards from Harry. The big wolves paced and whined and yipped, but were too fearful of us to come any closer to 'rescue' their pups. Harry tossed the bread to the furry little pups, and they attack the loaves playfully before devouring them. Then they reluctantly went back to their parents.

I was amazed at Harry's change in character. Just a few years ago, he would have shot every wolf he saw. And now, here he was, practically feeding them out of his hand. I liked the change. It was good to see Harry happy. He had mellowed out a lot over the past few years.

Over the summer, Harry fed his pups nearly daily, until the parents decided enough was enough, and moved the whole family. By fall, the wolves had left the valley to avoid the deep snow, and to find easier prey, perhaps caribou many miles away on the open tundra. Before they left, the adults grudgingly allowed the kids one last farewell to their human 'grandpa'. Harry glowed as he told me that he stroked the head of the smallest wolf. They sang to us that night, a mysterious, soul-searing melody that echoed through the mountains, and then they left.

The next day, before the snow fell, Harry flew to Bethel to meet the jet. Jillian was returning from Montana, where she had spent the summer fighting forest fires. That summer she had gotten another job offer from the smokejumpers, completed their rookie training, and seemed to be enjoying the job of her dreams. Now fire season was over, and she was headed home. She had sold her trailer in Bethel, and since Mike was doing time in prison, Jillian planned to spend her winter at White Bear trapping. She had used the money from the trailer to pay off Eddie's outstanding debts, and donated a large sum of every season's earnings to Search & Rescue crews, still feeling guilty about the massive search she had created as a teenager. She has donated probably a hundred times more than was needed over the years, but it was always like Jillian to go to extremes.

It seemed that my entire summer had been spent that year fooling with the malfunctioning phone unit. I was in great shape from hiking up and down that mountain, carrying backpacks full of tools. First, a moose had tripped over the line and pulled in apart. I followed the entire line, burying it under a few inches of tundra and making sure it all laid flat. The heater had problems, and I had to go up many times to bleed the fuel lines. The batteries grew weak in a calm spell, and I carried a small generator up to charge the batteries. Then it got very windy, and the wind generator advertised to withstand gusts up to 150 miles an hour shattered its blades. I replaced the wind generator blades several times over the summer. Then the line went dead again, and this time it was the experimental station in Chuathbaluk that was to blame. By the time that was fixed, the shrews had chewed through countless spots in the line. It was impossible to tell where all the damage was, so I replaced the majority of the line after finding hundreds of places they had chewed. All in all, it was a frustrating and time-consuming project for which I got little gain. When I was able to make a phone call, the sound was poor and I would usually hear an echo in the background. Harry kept putting more money into the project, but I was growing weary of it.

Harry, who was a certified airplane mechanic, had repaired Jillian's airplane for her the previous summer, and she flew it a lot. Unfortunately, in January 1999, she wrecked it again near Bethel in icing conditions. She worked for Henry briefly to make enough money for repairs. Then she was gone to Montana again, to hurl herself out of airplanes into forest fires.

Harry was delighted when his wolves returned to the same area and had another litter of pups. There were only three adults in the pack, so we wondered what had become of last year's pups. Perhaps they had starved. It didn't seem that there was enough food for them in the valley. But I supposed, since the snow was gone, they could catch rabbits, and perhaps they ate shrews.

The little shrews were of almost epidemic proportions some years. Our house was filled with the scurrying, squeaking, twittering little creatures. All of our food had to be stored in sturdy, airtight containers, usually five gallon buckets, or it would disappear within a few days. The shrews would carry off copious amounts of anything they could get their little paws on, and stash it where they saw fit. It wasn't unusual to put your boots on in the morning and find a handful of dried noodles, or even a shrew itself. When Eddie and Jillian were children, doing their homework at the kitchen table, it had become a game of theirs to fling school books at the shrews when the little vermin crawled over their toes. Nights were filled with shrews twittering, and loud gnawing and bumping as they tried to fit a dog food kernel through an impossibly small crack.

There was an old legend of a miner that lived near the big lake in the early 1900's. He had been alone a lot, and made pets of the shrews. One winter, someone dropped in to check on him since nobody had seen him in awhile, and they found him dead in his chair, covered with shrews. His bones were polished white from their nibbling. It wasn't clear if the mass of shrews had actually killed him, or had merely taken advantage of the easy meal after he was deceased. Still, that story usually came to mind when a furry little body ran across our beds!

None of the commercial mouse traps worked on the shrews, as they were too light to trigger the mechanism. The best trap seemed to be Eddie's history book. A few years ago, Jillian had suggested that it might be nice to have a cat.

"I don't like cats!" I said.

"Why not?" She asked.

I had to think a moment. "I don't know. They just don't really do anything."

Jillian looked very pointedly at Taxi, sleeping on her dog bed, and then shrugged.

I was spending much of this summer pulling and chopping brush that had grown along our airstrip. Between the encroaching bushes and the flooding beaver dam, there was much effort involved in keeping our little mountain airstrip functional. I was relieved when Harry finally decided that the mountain phone was too costly. Not having to constantly maintain that phone saved me a lot of time which I used to garden and care for the airport. Toward mid-summer and again just before the ground froze, I always mowed the grasses short on the strip, so grasses and plants wouldn't trap the winter snow. Then the field could blow clean of snow in the wind.

I was sewing a patch on my jeans one morning, when I looked out my window and saw something in the little cottonwood trees. Putting on my glasses, I saw that it was a young lynx. I watched it as it bear-hugged the tree and climbed up to the first branch, then stopped and looked apprehensively at the ground. As if deciding it had gone too far, the little kitten turned around on the branch. It sat there a long time, trying to figure out how to get back down again. The lynx tried going head first, but no, that was too scary. I chuckled, enjoying its antics. The lynx kitten waited awhile, and then started backing down, big feet wrapped around the tree in a death grip. When its stumpy little tail touched the ground, it let go of the tree and turned and ran away as fast as it could from those big scary trees. I wrote to Jillian in Montana, how that was the cutest little lynx, wouldn't one of those make a neat pet?!

When Jillian got back in the fall, she and I spent weeks disassembling the entire phone system, rolling up the line, and backpacking everything off the mountain. She cut some brush before the snow fell, but once the snow covered the ground, we stopped, so as not to leave sharp stobs to catch our snowshoes. Then it was full swing into beaver trapping.

Jillian flew to town whenever the weather was good, sometimes only once a month, for supplies. Harry waited in town for his Social Security check, stayed there a few weeks after, and then flew home. During the winter, sometimes it was two months before he came home. He tired easily, and getting the plane ready for flying was a physically demanding ordeal that often took all day. The engine had to be preheated for at least an hour, and frost or ice had to be scraped painstakingly from every surface of the aircraft. There was usually a great deal of shoveling involved also. Jillian and I helped Harry get his plane ready when he would leave White Bear, and most of the time Jillian would make a special trip to Bethel just to help her dad get his plane ready to come home again. It never was as simple as hopping in and flying to town whenever you felt like it.

One day in May not long before Jillian was to leave again for firefighting, we saw a spectacular sight neither of us will forget. It was warm in the house, and I dozed off on the couch, listening to the soft spring rain dripping off the roof, and the solid thunk of Jillian chopping wood. Jillian was singing and far away Taxi was barking incessantly at something. I was jerked awake suddenly by Taxi's panicked yowling, and Jillian yelling, "Bear! Get the gun!"

I sprang off the couch and snatched the rifle off the gunrack. Throwing open the door, I was nearly knocked over by Taxi, who darted past me and hid under the kitchen table. Stepping onto the porch, I saw the young grizzly, still running toward where Jillian stood with the ax, still intent on catching the dog, not seeming to notice Jillian. She stepped up on the log pile. The bear skidded to a stop and reared onto its hind legs, just feet from Jillian. She was between the bear and I, and I couldn't get a good shot without hitting Jillian. She lifted the ax high over her head and faced the bear fearlessly. I stared in fascinated horror, expecting the ax to swing down on the bear's skull or the beast to swat Jillian off her lofty perch. I wondered if she could feel its hot breath in her face. Then, the spell was broken, and the grizzly lowered itself to the ground and bolted away.

"Man, did you see that?" Jillian exclaimed. "Damn worthless dog is going to get one of us killed one of these days."

She came in the house and took her gun off the rack. "Well that was stupid of me, I should have kept me gun with me. Just haven't seen any bears yet this spring."

"Probably because that grizzly was in the area. They chase off the black bears, you know." I said.

Jillian stood on the porch, watching the brush. "There it is. See, look, it's leaving, it's halfway up that hill and still running. Hey, there's another one! Same size, probably two years old. The mom may still be around, too, so keep your eyes open."

I watched the two young bears lope up the hillside and cross over into the thicker brush, toward the last lingering patch of snow. Funny, I thought, I don't remember that big drift there yesterday, and it sure hadn't snowed recently. And then it moved.

Jillian saw it too. "Look, Mama, the white bear!" She whispered in awe.

We watched the big white grizzly through the binoculars, as she greeted her grown kids, cuffing the naughty one with a huge paw, and then they all melted into the dense brush. It was a rare and precious reminder of our unseen namesake who shared this lovely valley with us.

## Chapter Thirty

The lynx kitten nestled in Jillian's arms, its bright yellow eyes looking into mine searchingly, as if begging for acceptance. The long bushy tail swished softly. I felt my heart reaching out to the homeless little lynx. It looked disheveled and embarrassed, having soiled its kennel during the long and frightening flight in Jillian's airplane. I could understand the little creature's discomfort. Here he was, uncaged at last, meeting his new family, starting a new life, and his coat was less than perfectly groomed! Now, what kind of first impression is that?! No wonder he looked embarrassed.

"You can keep him in your room until he gets big," I said.

Jillian let out her breath. What did she think, that I was going to throw the poor little thing out into the cold? I went to get a damp cloth. Wiping his feet gently, I looked into the little lynx's eyes, and saw a warm gratitude and love.

It was March 2001. Jillian had just returned from an assignment doing a prescribed burn in Mississippi. She had overnighted in Anchorage, again in Bethel, and then flew home. Harry departed White Bear after he saw Jillian land safely, as there was a big storm moving in. As we unloaded the cargo, one particular box was making some plaintive yowls.

"It's a baby lynx." Jillian said when I asked what it was. "The Alaska zoo was going to put it to sleep because they didn't have enough room for it. I told them we have lots of room and we can raise it and let it go."

"Oh! Remember I told you about that little one I saw? I thought it would have made a good pet! How old is it?"

"Uh, I think, maybe three months old." Jillian said.

Now, as I examined the amazingly tame little feline, I was surprised at the softness of its paws.

"Doesn't it have any claws?! Did they declaw it? How will it hunt for itself?" I asked, alarmed.

"He has claws. They're just under the fur." Jillian gently squeezed a paw, and needle sharp talons appeared from the soft velvet.

"His back is pretty dark! Is he a Mississippi lynx?" I pondered.

"No, I got him from the Alaska zoo. He will probably turn lighter when he gets older." Jillian said. "I was planning to keep him in the shed with the chicken feed. Maybe he can catch some shrews before we let him go."

"Nonsense! It's twenty below! He's staying in your room until it gets warmer." I interjected.

Jillian smiled happily. Well, if this little lynx was anything as wonderful as Mitaka, of course it could stay here!

"Did it have a name?" I asked.

"They called him Max, but we can change it if you want."

"No, I like Max. It's a good name." I said. The lynx, hearing its name, turned its head and regarded me with soft golden eyes.

"Mew." It squeaked.

Jillian looked at me and quickly said, "Its voice will change when it gets bigger."

"That's OK, I think it's cute." I stroked its silky coat.

Jillian set Max down and started making a place for him. She put out a bowl of water, a bowl of cat food, and made a litter box out of two cardboard boxes.

"It's potty-trained to go in the box." She explained. She had brought extra kitty litter and food with her.

"I'm going to go start making supper. Max, guess what you're having tonight? Rabbit! I'll make you a welcome home dinner, and when you grow up, you can bring me rabbits in return!" I said, smiling at the lynx as it lay contentedly on Jillian's bed, washing its face with a paw.

"Uh, I don't think he will eat rabbit." Jillian said.

"What?! Of course he will! That's what lynx eat, you know." I told her.

"It's just that, well, they've been feeding him this cat food, and I don't think he has ever seen a rabbit."

I snorted. "We'll see. It's his natural food."

When the rabbit was cooked I cut a few small pieces off and put them in the dish. The lynx came over and ate them up with much relish. Jillian's jaw dropped.

"See? I told you he would eat it. I'm going to write to Joyce and tell her about this lynx! She will love it!" I said.

"No, no, wait! Wait." Jillian pleaded, looking uneasy. "I've got something to tell you. Promise you won't be mad?"

"How am I supposed to promise that if I don't know what it is I'm not supposed to be mad about?" I asked, confused.

"Mama, it's not a lynx kitten. It's just a cat." Jillian blurted out. "Look here. See the long tail? See the small feet? And this dark stripe on his back? I thought you were onto me when you asked if he was a Mississippi lynx!"

I looked at the cat again, and now I could see what was right before my eyes. Well, it had been over 30 years since I had seen a house cat, and this little tabby sure did bear some striking resemblances to a lynx.

"Why didn't you just tell me?" I asked, hurt that Jillian had tricked me.

"Because you said you didn't like cats. I didn't think you would give him a chance. I thought he could live in the shed. Sorry. I just wanted a cat to catch some of these shrews. He can stay in the shed and you'll never even know he's there."

"Nonsense! There's plenty of shrews for him in here." Being a cat instead of a lynx really didn't change anything. Max still needed a warm place to stay.

"I got him from the Anchorage animal shelter. He's three years old. Sorry it's not a lynx. I can't believe he ate that rabbit meat!" Jillian exclaimed.

"Joyce has cats. She can tell us what we need to know about them," I said.

Unfortunately, Joyce died of health complications soon after, before she got to meet Max. I was heartbroken to lose a good friend.

The cat immediately took over the entire house. He made use of every high ledge and window sill. He quickly made friends with Taxi, which shocked us all, as the dog was used to chasing everything. The poor old dog developed painful episodes of shaking, and when these occurred, the sweet little cat would sit close by to comfort her. Even Harry decided he liked Max, so the cat had secured a permanent place in our house, without fear of banishment to the shed. He was very friendly, and loved to snuggle on my lap while I was reading or in my bed at night. I had never known how peaceful a purring cat could make a person feel. The best part was that the shrews started to vanish from my house. Max would stalk them with all the intensity of a lion stalking its prey. In the morning I would find little gifts by the kitchen stove, where I warmed his cat food for him.

After having adopted the cat, Jillian became aware of the plight of millions of homeless animals across the country. She started volunteering at an animal shelter in Montana when she wasn't on fires, taking dogs for runs with her. Since the shelter was close to the smokejumper base, she integrated the 'dog jog' into her required daily physical training, and got a good portion of the crew involved also.

Over the years, I have learned a lot from Max, the first thing being that things aren't always what they seem, and that sometimes one has to set aside one's preconceived prejudices and be willing to see things in a different light.

*Max Cat*

# Chapter Thirty-One

"Oh, shit, oh man," Harry moaned.

He was in agony with his latest attack of the gout. I did my best to make him comfortable. But even the weight of a sheet upon his swollen foot was excruciating. I went in our room to check on him and see if there was anything I could bring him. Max followed me in, and jumped on the bed, nimbly avoiding Harry's foot. I reached down to pick him up, just so he wouldn't accidently step on Harry.

"No, no, leave him there!" Harry said quickly. "That's my little kitty cat, aren't you, Maxie cat?"

"Can I get you anything?" I asked.

"No, I'm fine." Harry was petting the cat, and seemed more content now.

I left, and went back to sorting the berries I had just picked. I separated out the leaves and stems and other debris. Then I put the good berries in quart jars, filled them with boiling sugared water, and set them in the canner kettle. After it came to a boil, and boiled for twenty minutes, I took the jars out of the kettle and set them on the kitchen counter. As they sealed, they would make a little ping. Sometimes one wouldn't seal, and I would still be able to salvage the berries for use within the next few days. Sometimes a jar would break, and those berries would be wasted, as it was too dangerous to try to strain them from the broken glass. It was incredibly disheartening when this happened, as a lot of hard work had gone into preparing the berries to this degree. Normally the berries were scattered far and wide across the tundra, and it took hours of walking to find enough to fill one quart jar.

This batch all sealed, and I smiled to myself as I labeled them and set them on my shelves. Glancing out the window, I saw something scurrying in the yard. Was it one of my hens, escaped from her coop the last time I went to check eggs? I had better get it inside before Taxi found it! Slipping on my boots, I went out to catch the hen. But as I got closer, I saw that it was a ptarmigan, and she had a little brood with her. I watched the fluffy chicks darting around, and the parents trying to herd them down the trail. One fluttered and tried to fly, but its stubby little pinfeathers could not hold its weight, and it fell forward onto its breast clumsily. I laughed, and the sound sent the birds scurrying for cover in the brush.

I thought about Silver Cloud, my fluffy gray Cochin hen, who was trying to set on some eggs. I had made her a secluded nest of her own away from the other hens, and she sat persistently on six eggs. I carefully picked her up and set her on the floor with the rest of the chickens twice a day during feeding. She was quite gentle, and would certainly make a good mother. Another week, I thought to myself, and we will see if anything hatches. I went back inside and checked in on Harry, who was now snoring loudly. Little snores came from the chair in the corner, where Max had rolled himself into a feline pretzel. I smiled and went to start dinner.

Harry's gout attack lasted a few weeks. During the time he was sick, I didn't leave the house for more than a few hours, just in case he needed anything. I didn't like to see him suffering, but sometimes I was sure he played upon my sympathy more than was needed. He loved being waited on, and I didn't particularly mind for a few days, but now my chores were backing up, and there was much to do before winter.

When the weather was nice and sunny, I split the winter's supply of firewood and stacked it inside on the porch. Harry had bought a hydraulic log-splitter, and it saved a lot of time and blisters, once I got the engine running. He had shown me how to fix it, and every summer, I got it running and spent a few weeks splitting wood. On sunny days, I also cut and dried hay for the hen's bedding, storing it for winter in one of the sheds.

*Silver Cloud and her chicks*

One day, when I went into the henhouse, I was greeted by Silver Cloud's fussy clucking, and the sound of chirping. Parting her thick plumage, I saw a newly hatched baby chick, weak and sodden, lying under her. I was in awe at the precious fragility of new life. Silver Cloud only allowed me a small peek before she settled back down on the little chick, insisting in her mother hen voice that it needed to be kept warm. It looked so small and helpless, I was sure she would crush it with her big feet. I had to remind myself that hens had been hatching chicks for as long as they existed. The next day, the little yellow chick was dry and fluffy and very healthy looking. Two more hatched, and Silver Cloud did a fine job mothering them without any of my advice. I kept them separated from the main population until they were nearly full grown, as the other adults had little tolerance for the newcomer. The chicks were very cute, and delightful to watch, so I spent a good portion of time in the chicken coop. It also gave me a bit of relief from Harry's often overwhelming neediness.

In mid-September, Harry came back from the airport, and told me he had just shot a moose. He had just left a few moments ago, so I didn't know if he was joking. But I gathered my knives and went along with him. Harry had dropped a big bull moose right at the edge of the airport. We could drive the truck right up to it. It was a very easy moose to butcher, and Harry offered to store the meat in his freezer in Bethel, to save me the work of canning it. He even helped me package and label the meat. The next day he flew the majority of the meat to town to freeze. It was the easiest moose I had yet to butcher and prepare for storage.

A week later, Harry was returning home when he wrecked his plane. It was a bright, sunny day in late September. The sun beamed down intently, as if knowing soon it would be banished below the horizon for months. Harry had called on the radio earlier, and told me he would be home by one in the afternoon. I waited for him at the airport. The sound of his plane reverberated through the mountains as he crossed the last ridge and started to descend. I saw him set up for landing, and then turned to fetch the chock blocks for the wheels. It was a lovely day, and there wasn't much wind, so I had no concerns for his safety.

The next moment I was sprinting toward the airport, the grating scrape of ripping aluminum filling the air, followed by an earth-shaking thud. Horrified, I saw that Harry's airplane was standing on its nose it the bushes to the left of the airstrip. I ran towards it, not knowing what to expect, hoping that Harry had survived. By the time I got there, Harry had opened the door, but was pinned against the dash by the cargo. The heavy 55-gallon drum of diesel fuel had broken its cargo strap and broken the seat rails as it slid forward. Oh, shit, was it going to catch on fire?

"Dolly! Go get a pry bar, and a ladder, so I can get out! Hurry up! Dammit! Owww!" Harry gasped.

Relieved that Harry was alive, I ran back to the shop and grabbed a pry bar and a ladder, and on second thought, a fire extinguisher. Panting from the effort, I carted the tools to the wreckage. Harry was squirming impatiently. I shoved the bar under the barrel and lifted it just a little ways off the seat back. It was at an awkward angle and I couldn't get much leverage. After much grunting and cussing, we managed to get the fuel drum shifted just enough for Harry to squeeze past. I set the ladder up for him in the uneven terrain, and held it steady as he climbed down.

"Whew! Thanks Dolly!" He said shakily as he walked around the plane surveying the damage.

The plane was practically totaled, but I was more concerned about Harry. How could he not be hurt?

"I'm fine." He insisted.

He was limping a bit, but otherwise seemed to be OK.

"What happened?" I asked.

"I got down over the trees and the sun was in my eyes, lost the strip for a minute. Landed just a few feet to the left. Damn it."

The fuel tanks were leaking and I was still concerned about the plane starting on fire. Harry went back to the shop and started tinkering with the front-end loader. He had bought it at an auction a few years ago, and brought it to White Bear to clear snow from the airstrip in winter so he wouldn't have to use skis on his plane. It had been an exhausting and time-consuming ordeal getting that piece of machinery across the mountain ranges, but once it was here, it proved to be valuable. It was far more comfortable for Harry to operate than the old D8 cat, and the cabin was heated.

We hooked some cables to the plane and gingerly pulled it back out onto the airstrip. Harry sighed and swore at the damage. It would take a lot of work and parts to get the plane flying again, and with our meager income, that didn't look possible. He was pretty depressed about it for a few days, and finally agreed to let me tell Jillian. We now had a satellite phone that worked sporadically whenever the satellites were in the right alignment. I would normally get cut off several times in a short conversation, and sometimes have to wait hours for a signal to return. It was very costly, being considered an international phone call, so no one other than Jillian called me. I left the phone on between six and seven every night, just in case Jillian wanted to call. She called me two days after Harry's accident, and upon hearing of the crash, offered to come home. She had just gotten off a fire assignment, and would likely be laid off next week, so she did not take no for an answer.

A few days later, Jillian flew over in her 172, picked her dad up and took him to Bethel. Upon return, she was setting up for landing, when I heard her apply full power and fly over high. I rushed out to look if there was a bear or something on the strip. Still pretty shook up about Harry's accident, I turned on the handheld radio and called Jillian.

"73 Lima, the wind is about twenty-five from the south." I said.

"OK. The sun's too bright, I can't see the runway down low. I totally see what happened to Dad. I'm going to circle up high for a bit and wait for a cloud."

As luck would have it, there were no clouds in the clear blue sky. After a while, Jillian came back on the radio and said she was going over to Aniak to set down until the sun went behind the mountains. An hour later, she returned and landed uneventfully.

"Dad was telling me about somebody he knew that crashed into a mountain landing with the sun in his eyes. A year later the guy's son died in the same place, doing the same thing." Jillian said.

Harry borrowed money and started gathering parts to fix the plane. Meanwhile, Henry graciously let his dad borrow one of his Cessna 206s. That plane was a corroded rattrap, and Harry swore at it up one side and down the other. It always made me nervous when he took it to town. For one thing, the junker would never start, and he would have to hand prop it. Harry made me sit at the controls and hold the brakes, a task that made me edgy. I always forgot which way things were supposed to go, and didn't want to screw up and see Harry injured because of a mistake that I made. When Jillian was home, she would prop start Harry's plane for him, and that made me nervous too, fearful of her stumbling and falling into the prop and being chopped into a hundred pieces. Harry started working on the plane, but there was just so much wrong with it, he was overwhelmed.

Over the next several years, Harry used Henry's plane, and started rebuilding his own. He got partway into it, and then decided he needed to build a hanger to work on it. He had several Sky Van loads of prefab hanger pieces flown up, before losing motivation and running out of funds to finish that project also.

In the early part of 2004, Jillian was recovering from a major knee surgery as a result of a bad paraglider accident. She was working hard to build up strength so she could go back to smokejumping in the spring. The smokejumpers required an arduous physical test every season, just to have their job. Jillian signed up to go to the late refresher in June to give herself more time to heal. In late May, she returned from a checkup in Anchorage, got in her plane, and flew home.

Hearing her plane passing overhead, I rushed outside with the radio.

"73 Lima, is that you? You're early!" I said. Jillian was rarely ever early, as she tried to cram a week's worth of chores into a few hours of time.

"Yeah. I hope you don't get mad. I got myself a present from the zoo. Is the wind from the south?" She answered.

"Roger, roger, the wind is south about ten."

I wondered what Jillian had been talking about. I guess I would find out soon enough, and shouldn't distract her while she was landing. The zoo? Oh, she probably got another animal of some sort. The year before, she had rescued three big white domestic geese. They now lived in luxury, having their own little shed and pond to swim in.

I hoped it wasn't a horse! Jillian had wanted a pony when she was a little girl, but that was so long ago. I hadn't thought she still wanted one. Oh please, don't let it be a horse! I could imagine long summer days filled with cutting hay from between the alders, back-breaking labor for little reward. I had been a little relieved when the last of the cows had died. Oh, I hope it's not a horse, I thought as I turned the last corner of the trail to the airport.

And there it was, a small black pony, nibbling grass near Jillian's plane. Oh well, I sighed resignedly. But why such a small pony? What good would it be? Could it pull wood or a cart or a sled? Maybe it would grow bigger. I stopped the truck and got out. Jillian looked at me apprehensively.

"Come here, dog." She called.

Dog? That's an odd name for a pony, I thought. Then the creature turned, and walked toward us, long, white-tipped tail swishing softly. It walked up and sat at my feet. I just stared at it for a second. It was not a pony. It was a very large dog! It extended a paw, with white-stockings with black polka dots.

"He wants you to shake his paw." Jillian said.

I took the paw in my hand, and the dog smiled up at me. His soft brown eyes spoke of a gentleness that belied his great size. He turned his head to the side politely, and coughed.

"He got a little bit airsick on the way home." Jillian said. "You're not mad, are you? I just thought Taxi is pretty old, and we needed a good guard dog. He seems nice. If you don't like him, I already have two people who want him."

"We'll see." I said. "I'm glad it's not a horse."

"A horse?!" Jillian cackled. "Why would I want a horse now? That's something I wanted when I was a little kid!" She patted the dog's head. "He IS almost as big as a horse though."

"What kind of dog is he? You didn't get an expensive purebred, did you?" I asked.

"NO WAY!!" Jillian snorted. "Purebreds are for rich snobs that just want a piece of paper to wave around and brag about. Nope, this here is a blue collar working dog, not some hoity-toity purebred! As if! Nope, I got him from the same place as Max. Anchorage animal shelter. They said he was part Swiss Mountain Dog. It's like a Saint Bernard."

"What's his name?" I asked.

"They called him Leo, but that's not his real name. He was an unclaimed stray for two weeks. We can name him whatever you want."

I looked at the new addition to my family, not disapprovingly. He was large and powerful, with a striking coat of black and white. He seemed obedient and mild-mannered. I just hoped he would get along with Max and Taxi.

"We have to introduce them slowly," Jillian explained, as she made the big dog a comfortable nest in a corner of the porch. She put out food and water and several old sleeping bags for him to lie on. Then we briefly let him explore the house. Taxi whined peevishly, and the big dog ignored her completely. Max came over, interested, and the dog turned his head away.

"I think he will be fine with the other pets. We just need to keep him on the porch a few nights until they get used to him, so they don't feel crowded or replaced." Jillian said.

We played a little game with our new dog, calling out names that might suit him. He fell asleep during it, so we didn't feel like we ever got close to his original name.

"He's a Mountain Dog, so he needs a mountain name. How about Denali?" I suggested.

"That's perfect." Jillian agreed.

Denali's tail wagged. He seemed like anything would please him. But that night he whined and cried until I sneaked out to let him in. Once in the house, he lay quietly in a corner and didn't stir again for the rest of the night. And so his imposed banishment ended, and the other animals accepted him without incident. For such a big dog, I was amazed at how little room he took up in the house. He was far less clumsy than I, and never knocked anything over. He was content to lie on his bed, and he didn't pay much attention to Max or Taxi. He never made a sound unless there was a bear in the yard. And, unlike Taxi, he was fearless when it came time to protect his family.

## Chapter Thirty-Two

The loader wouldn't start. It was a last ditch effort to clear the snow off the airfield, so Harry could get to Bethel. He had been home a month already, and was nearly out of his medicine. The day before he had planned to leave, the winter storm set in, and it dumped nearly three feet of snow overnight. There was another big storm forecast to hit tonight. Today would be Harry's only chance to leave for maybe another month. If only the darn loader would start.

"Fuel filters." Harry said, among other cuss words, after he spent precious hours dismantling the loader that morning. "And I don't have any spares. Damn it!"

I had to take the snowmachine back to the house to call Jillian, so I left him to swear at the useless piece of machinery, hoping he could find some way to fix it while I was gone. Jillian had returned from smokejumping that fall to find the White Bear airstrip already snowed in, with no chance of getting home in her wheel equipped Cessna. She was staying at Henry's house in Bethel, waiting for her dad to plow the strip, or the wind to blow it clean so she could get home and start trapping.

"KYH6, White Bear." I called.

"Hey, there you are. I was starting to worry. How's the weather?" Jillian asked.

"The weather is good. We can't get the loader started. Your dad said he needs new fuel filters. I don't know if he can get it started. He's almost out of medicine. He only has enough for today, so we were hoping he could leave today."

"OK, well, I can do an airdrop. I can get the filters. Could you tell me what model or serial number or something?" Jillian asked.

"No, no, that's OK. No, I don't know what kind it is. Oh, wait, here's the manual right on the kitchen table." I read of the numbers she wanted.

"OK. I'll be flying over at two. I already packed some boxes up last night, and I saw Mickey in the store this morning. He said he would help kick boxes out for me."

"Oh, I don't think you have to do that. Your dad will probably have the strip cleared before you get here. He's pretty good at fixing things." I said.

"Well, you know how things go, and there's another big storm coming in, so I'm coming up with Dad's medicine anyway, just in case he doesn't get it going. He shouldn't go without insulin, you know." Jillian reasoned.

"Yeah, I know. Just be careful."

"See you at two!"

I left the dogs home, so they wouldn't get in the way. Taxi was too old and crippled to make it through the deep snow, and I wasn't sure if Denali would try to chase the plane, so I left him home, too. He laid back down on his bed obediently, without whining, when I told him to stay. I went back to the airstrip, hoping to see Harry plowing the airstrip, but he was still fooling with the loader.

"Jillian is going to airdrop some filters and your medicine." I reported.

Harry was less than pleased at that bit of news. Although Jillian had previously done several successful airdrops, he did not like her doing them. He thought it was dangerous and there was a big chance of losing the cargo. He had tried it once long ago, and the cargo smashed badly. Jillian had an entirely different system, adopted partly from her smokejumper paracargo background. But she didn't use parachutes, instead flying very low to the ground at a slow speed, and having a passenger throw securely packaged boxes into the biggest snowdrift. She was pretty adept at it, and managed to throw pumpkins out, unpackaged, one Halloween and they landed intact.

"The trick is getting really slow, right above stall speed, so you can get the door open." Jillian explained.

But that could be very dangerous, if you were low, just feet off the ground, so Jillian would line up with the airstrip and use it as a safety net, of sorts. Although the snow was deep and the plane would flip, at least the area was downhill and clear of trees.

There she was now, crossing the mountains, the plane bouncing along in the updrafts of the incoming storm.

"73 Lima, the wind is calm on the ground." I said.

"Whooo-eeee, it's not very calm up here! It's like a fart in a frying pan," Jillian laughed as she bounced along. I could tell by her voice that this was going to be 'fun'. "Fun' for Jillian usually made me cringe in terror.

"Be careful," I warned as the plane started up into the narrow box canyon.

"Yep. Coming in 'live' on this run."

The plane dropped lower, making the steep turn and disappearing behind the ridge. The engine was idling now, and I held my breath, listening for the sound of it again, straining my eyes to see it. It popped up over the rise, low, appearing to be almost on the ground, following the curvature of the mountain as it glided toward the airstrip.

"Up, up, up!" I fussed under my breath. "Come on, that's too low."

But it was setting up to be a normal approach, as Jillian always did get pretty low on airdrops, so as not to smash the cargo. It just looked faster than it should for some reason. The plane whistled past, and suddenly veered wildly to one side. Something was wrong! Oh no! I found myself running across the tundra towards it, willing it to lift and straighten before it slid sideways into the mountain. I could imagine the grinding grating crunch of metal as it hit, could see it smash itself to smithereens upon the steep slope. No, please, no! I didn't want to watch. The plane continued to slide sideways, engine screaming for purchase. I turned my head away. I could not watch. The sound of the engine ceased, and I braced myself for the explosion. But then it surged again, powerfully, and I looked up hopefully, and let my breath out. The little brown Cessna was climbing out and turning back toward me.

I grabbed the radio. "Is everything OK?" I asked.

"Yeah." The 'fun' was out of Jillian's voice now, replaced by a cautious tone. "Yeah, everything's fine. We just caught a huge tailwind and couldn't get slow enough. The box got stuck in the door.

*Jillian airdropping supplies and medicine with Cessna 172*

Are you sure the wind is calm down there? I had a fifty knot tailwind."

"The wind is still calm on the ground." I said, but could see the snow whirling off the mountaintops now. The plane tossed wildly in the wind above me.

"We're switching up the pattern, dropping uphill to the south." Jillian stated.

"No, no. Your dad said not to try it, go back to Bethel!" Harry was nowhere nearby, but it was a last ditch effort to make Jillian see the risks of this operation. Jillian tremendously respected Harry's advice about flying.

"Uh, we're going to try one pass and if it doesn't work, we'll go back. I'm staying higher, so keep an eye on where these boxes land." She said, barely understandable through the turbulence.

I didn't like it at all. She was dropping uphill and had to make a steep turn to get out of the canyon. I didn't know too much about flying, but it seemed dangerous. I couldn't watch. I didn't care about those stupid boxes, I just wanted it to be over, and Jillian to fly safely away. I sat on the snowgo seat and waited, listening to the plane struggling through the wind at full power, listening to it speed past and come around again. After a few passes, I hear the plane a lot higher, and turned the radio on again.

"OK, you got, uh, hey Mickey, how many did you throw? Nine, I think. You got nine boxes down there somewhere. Good luck finding them all. We're headed back to Bethel." Jillian said.

The plane climbed, as if to go out over the mountains to the south, but the wind caught it and threw it violently toward the ground. Unable to climb, it turned very steeply, nearly inverting itself, and the wind caught it again and carried it out of the canyon.

"Call you at six." Jillian said as they zoomed past.

I went out across the snow covered tundra at the airstrip's end, looking for the bounty that had just fallen from the sky. I was relieved they had left safely, but still a little bit upset at Jillian for risking her life so dramatically. There was nothing we needed that badly! Well, maybe Harry's pills and his insulin.

I found a few boxes, punched deep into the snow, and loaded then onto the sled. They were scattered about, and not in the typical small area that Jillian usually airdropped. I heard Harry drive up on the snowgo.

"I'm going up to the house. I've had enough for today. That storm is moving in." He looked tired and haggard.

It was only a short time after Harry left, that the storm hit the ground in full force. The wind that had driven the plane so relentlessly, now nearly knocked me off my feet. My eyes watered with the stinging spray of snow. I was relieved to find the last of the nine boxes, now nearly buried under the snow. I hurriedly lashed them onto the sled and took off for home, hoping Harry had made it back.

At home, I carefully unpackaged the boxes. Fresh fruit, wrapped tightly in loaves of French bread, was bruised slightly, but looked delicious. There was cat treats, dog food, ice cream, candy and bacon, but where was the medicine and the fuel filters, and the mail?

Harry was livid. "I knew she would lose it! Darn it, I was expecting important things in the mail!"

"Maybe she forgot a few boxes in Bethel." I reasoned. It looked as if she had stayed up all night, carefully packaging the treats so they wouldn't be smashed.

When Jillian called at six, she was apologetic. "Oh man, I probably miscounted boxes. Maybe we threw eleven instead of nine. I kept making more, and lost count. We threw everything, it's not here."

"That's OK. I'll try to find them tomorrow. It's really storming right now! I'm glad you made it back to Bethel."

"Yeah, Mickey was, too! He wanted out of there fast, so he shoved about four boxes out every pass. Look farther up the canyon. Take Denali." Jillian suggested.

The next day the blizzard was raging outside. I decided to leave the dog at home and run down with the snowmachine to look for Harry's pills. He sure looked pale this morning. The windblown snow was blinding, and I ran off the trail and got stuck several times. By the time I got to the drop area, I realized it was pointless to look for the boxes. They were now buried under many feet of snow. I would not find them until the spring. I looked anyway, futilely, thinking of Harry's dire condition. Just before dark, I gave up and went home.

"Why didn't you take the dog?" Jillian scolded me that night on the radio.

"The snow is so deep, I thought he would have a hard time. He doesn't like to run with the snowgo, either. Maybe someone hit him with one or something." I answered.

"Take the dog tomorrow." Jillian insisted.

Harry looked even more feeble the next morning, and I hesitated to leave him. The storm was still raging outside. No, I needed to try to find the boxes. I dressed warmly and strapped on my snowshoes.

"Come, Denali." I called.

Denali got up, smiling happily at being invited, and followed me down the trail. His previous owner must have taught him to stay behind, as he kept an even distance between us. When I reached the airport and stopped, he came up and pressed his forehead against my hip.

I stroked his broad head and told him, "We need to find something under the snow."

With that, I started punching a stick through the drifts, hoping to feel a box underneath. Denali watched with interest, and then wandered off. I worked in ever widening circles. What would happen to Harry if I didn't find his medicine today? It would take a week to order replacements from Anchorage, and then would the weather be good enough to do another airdrop? I would never find the boxes, and Harry would die. It was a hopelessly large expanse that I had to cover, and I could easily walk right over a box and never know it was there under five feet of fresh snow. I should probably go back and take care of Harry, and make him comfortable.

Turning dejectedly to leave, snow spraying my glasses and wind sucking away my breath, I called to the dog. Strange, I thought, he is usually good about not running off. Then, looking back, I saw him, or rather his hind quarters sticking out of the hole he was digging. I rushed over and fell to my knees besides him. I couldn't believe what I was seeing. A cardboard box, buried under the snow! I hugged Denali, telling him what a good dog he was, and then crawled down in the hole and dug out the precious box. Hopefully it was the right one, with the medicine! There should be one more, but did I dare to hope we would find it.

"Denali! Good boy! Go find another one." I waved my arm out across the tundra.

He looked at me quizzically with his intelligent brown eyes, and then turned and ambled away, nose to the ground. A few hundred feet farther, he stopped, and started digging enthusiastically. I ran over and helped him unearth the last box.

I gave him a big hug. "What a wonderful dog! Let's go home now!"

We had the missing two boxes! But Denali didn't think the fun was over. He was a short ways away, digging again. I went to check, and couldn't believe that he was unearthing yet ANOTHER box! Wait a minute, Jillian had miscounted again. Maybe there were more? I decided that there had to be at least one more, since Jillian had seemed sure that it was an odd number. Denali agreed to that idea, and scoured the side of the mountain, finally discovering the last box several hundred feet away in a thicket of brush. Finally deciding we had the last of them, we went home.

Denali enjoyed a barrage of praise and extra treats, having proven himself to be worth his weight in gold. He had undoubtedly saved

Harry's life. There is no way I would have found Harry's medicine before spring. Harry regained his strength and a week later when the weather finally cleared enough, he installed the new filters and added the fuel deicer Jillian had thought to send along. The loader started right up. The days were pretty short now, so he was only able to get half of the strip plowed.

It was narrow, with huge berms on both sides, but he said, "Tell Jillian she can come up now."

Jillian landed uneventfully on the very short strip just before dark. Denali, who hadn't seen her for six months, was delighted, and she made a big fuss over him.

"Pretty good dog, isn't he? To think he would have been put to sleep! Well, he sure earned his keep!"

I agreed with her wholeheartedly! Denali was the best dog we ever had. Jillian later trained him to guard the geese and chickens. The gentle giant would lie in the yard contentedly while my hens pecked mosquitos from his back. If a hawk or fox dared to come near, he was on his feet instantly, protecting his flock. He was so well-mannered, we could take him along on the trapline. I shudder to think of all the other wonderful dogs and cats put to death each year in our shelters, and wish more people would consider adopting a pet rather than buying one.

*Denali, our very special mountain dog*

## Chapter Thirty-Three

My feet went out from under me so fast I didn't have time to think about catching myself. I fell hard, knocking the wind out of my lungs. My elbow throbbed painfully from where it hit a big ice chunk. Oh no, I thought, I hope I didn't break it! Beside me, the gallon jugs of water I had so painstakingly extracted from the creek through the thick ice lay spilled over the snow covered ground.

I had been snowed in for nearly two months. Harry was stuck in Bethel. The skis for his Cessna 206 were broken and far too expensive to repair. Jillian had returned from smokejumping and made several airdrops, so I was well-stocked with supplies. But, if my arm was broken, there would be no way for anyone to pick me up, except for perhaps an expensive helicopter extraction. And who would take care of the animals and the homestead?

I flexed my arm gingerly, and decided that the bones were possibly chipped, but not completely broken. I was angry at myself for not wearing my ice cleats. The ice under the snow was impossible to see and very slippery. Now, I would have to refill my water jugs all over again, with my hurt elbow. Well, no use crying over spilled water, I thought as I picked myself carefully off the ground. I gathered up the jugs with my good arm, and waded through the snow to the 'water hole'. I had dug a tunnel down through the snow to the creek and chopped a small hole through the ice. I used a long handled ladle to reach the water, which I painstakingly transferred to the gallon jugs. It was a time-consuming task, so I would usually get enough water to last me a few days each time.

Now, as I refilled my water jugs, avoiding usage of my injured arm, I wondered when Jillian would get home. She had gone to Fairbanks, where she was picking up a ski plane she had bought with her summer's wages. She had told me it was an old plane, and it hadn't flown in a long time. It was taking longer than anticipated to go through its mechanical inspections and install the skis, so she was camped out in the trees outside of town, waiting for it to be declared airworthy. She called me on my satellite phone occasionally and updated me on the progress.

I finished trickling the ice cold water into the jugs, and made several trips carrying them back to the house, avoiding using my hurt arm. I steered clear of the icy patch, and once in the house, I found my ice cleats and put them on. When I finished, I peeled off my shirt and looked at the damage. I was relieved to see that there were no bones sticking out, and the skin was not broken, but the elbow had swollen considerably. I had an aloe vera plant that Jillian had given me for my birthday years ago. It had flourished and was now of Boone & Crockett proportions. The aloe was my old stand-by, if anyone in the family had any ailments, I was quick to peel a leaf and apply it to the injury. Soon Harry began teasingly calling me 'Dr. Aloe' whenever I came his way wielding a leaf. Now I took a leaf from the big plant, peeled one side so the gooey inner flesh was exposed, and wrapped the cool soothing remedy against my elbow with an Ace bandage. Max watched with interested concern, and when I laid down that night he gently curled his body around my elbow, as if protecting it from further harm. The next day, my arm was colorful, but much less painful. I kept applying fresh aloe leaves for the next several weeks, and it healed without further complications.

At noon one day, Harry informed me that Jillian was in McGrath on her way home with the ski plane. She flew over White Bear a few hours later, the tiny silver plane glinting in the pale afternoon sun before it touched down. My arm was still a bit sore, so I took longer than usual to pull the snowgo out, hitch up the sled, and meet her. When I got there, the plane was parked in the tiedown, and Jillian had the cowling off, looking concerned.

"Hi, welcome home." I gave her a hug. "What's wrong?"

"Ran out of oil. Engine was running fine, and I don't see where it's leaking from. Got the phone with you?" She asked.

*Jillian's Cessna 140 on skis*

I handed her the sat phone. "What kind of plane is it? Is it a Super Cub?"

Jillian laughed. "No, it's not a Cub. Not on my salary! Cubs are really expensive, I could never afford one. Nope, this is a 1946 Cessna 140. Got it cheap. Hasn't flown in fifteen years, but we did some work to it, and it runs great. Just don't know about the oil problem, can't see where it's leaking."

She called a mechanic friend, and fooled with the plane a bit, but decided she didn't know enough to work on it. The next day Henry put his Cessna 185 on wheel skis, and brought Harry up and took Jillian back to Bethel with him. He landed uneventfully, but had to make several tries to get airborne with the deep snow and extra drag of the wheel skis. It was frightening to watch, as both of my children were in that plane. I was very relieved when they finally lifted off safely, and flew back to Bethel.

Harry plowed the field with the loader, and the next day, Jillian came home with her Cessna 172. After about a week, she took Harry back to town, and came back again. She was home when the next big storm blew in and the field was snowed in again.

"Mama, I going to fly the ski plane to Bethel, and have someone work on it." She said.

I was less than excited about her taking off with the broken plane, but she insisted it was running fine. She did several test run-ups of the engine and decided she could make it to Bethel if the oil tank was topped off. I watched the tiny plane lift off easily and fly away. A few days later she was back, and flew that plane the rest of the winter. She had watched the mechanic install the skis, and became very proficient at switching from wheels to skis by herself. That little 140 turned out to be a good plane, and hauled a lot of supplies to White Bear over the years. And the best part about it was it was light and easy to turn around in the deep snow.

That summer, as I was panning for gold, I found a lovely stone. I had found other interesting rocks in the past, but this one had symmetrical facets and a nice sheen. I didn't know what it was, so I sent it to Jillian to identify. She took it to someone in Montana, and they told her it was a garnet, not particularly valuable, but beautiful. In all my years of gold panning, that was the best thing I had found. I rarely ever found as much as a tiny fleck of gold, but it was fun looking for it, and I did it with a pick and shovel, in a manner that did not disturb my beautiful, pristine mountain valley.

I was facing a very difficult dilemma that year. Taxi was now seventeen years old, feeble and blind. I could tell the amount of pain she was in when I carried her outside daily to go to the bathroom. I knew the biggest kindness I could do for my dog would be to put her down, but Harry was adamantly opposed to that idea. It was as if, now that he was aging, he could see his own self in the old dog. He had always liked Taxi a lot, and we had spent a great deal of money shipping her to the vet in Anchorage a few years ago when she was sick. I knew that I needed to put Taxi down this summer, before the ground froze, so I could dig her grave. But I kept putting it off, telling myself she needed to live one more day. Harry was at home most of the summer, so there was never any good opportunity to do the dreaded deed without his knowledge.

One day in late August, Harry was off to town, and I realized with a sickened feeling that if I was going to relieve Taxi of her painful existence, now was the time. I argued with myself, but deep inside,

I knew the task had to be done. I carried the old dog out to the truck and laid her on the seat. I brought her dog bed and some blankets, and went back in the house to get a rifle. Which gun should I use? My familiar old .22 sat on the shelf, and I reached for it, and then hesitated. No, I didn't want to look at that gun later and remember that I had used it to kill a dear old companion. I took a rifle off Eddie's gun rack, dusty and neglected, and left before I had second thoughts. I drove the truck as slowly as I could to the airport, the old dog whining painfully at every bump we hit. She was so weak, she could barely lie on the seat without falling to the floor, so I held her there with one hand as I drove.

I remembered all the good times we had, picking berries out on the tundra, Taxi racing with the wind, chasing anything that moved, and tears ran down my cheeks. When I got to the airport, I gently lifted her out and laid her on her dog bed. Then I set to work digging a grave, postponing my dreaded task until there was no excuse left.

When I finally ended her suffering and laid Taxi to rest, I knew that I had done the right thing for her. It was such a difficult thing for me to do. I told Harry that night on the sat phone that she had died that day, of another stroke. We reminisced on old times, telling each other that she had lived a very good life, longer and with more freedom than most dogs.

The powerful winter storm that ripped through the valley in December knocked over several of the cottonwood trees, and tore off some of our roofing. The wire for our radio antenna had been connected to one of the trees that broke in the storm. When the wind calmed somewhat, Jillian went up on the roof to survey the damage. After fixing the roof, she started rerouting the antenna. It was almost dark when she came down.

"Mama, can you come up and help me hold the wire while I nail it?" She asked.

I put on my thin jacket and rubber boots and clambered up the ladder to help her. It was still pretty windy and I briefly thought of going back down for a thicker coat. But this won't take long, I thought. A few minutes later, we were done. Just then, a powerful gust of wind hit, and we both heard a loud thunk.

"Oh, shit! I hope that wasn't the ladder!" I groaned.

Walking down the slope of the roof, I saw that it was indeed the ladder that had fallen over, trapping us on the roof, with the wind picking up and night approaching.

"I always tie the ladder to those two nails on the roof, just so that doesn't happen!" I lectured Jillian.

"Yeah, I know. I forgot to do that. Too late now."

Jillian scouted out the safest place to get down. The roof was high, probably twelve feet in the lowest place, since the building was set up on several feet of blocks to make it level. There was not much snow cover on the ground. What were we going to do? It was nearly dark now. Harry was in Bethel, and he wouldn't be concerned if he didn't hear from us for several days, as he was having frequent problems with the old single-side band radio.

"See that snow drift there? I bet I could just jump over into that and do a good roll, and I'd be fine. I'll put the ladder up for you."

I opened my mouth to say, no, don't, that's too far, you'll hurt yourself, but it was too late. Jillian disappeared off the roof, and a second later I heard a thud, and a loud snap. I rushed to the edge of the roof and looked down. Jillian was on the ground holding her ankle.

"Ice." She gasped. "The snow drift had a big chunk of ice in it."

"Oh no! Did you break your leg?" I asked, but I already knew the answer.

"I don't know. Give me a minute. Probably just sprained, that's all." She stood up, and fell over with a whimper.

"Oh no." I cried. What could I do? Nothing. I was still trapped on the roof.

"Just hold on. I'll set the ladder up for you." Jillian said.

She dragged herself around the building to where the ladder lay. I couldn't bear to watch, so I started gathering tools. I heard the ladder rattle against the siding of the house, and hit the ground, then Jillian's frustrated swearing, then she tried a few more times.

Finally I heard her yell, "OK. It's up. Come on down."

I scrambled down and helped Jillian into the house. She held onto my shoulder and hopped on one foot until we got inside, then plopped into a chair. She pulled out her knife and cut her boot off. The ankle was swollen and lumpy, but no bones were sticking out.

"You should go to a doctor. That looks broken." I said.

"Nah. There's no bones sticking out, so the doctor probably won't do anything anyway. I can't afford anymore medical bills. They would probably just say to stay off of it for six weeks." She said.

"What if it sets wrong? You might not be able to run again." I worried.

"So then we will set it. Can you grab me a couple willow sticks and an ace bandage?"

I went outside and cut a few sticks, grabbed a leaf off my aloe, and the bandage. Jillian pulled her foot around to where it should have been.

"Does that look straight?" She asked through gritted teeth.

"I don't know. I guess. You really need to go to a doctor. You make your living on your feet, you know." I said as I wrapped her leg tightly in the bandage.

"Quit nagging. I can't go anywhere tonight anyway."

It was true. Besides, the last storm had drifted snow across the airstrip in hard ridges, so it was unusable for either wheels or skis. Jillian's 140 was at the airport, on skis. There was no way she could fly it with a broken leg, especially since it was on skis. The ski plane did not have brakes, and a pilot would usually have to get out several times to push the tail around on a narrow strip, to maneuver it in the right direction prior to takeoff.

Jillian did not want me to tell Harry about the accident that night. "We don't need to make Dad worry. There's nothing he can do about it right now anyway."

She was right. There was nothing anyone could do until the morning. She used the back of a chair to hop around the house, and didn't seem to be in that much pain. Max stayed close to her, and his company comforted her a great deal. Then, as if realizing that I needed comforting too, the cat nestled close to me. His presence soothed my anxious mind, and I was able to get a few hours sleep.

The next morning, Jillian was pale and shivering and cranky.

"I think you should tell your dad," I said.

"Dammit, quit nagging at me. He can't do anything anyway, the airstrip is bad. I don't want to tell him. I don't want him to try to come up in the 206. He'll wreck it in those drifts." She said as she pulled on her parka.

"Well, you need to get that looked at. We should get a helicopter to pick you up." I insisted. The wind had picked up again, and was too strong for a plane to land.

"You're just going to keep nagging for six weeks until this heals, aren't you?! Shit, I might as well get out of here before I go nuts listening to you!" Jillian snapped.

"I'll call Henry and have him arrange a helicopter then," I said, relieved.

"OK. Have him bring some crutches."

I called Henry at work on my sat phone. He answered right away. He was calm and concerned, and very helpful. Henry was always level-headed in an emergency. He would call me back in fifteen minutes, he said.

The phone rang ten minutes later. "Tom is bringing the helicopter up. We will be there in an hour."

An hour later, Yukon Aviation's Bell helicopter landed in our front yard. Jillian hopped out on crutches, and they departed as quickly as they came. An hour after they left, the weather became too bad for even a helicopter to fly in. They had left just in the nick of time. I fussed around the house a bit, waiting for news from the hospital. Harry later reported that Jillian spent five hours in the waiting room before she was seen, and then the doctor wasn't on duty, and no one could read the xrays. The only information the nurse had was, "You broke all your leg-bones."

Since they couldn't set the leg there at the Bethel hospital, Jillian had to go in to Anchorage, where she got numerous screws installed to repair the four places the leg was broken. Two months later, she was back at home, flying the ski plane, trapping, and getting in shape for smokejumping again. Since she was not insured, she had overwhelming medical bills to pay.

Jillian laughed it off. "Too bad I wasn't born Native. Just means I have to work harder to pay for everything, I guess. I just hope I can run fast enough this year to keep my job!"

I flew over to Aniak a few times with Jillian that spring so she could run on the roads there. The great thing about Aniak was that now they had a dental therapist stationed there, and he could do any dental work a regular dentist did. I was able to get some of my teeth worked on while Jillian ran all out to strengthen her legs. We usually filed a flight plan, but we never did tell Harry about our excursions, to keep him from fretting.

## Chapter Thirty-Four

The valley was thick with smoke. The night before, I had detected a faint whiff of wood smoke on the breeze. Now, the sky was obscured, and when the sun rose above the mountains, it hung blood red in the thick gray haze. Where was the fire? Was it merely smoke drifting in from the big fires all around the state, or was there a raging inferno racing towards our home? I climbed the mountain overlooking the valley, peering down through the smoke, hoping to detect the source, and locate the fire. But the visibility was so restricted that I could not make anything out. I wished Jillian were here. She would know what to do. Ironically, our home-grown firefighter was off in Oregon, fighting fires there.

"You should call someone and report the fire." Harry suggested, sensing my worry.

A good deal of my concern was about Harry. Although he was in fairly good health now, breathing the acrid smoke could not be good for him, and if he were to get sick, how would I get him to a hospital? If the fire were to race up the valley, it could cut us off from the airstrip. And Harry, with his bad leg, was in no shape to outrun it up the side of a mountain.

I picked up the phone book and tried to find a number to call to report the fire. But after dialing several numbers and just getting automated recordings, I grew frustrated. The phone signals were bad today, and I got cut off several times, which further increased my frustration.

"I can't reach anyone." I told Harry.

"Keep trying! We have to do something quick, before we get burned up!" Harry said impatiently. "Maybe you should call Jillian. She probably knows what number to call."

Yes, I thought, I should call Jillian, she will know what to do. But would she have her cell phone with her, or would she be out in the field? I picked up my sat phone, and fooled with the antenna until I finally got a signal. Jillian answered on the first ring. She was in the smokejumper loft, packing a parachute for her next jump.

"Man, I wish I was there! OK, read me the lat-long off the back of the phone and I'll see if there's a jump plane anywhere close by." Jillian said.

She had taped a list of emergency phone numbers and the coordinates to the homestead on the back of the sat phone before she left. I read them off to her, and she told me to leave the phone on and she would call back.

Five minutes later, Jillian called back. "There's a jump plane near Aniak. They're going to head your way and see what they can do about putting out that fire. I wish I was on that plane!"

About twenty minutes after Jillian called, a plane flew over. I tried to call it on my handheld aviation radio, but the plane must have been on a different frequency, as it didn't answer me. It tipped a wing, and started circling. It seemed as if it circled a long time before two objects fell out to the north of the house. I watched in amazement as parachutes blossomed out and the two men floated softly downward and drifted back, landing on the tundra just above our house. I ran up to meet them.

"Watch out, there's cargo coming in," one man warned, pointing to the sky.

Two more objects fell out under smaller canopies, and thudded into the ground close by.

"That's our firefighting supplies," explained the man.

They introduced themselves as Mike from the Fairbanks base, and Rocky from the Montana base. And yes, they both had worked with Jillian many times in the past, and were delighted to see our home.

"Where's the fire? Why did you jump right here, and not by the fire?" I asked.

"The fire is about three miles away, down in that valley below your airstrip." Mike informed me. "We saw it from the air yesterday, too, but we couldn't get approval to put it out. It's in a different fire management zone, and the officials just want to let it burn. It's frustrating for us, because we can put these fires out fairly easily when they're small, but the officials don't think it's necessary until the fires get big, and then it's more costly and dangerous to stop the fire."

"So what are we going to do?" I wanted to know.

"We told the powers-that-be that there was a home in danger, and they finally gave us permission to jump here and do structure protection. We will try to stay here as long as they let us." Rocky said.

The smokejumper's presence was a great solace. They were professional and well-informed, and I felt safe with them around to protect us from the fire. I invited them down to the house and showed them around. Harry thought it was pretty amazing that the smokejumpers had gotten there so quickly.

"Half an hour after you called Jillian five thousand miles away, there's jumpers on the ground!" He exclaimed.

"There were over 800 lightning strikes in this area last night. We were out patrolling for smokes near Aniak when the Fairbanks base called and gave us the coordinates to come here, so we weren't far away." Rocky told him.

The two men looked over the house and surrounding buildings, showing me where they would set up pumps and hose if the fire came in our direction. I drove them to the airport to see if we could see the fire from the end of the trail, but the smoke was too thick and the curve of the mountains blocked the view. The sky was dark with a new storm. Lightning ripped across the sky and thunder rattled the truck windows. I wondered how many new fires this storm would create, and was again grateful for the smokejumper's presence. By now it was after midnight, but still daylight. When we got back, the men set up tents on the tundra, declining my invitation that they stay in the house.

The next morning I made coffee and breakfast, and Rocky came down to join us, and a little later, Mike came in also. They wanted to try to see if any new fires had started, and if the wind had pushed the big fire any further up our valley. I handed Mike a pair of long range binoculars and Rocky a 30-06 for bear protection, and showed them where to hike up the closest mountain to avoid going through all the brush.

"Take Denali along, too." I told them. "He will tell you if there's a bear around, and he loves going up the mountains."

They took off up the mountain with their backpacks of fire gear, and I went back to the house. Harry decided he should go to Bethel while the weather was clear. His Social Security check should be in the post office soon. He was currently without a plane, as the ratty old 206 had broken down, and Henry was trying to sell it. I called Henry on the sat phone, and begged him to come up and pick up his dad. He said he would be here in a few hours. Henry did not like to fly to White Bear. Over the years his visits became less and less frequent. He made a lot of excuses, the main one being that we did not have a wind sock, and he couldn't tell which way the wind was coming from. I was hesitant to put up a wind sock because of the amount of maintenance it would require, and the fact that every year I heard of aircraft accidents caused by a pilot trusting a malfunctioning windsock. I always told pilots on the handheld radio which way the wind was coming from, so I couldn't see why Henry needed a windsock after so many years of landing here without one. I was surprised and very pleased when Henry agreed to pick his dad up this time, and save us the cost of an expensive charter.

Rocky and Mike came down from their hike up the mountain, and told me where they had seen new fires. Unfortunately, the fires were in an area where the 'powers-that-be' wanted to let them burn. The wind had pushed the main fire a bit closer, but now it was headed the opposite direction. When they had radioed in to their dispatch office from the top of the mountain to report the fire status, they were told that they were needed in Fairbanks, and to pack their gear and meet a helicopter in two hours. Rocky and Mike were as disappointed as I was. I wished they could stay until the big fire was completely out, and the danger was past. Mike was annoyed with the officials that made the decision.

"We could have put that fire out in three or four days." He said.

Since they had a bit of time before their helicopter arrived, I took them to the hotsprings. On the way, Rocky saw a small black bear, even before Denali saw it. It went running off and we continued on our way, trading stories. Rocky had worked with Jillian in Montana, and told me that everyone there missed her a lot. She had transferred to the Oregon base this summer, because the jet travel was twelve hours shorter, and she could get home faster if we needed anything.

"Why doesn't she jump out of Fairbanks? That's closer." Mike wanted to know.

"Jillian keeps putting in for the job but hasn't gotten it yet." I said.

"Yeah, the BLM is taking some budget cuts now, so we probably won't be doing any hiring for awhile." Mike confirmed.

When we got back, the men started packing up their tents and gear, and I started getting Harry's things ready for town. Henry would be arriving shortly, and I wanted to meet him at the airport so we wouldn't keep him waiting from his busy schedule. I thanked Rocky and Mike for jumping in to protect our home.

"It's no problem. We take care of our own." Rocky said. The smokejumpers were a close-knit group, and they all saw Jillian as a sister.

"It's just too bad we couldn't put out that fire," lamented Mike.

He handed me a list of telephone numbers. "Here. These numbers will get you directly to a dispatcher. If that fire gets any closer, call right away, and we will come back. I hate to leave you alone with that fire in this box canyon! I'm going to talk to someone in the McGrath district about doing a patrol flight over this area every day. I think you are safe right now, but if the wind picks up, call us right away."

He went on to explain that the jump list rotates and the chances of Rocky and him being on another fire together would be slim.

"But you can trust whoever jumps in to do the best they can for you. We are all family." Mike said.

I was beginning to see the draw this job had for Jillian. Not only was it an exciting outdoor profession, filled with hard work, danger, and travel, but also the brotherhood and support of the smokejumper community was a compellingly strong bond.

Rocky and Mike both gave me warm hugs goodbye, and stayed to wait for their helicopter as I drove Harry to the airport to meet Henry's airplane. Henry was a bit late, and told me of all the fires in the area. I warned him to look out for the helicopter, inbound soon to pick up the smokejumpers. He was in a hurry so Harry got in and they took off.

By the time I got back to the house, the helicopter had come and gone, taking Rocky and Mike with them. I felt a twinge of fear, Henry's voice echoing in my mind, "There's a lot of fires at the bottom of this valley." But then I reached into my pocket and pulled out the list of phone numbers that Mike had written out for me. I felt warm and assured again, with the knowledge that help was now just a phone call away. The next day the rains came in torrents, and washed away most of the fires. It rained much of the summer, and I did not need to call the smokejumpers back. Later, Rocky sent me a lovely photo album of pictures he had taken during the short time he was at White Bear.

It was an honor to meet some of the brave men who risk their lives protecting our backcountry forests. Of all the pictures Jillian sent and stories she told of her summer's labor, it wasn't until Rocky and Mike jumped into our homestead that I truly understood the magnitude of this heroic occupation.

# Chapter Thirty-Five

The letter I received June 30th, 2009 turned my world upside down. It destroyed our peaceful existence, filled our lives with fear and worry and despair. Ultimately, it killed my husband.

Henry had dropped off the mail when he picked Harry up from White Bear. He was in a hurry, so I did not have time to sort through the mail before they left. Later that evening, after my chores were done for the day, I sat down to read the mail that had accumulated over three weeks. It was a much anticipated event, as I loved getting news from friends and family. At first, I set the envelope from BLM

*White Bear Homestead*

aside, believing it to be a receipt for the water rights I had paid last month. After reading the remainder of the mail, I opened the letter, planning to file the receipt in its folder.

My jaw dropped and I almost had to pinch myself to make sure I was not dreaming. But, no, this nightmare was real. The BLM letter was not a receipt. It was a notice that they were conveying several large parcels of land to the Chalista Corporation. Among the parcels was a huge block of land completely overlapping our homestead. It was mixed in with several other large parcels, some nearly 20 miles away and others as far as Sleetmute. Reading further, I saw that I had 30 days to appeal the BLM "Decision" to convey the land. I looked at the postmark, nearly two weeks ago, and realized that I needed to do something, fast! But now it was the 4th of July weekend, and no business office would be open. What could I do from here?

I worried and paced all weekend. Why did Chalista want our homestead? We had no idea they had ever filed for land over the top of our homestead. Harold Corbin had shown me the map of their selection of 20 acres over two miles away, and the BLM had confirmed that location by retracting one of our mining claims whose border overlapped Chalista's selection. But how did that 20 acre claim suddenly inflate to cover 6500 acres?! The new selection now covered the entire White Bear valley. I was completely blindsided. I had no information at all about Chalista's selection. Why had they kept it secret from us? How could I appeal, if I didn't even know exactly what I was appealing?

On Monday, I called Martin, a trusted Bethel lawyer. Yes, he said, he could help me do an appeal, but he warned me that land issues weren't his forte. We made a plan that the next morning at 10, Martin would let the answering machine pick up my satellite phone call, and I would dictate what I wanted in the appeal. His secretary would type it up and send it to the Board of Appeals. I frantically wrote up a statement, outlining how the massive land selection covered our property and threatened our existence. I made several phone calls, trying to get more information from the BLM, but they were very tight-lipped, and referred me to their lawyer without answering any questions.

The next morning, I dictated my appeal to Martin's answering machine, assuming his secretary would have it done by the afternoon. But it was nearly a week before she got to it. Time was running short. When she finally got it done, Harry went over to the law office to sign it. He was very distraught over the whole ordeal.

"Dolly, my entire life's work is being given away to the damn corporation." He told me over the phone that night. "They'll get whatever they want, because they are Natives. It doesn't matter if what they are doing is wrong. The BLM is just going to kiss their ass and give them whatever they want."

"We will do everything we can to fight this. There is always hope for justice." I tried to convince him, and myself.

There wasn't much else we could do now but wait, and hope the appeals office would see the conflict this selection was creating. I called the BLM solicitor. He was condescending and insisted that the Chalista selection would not affect us. He begged me to withdraw my appeal. It was obvious he did not understand that the parcel of land that Chalista had selected contained the natural hotsprings which we used to heat our house. The hotsprings is the very lifeblood of our existence. How had it become available only for Chalista's selection, and not for ours? How had they been exempt from the Geothermal Act of 1970, which stated that all land within one quarter mile of a natural hotsprings was reserved to the United States? We had to comply with numerous regulations to utilize the hotsprings waters, now it was just going to be given away to a big corporation?

The ordeal had an overwhelming effect on Harry. A few weeks after the letter came, Harry ended up in the Bethel hospital. He had suffered a stroke, no doubt escalated by the stress and fear of the possibility of losing his home. I called him every day in the hospital. Jillian was fighting fires all over the country, but had made arrangements to come home so I could be with Harry.

But Harry wouldn't hear of it. "No! Tell Jillian to keep working! We need money to pay the lawyer. And you just stay home. There's nothing you can do here, they are taking good care of me."

Now, in addition to worrying over the appeal, I was very concerned about Harry's health. He was in the hospital nearly two weeks, and as soon as he could leave, I arranged for him to charter up to

White Bear in a small plane. When I helped Harry out of the Maule, I was surprised at how much he had aged in the past few weeks. But his face brightened at the prospect of being at home. Here he was, surrounded by the fruits of his lifetime's grueling hard work, in the golden years of his life, but now he had to live in fear of losing it all.

"We will get through this," I told him, as I hugged him tightly.

Harry's health improved a bit, and he was able to walk around with the help of a cane. He was grateful to be home, and thanked me every day for paying for the charter. But the fear and doom of losing White Bear still lingered in his mind, and ate away at his peace.

Over the next few months, I wrote many letters, and spent thousands on the expensive sat phone calls trying to get more information on Chalista's selection, and the grounds for BLM's decision to convey the land. Jillian also made a lot of calls whenever she was not on fire assignments. She had sent in a letter of statements backing up my appeal, and had been in contact with the Board of Appeals in Virginia. She returned a bit earlier than usual that fall, foregoing her typical few weeks of travelling. When she got home, bringing the mail, and all the information she had gathered, we sat down to sort it out.

We learned that, in 1988, when Peter Lott and the two men came up in the helicopter, they were actually certifying the White Bear hotsprings as a Native "cemetery historic site", instead of the old Tuluksak hotsprings. The old Tuluksak hotspring had no value to Chalista now that it was closed up, and the White Bear hotsprings did have value, since we were living here and using it. The Chalista Corporation had moved its 20 acre selection from two miles away, and increased it to 40 acres over the White Bear hotsprings and our homestead. Chalista had filed for two separate parcels; one being the 40 acre hotsprings plot, which had been rejected in favor of the larger 6500 acre plot that covered the entire valley. So, their "cemetery historic site" seemed irrelevant, since it had been rejected anyway. Still, we needed to get more information on that. Why hadn't we been informed, since it was overlapping our homestead? Why was it kept secret?

In November of 2009, we got a notice that BLM withdrew from the conveyance of the 6500 acre parcel, stating that it was in error, as the parcel wasn't even available for selection under those land laws.

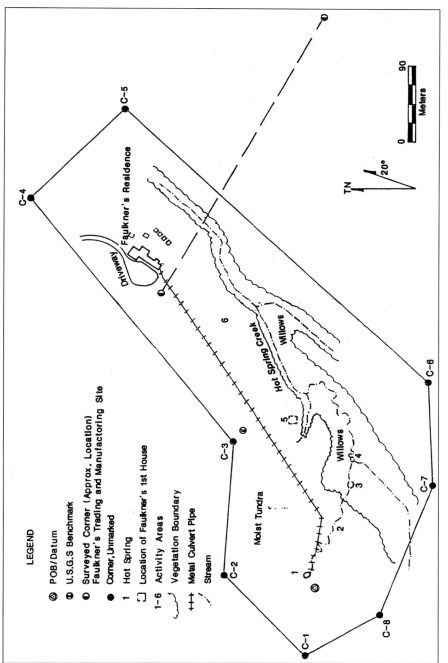

*Chalista's claim over our home*

They never offered to pay for our expenses created by their mistake. At first we were relieved, that the battle was over. But no such luck, the BLM now informed us that they were planning to convey the 40 acre "cemetery historic site" to Chalista. We thought that selection had been rejected?! Now, how could they come back and use it again? We desperately needed more information on this supposed "cemetery historic site". But everywhere we turned for answers, we came up empty-handed. Both the BLM and Chalista were very close-mouthed about this particular selection. I wrote a letter to the Senator, and requested documents through The Freedom Of Information Act, and finally documents started trickling in. But, some of the documents are still being withheld.

I was horrified when I saw the map Chalista had drawn of their "cemetery historic site". It covered only the areas of our usage; the headwaters of the hotsprings, our entire pipeline down to our house, and even our HOUSE itself! Everything was drawn and labeled, our house, shop, and buildings. Of millions of unoccupied surrounding acres, why had they specifically chosen the areas that would most conflict with our usage? Reading through the documents, I saw that they had certified the "cemetery historic site" through a process of taped recordings with Native elders. These were supposedly on file with the University of Alaska, but we were told that they were in Yup'ik and were never transcribed to English. Jillian got copies of the tapes through the Bethel library and we took them to a friend whose wife could translate.

Meanwhile, we researched as much as we could about the very hush-hush "cemetery historic site". When we got the documentation we were surprised to read their justification:

"Old village site for spring, fall, and winter use. The reindeer corralling area. Hot Spring was used as cooking food, most of all it was used as medicinal purposes and sauna long ago. On this land there are 1 or more graves."

None of this made any sense. Over the years we had several archaeologist and geologic surveys of this area and none had never uncovered any "old village"! If this area was so important to Natives, where had they all been over the past 40 years? There was no sign of anyone when we got here. Over the years no one had ever made the long journey 45 miles from any river to "use" the hotsprings. The closest reindeer corrals were documented as being on Bear Creek, where there also was a hotsprings, long ago destroyed by mining, and Bogus Creek, where there also was an old hotsprings. Cooking food? In 140 degrees? It was unbelievable. Medicinal? Wasn't the water analysis toxic? We had chickens and cows die from drinking it. I had never seen anyone drink it, or "bathe" in the hotspring's tiny trickle in the entire time we were here.

What about the "grave"? Where was it? We had never seen a grave here, other than Eddie's grave. Over the next year, through much research, we learned that there was an old legend of a man who went up to a hotsprings and might have been killed by bears, but his body was never found. His camp was shredded, and searchers assumed he had been eaten, although they never found his rifle. A man in bear country never goes far without a rifle, so apparently he wasn't near his camp. The exact location of the hotspring was a mystery, as was the location of the man's body. So THAT constitutes a "grave"?! No wonder Chalista had wanted to keep it a secret, so no one would question it!

We had much more difficulty and expense than we anticipated in translating the tapes. Many of our Native friends were not fluent in Yup'ik. One translator charged us thousands of dollars to translate a 40 minute tape that was mostly in English. But for every disappointment, there was another person who would surprise us with their kindness and generosity. Eventually we got all the tapes translated and typed out. We found that all of the people interviewed had been asked questions about several sites at the same time, and there was much confusion on exact locations, much rustling of maps and people saying, 'I got this wrong, no, it's here, not there."

When we got to the tape of Peter Lott, I finally understood why he had so tearfully apologized to me so many years ago. The entire certification had hinged on his testimony. Over and over on the tape, he had mentioned the Bogus Creek hotsprings, and they brushed him off and led him on with what they wanted him to say. They had drawn "activity areas" on a little map, marking our house, because we had let Peter Lott stay there with us. Who knew having a houseguest would entitle them to later take away your home?!

Supposedly, the "historic" usage of the hotsprings was that the Laplanders had herded reindeer in the past, and often stopped to cook a reindeer leg in the water, and to bathe. There were a lot of flaws with that, the first being that Laplanders, or Sami, were of Finnish descent, not Alaskan Native. This narrow box canyon did not offer much grazing for reindeer. Water needs to be above 212 degrees (boiling) to cook meat. If it had been used as a corralling area, it would have had a large stack of bones and antlers, such as the old Bear Creek corral, were the Sami herded the reindeer to feed the miners, and there was a very hot hotsprings, hot enough to cook meat. The historic usage report also stated that this hotsprings was used frequently for bathing by miners. Once again, the miners were not Alaskan Natives, and the Bear Creek or Bogus Creek hotsprings were both much closer to the mine than the White Bear hotsprings.

Nearly all of the natives interviewed did not describe the White Bear hotsprings correctly. Instead they parroted a 1917 geological report that may have described a different hotsprings entirely. It was obvious by their description that most of them had never been to the White Bear hotsprings, and nearly everyone admitted it. One man claimed that plants grew at the hotsprings all year around, enough to feed an entire village. It was a ridiculous statement, as plants need sunlight to grow, and with only 3 hours of sunlight, nothing grows in winter at the White Bear hotsprings. The banks freeze solid in the winter, so obviously he had never been here. Still his word was taken as 'fact'. The report claimed that the White Bear hotsprings was so well known, natives everywhere called it "Puqla". What the researchers didn't say was that "puqla" is the Yup'ik word for "hot" and you can't even begin to say "hotsprings" in Yup'ik without using the word "puqla".

Jillian had a brief talk with Chalista, to see if we could resolve our issues and come to a peaceable agreement. But Chalista was unfriendly and aloof, and Jillian said she got the feeling they wanted to make trouble for us. She had spoken to their chief lands director, Julie MacFee, and the woman had been very passive-aggressive and dishonest.

"First she said they had no intentions of developing the area, because they can't under regulations determined by that type of lands selection," reported Jillian, "then with the next breath she says it will be ten to fifty years before they develop the area, so it shouldn't affect us. What a two-faced double-speaker! I don't trust anything that woman says. I will still be living here in fifty years, so how could that not affect us?"

"We tried to reach a peaceable resolution, but if you don't think this corporation is trustworthy, then we need to do what we can to fight it." I said.

"No, of course they aren't telling the truth when they say they mean us no harm. Why would they specifically file over our house and our pipeline? There's a lot of land in every direction."

"I don't know. I scares me." I said.

"It would be different if the area truly was a Native usage area. But it's not. No one was interested in this place until we started building the lodge, then they thought they could make money off us, so they filed over the top of us. Julie said to me that our being here kept the Yup'ik people from their traditional places. Which Yup'ik people exactly?! What are their names? As long as we have been here, I have never seen anyone come up here. It's not as if thousands of people instantly knew we were living here and stopped coming. If it were truly a traditional place, we would have seen people coming by over the years. There would have been traditional sod houses here too." Jillian reasoned.

"I think people just got jealous when Peter Lott told them we brought him and Martha up here and fed them. Then EVERYBODY wanted the same thing, for free, but of course we can't afford to cater to everyone. I just wish people wouldn't be so dishonest and try to get something for nothing. We've worked very hard for what we have. I think other people should work hard for things too, instead of trying to steal it away from the hard working citizens." I said.

"What's this about Native heritage? I was born here too. Where's MY heritage? Do I have to work hard all my life just so that someone who has never even seen the hotsprings takes it all away and says they are entitled to it? The Yup'ik people never gave anything back to the Aleuts or the Athabaskans, or any of the other people that were in Alaska before them! They took away other people's land, call themselves the "First People" but they were really the "Last People".

They stole land away from the Indians and drove them south. People as far south as Argentina crossed the Alaskan land bridge, long before the Eskimos." Jillian said.

"It's not the Yup'ik people's fault. It's a human trait, as old as the human race. It has happened all across the world. But if we want to make the world a better place, then everyone has to follow the same rules, not just people of certain races." I said.

But it didn't seem that Chalista had to follow any rules at all. The legal description of a 'cemetery' is "an area where six or more bodies are buried", yet Chalista could claim a 'cemetery' over the possibility that maybe someone might have died in the general area. No one else could own the land surrounding the hotsprings, but they think they can. They didn't need any physical evidence on the ground, and reports did not have to match actual facts, and they could claim land without a survey, over the top of the home we had lived in for over 40 years.

I cannot begin to describe the ongoing agony and mental anguish my family has suffered and continues to suffer from this injustice. As our legal battle continues, I plead with readers for support and advice.

# Chapter Thirty-Six

The encounter was so sudden, it took my breath away, and for a single moment I stood frozen, staring into the grizzly's eyes. It was so close I could reach out and touch its shaggy bronze fur. I had just stepped out of the henhouse, and the bear had been on the other side of the door. My rifle was just a few steps away, in the feed shed, but the bear was between me and the rifle.

The next seconds were an explosion of activity. From the corner of my eye, I saw a big black beast, all fangs and bristling hair, lunging for the grizzly's throat. The bear wheeled around, nearly knocking me over, whites of its eyes showing in terror as it galloped away. Still snarling, Denali matched the bear stride for stride as they raced off through the brush and across the creek. I heard the branches snapping and the water splashing and the bear grunting.

"Denali! Denali, come!" I shouted, my heart hammering hard now with fear.

Denali is a huge dog, but he was less than a quarter the size of the grizzly. It could kill him with a single swipe of its paw. Still, he had shown no hesitation to protect me. I hoped Denali was OK, and the bear didn't get him. I did not want to go into the brush after them, and now I could no longer hear the dog barking, or the brush cracking. Please, please, don't let the bear kill him, I begged. Denali doesn't normally bark much, even when he is after something, I reassured myself, so maybe he is on the way back. I found one of the hens that had escaped out of the door during the commotion, and recounted to make sure I had all seventeen.

"Denali!" I shouted again up the hill where I had seen him disappear. He normally did not chase animals past the boundaries of his yard.

Just then I heard a heavy panting and turned, gripping the rifle tightly, scanning the brush. Willows parted, and my beloved dog stepped out, muddy and panting, but unscathed. I gave him a big hug and told him what a good brave dog he was. He smiled back and wagged his white-tipped tail happily. We went into the house to start breakfast.

"Dolly! Dolly! Is everything OK? Who were you yelling at? Is it Chalista? I told you they were coming to take White Bear away! Dolly, are you OK?" Harry's frightened voice came from the bedroom.

I rushed in to console him. "No, no, it was just a bear! Denali chased it away. Chalista isn't here, no one is taking White Bear away."

"They will come. I'm telling you. They're going to take it all away. A bear, you said? Where's my little puppy-dog?"

Denali walked in and Harry reached out to pet him.

"Do you want to go sit in your chair while I make breakfast?" I asked Harry. He needed help getting up sometimes now.

"I suppose so." He said.

I helped Harry to his chair in the living room, and started cooking our meal. Reflecting back over the summer, I realized it had been one of the most stressful times of our lives. The impending conveyance of the hotsprings which we used to heat our home threatened our very lives here in this remote rugged wilderness. Every day was a struggle, even small chores seemed overwhelming. Often, I stopped and asked myself, why even bother? Why pick berries, why patch the roof, why split wood? Chalista was going to get everything we have worked all our lives for. Why even go on? Even my son's grave was threatened by the proposed conveyance. No one was listening to us, no one cared if the phony reports did not even match what was actually on the ground. I had written hundreds of letters and spent thousands on sat phone calls, and still, no one understood or cared. The stress had taken its toll on all of us. Harry had gotten weaker, and was continually fearful of losing his home. I was tired and depressed, and Jillian had been hesitant to leave for firefighting this summer. But we needed money to pay for the upcoming court battle, so I convinced her to go. The fear of losing White Bear was taking a big toll on Jillian too, so I thought she needed a diversion.

"White Bear is all I have to look forward to. I've worked hard all my life for this place. If Chalista ends up with it, I will have nowhere to live when I retire." Jillian lamented.

Jillian worked hard for a living, and lived simply on her $25,000 salary. We all lived below what most people call the poverty level. How would we afford to pay for a lawyer? It could cost hundreds of thousands. It could drag out for years and years, long beyond my lifetime. Jillian would be left with debts for the rest of her life. It was not fair to any of us. What could I do to secure our home that we had worked so hard for? Take it to the people, I thought. Let everyone see this civil injustice. Maybe someone out there, one reader, will know something, some way to make a difference. And that was the birth of this story, my first book.

I continued to write letters. The BLM deferred the survey that summer when I explained that Harry's health was very poor and it would have a detrimental effect on him. That was the first indication of compassion from BLM. Their decision to defer the survey could also have been influenced by the fact that we denied them usage of our private airstrip, but I would like to think more optimistically and take this opportunity to praise the BLM for their understanding.

Jillian hired a lawyer who specialized in land issues. He was very expensive and came with a partner, who was equally expensive. In less than a month, Jillian had spent her entire year's salary on the lawyers. But, they were very knowledgeable, and showed interest and professionalism in our case. Finally, someone seemed to understand! It gave us a small glimmer of hope. They had meetings with several government officials, none of which resulted in anything, but at least now, someone was listening to us.

Harry was very fearful of being sent to a nursing home. He wanted, more than anything else, to live out the rest of his days surrounded by comfortable, familiar things. Although it was an increased workload for me, I understood completely and did the best I could to honor his wishes. Things took longer to do, and I could not stay out in the garden or go picking berries as long, for fear that Harry would need something or fall while I was away. He had fallen once already, getting up off the toilet, late that summer. I rushed to help him up, but he was too heavy for me to lift, and he was too weak to help me.

"What should I do? Should I call someone to help?" I asked Harry fearfully.

Who could I call for help? Henry had stopped flying nearly a year ago, and wanted nothing to do with his dad since Harry had been in the hospital. Jillian was probably out on a fire somewhere. Who else could come and help us?

"No, no, no! Dolly, don't call anyone! I don't want anyone to come and take me away to a nursing home. I'm just fine right here. I'll be stronger tomorrow, I'll get up then." Harry insisted.

It was already getting dark, so having someone fly up to help wasn't an option. I gathered several blankets and quilts, and made Harry a bed there on the bathroom floor.

"Thank you. This is real nice. I'm good right here." Harry said when I asked him if he was comfortable.

I went in the kitchen and fixed him his favorite macaroni and cheese with Spam. He ate most of it, and thanked me again. I couldn't sleep well that night, worrying about Harry. I checked on him several times that night. In the morning, I tried a few more times to get Harry up, but he was still too weak. I came up with a plan. Digging through some boxes that my friends Mike and Roma had sent me, I found some heavy duty eye bolts. I screwed those into the ceiling above Harry, and then dug through some scraps of sturdy canvas and nylon straps. I bent over my sewing machine, working the foot treadle feverishly until the big sling took shape.

"What are you making?" Harry wanted to know.

"It's done! I think this will help you up," I said as I showed him the sling.

I tucked it under him and hooked the nylon straps to one end of a come-along winch. The other end I hooked to the eye bolts in the ceiling.

"Ready?" I asked.

"OK, let's go." Harry said, grabbing the sides of the sling to help himself along.

We had to readjust the sling a bit, and then I carefully winched Harry up enough to slide a chair under him.

"Holy cow, it worked! Now isn't that something! Dolly, you're pretty smart after all." Harry said, relieved.

He sat there a few minutes, and then he was ready to go to his bedroom. It was far easier now to pull him to a standing position and help him along. Harry recovered his strength considerably over the next few days. Jillian came home the following week, and brought Harry a walker. It put my mind at ease considerably knowing he was less likely to fall down when I was out of the house.

Jillian had been filling out tons of paperwork, trying to get her dad some more medical assistance under the Personal Care Attendant program paid by Medicaid. It was an almost overwhelming amount of paperwork, and Harry had to be seen by a program manager. The airstrip had too much snow for a wheel plane, and Jillian's little Cessna 140 ski plane could not safely take off with the weight of another person from the short White Bear airstrip. The Medicaid program manager finally got a ride up in a chartered ski plane, and after a few more months of paperwork, Harry was allowed to hire a Personal Care Attendant. There were no actual requirements for the job, other than a clean background. I thought it would be a perfect job for a Native person from one of the villages, and Jillian hung up several flyers around Bethel. But no one from the villages wanted to work, and especially not to be so far from their own families. Time was running short, as fire season was rolling around again, and now Harry needed nearly constant care.

Our days were filled with Harry's care. He had weakened again, and was now bed-ridden. Jillian and I divided the chores, and she would get upset if she thought I was doing 'her' chores. She scrubbed her dad's laundry at least three times a day, cooked his meals, and helped me feed him. It took both of us to sit Harry up in his bed so he could eat. I would hold him steady and help him eat. Harry enjoyed sneaking some of his food to Denali when he thought I wasn't looking. He seemed to be comfortable, and still thanked me nearly daily for my assistance. Jillian had asked him once if he wanted a ride to Bethel with her.

"Hell no!" Harry had said adamantly.

A doctor who had a ski plane flew up once, upon our request to check on Harry, and had lauded us for our care. It was a comforting thing for me to hear, as I had no medical background, and wanted to do the best I could for my husband. We advertised for a PCA on Craigslist, but the allowed number of paid hours was too low to interest anyone. Jillian told me she would stay home to help with her dad if no one applied for the job. When she did fly the 140 to Bethel for supplies, she had to make a return trip the same day in order to help me with Harry. It did not leave much time for anything in town. She would refuel the plane, go to the post office and the store and come right back.

Jillian would often have to return in bad weather or near dark. I worried about her flying that winter, particularly since none of us had been getting much sleep. Harry had been sick the past few days, and we were all exhausted. There had been a particularly bad storm for a few weeks, and Jillian had not been able to fly to Bethel. Harry was getting low on medicine and there was another big storm rolling in. As soon as it got light, we took the snowgo to the airport and started scraping ice off the Cessna 140 and preheating the engine with the small generator and diesel space heater.

"I don't think you should go today," I said, watching the clouds billow over the mountains. "That storm is supposed to hit tonight. You might not be able to get back before dark."

Jillian looked at the sky. "I might make it, if I hurry."

I wanted to say, 'might' isn't good enough, but she was already getting into the little plane. The engine turned over and fired off smoothly, and the plane slid forward over the drifted snow. I jumped on the snowgo and followed her to the end of the airstrip, where it was too narrow for the ski plane to turn around by itself. Jillian got it turned partway, and I hopped off the snowgo and gave the tail a little push, grateful that it wasn't a heavy plane. It spun easily around and I saw Jillian glance back to make sure I was out of the way before adding full throttle. The plane surged ahead, spraying snow before it lifted off and flew away. I went back home and checked in on Harry.

Two hours later, I went back to the airstrip to wait for Jillian to return. The weather, thankfully, was still OK, although the wind was picking up a bit. Jillian was late, which wasn't unusual, so I didn't worry much at first. Then, as darkness started closing in, I began to worry. The old plane was not equipped with lights. Perhaps something went wrong? Last month the plane had sprung an oil leak, and the engine had started on fire on the way to Bethel. Jillian had fixed it and returned home, but she was late then, too. I should call the control tower in Bethel, and see if she took off. I pulled my sat phone out of my backpack, where I had it wrapped in several wool socks to keep it warm.

"Hello, this is Dolly at White Bear. Can you tell me if Cessna 89290 took off from the Kuskokwim River?" I asked.

"Yes, she took off about an hour and a half ago," the air traffic controller answered.

I thanked him and hung up. Jillian should have been here half an hour ago. Perhaps she had turned around to go back to Bethel for some reason. Maybe the weather was bad, or something was wrong with the plane. I decided to stay at the airport until dark. Just then I hear the vibrating hum of the plane's engine. Looking hard, I could make it out, higher than normal, its gray metal barely discernible from the darkening landscape.

"Cessna 290, the wind is from the south." I reported on the radio, relieved that the plane had finally shown up.

"OK. Sorry I'm late. I'm going to fly over, and I want you to tell me if my right ski looks OK. I can't see it from in here." Jillian said.

The plane flew over low and circled. The ski looked OK to me, but I wasn't sure what I was supposed to be looking for. I said as much to Jillian.

"Good enough. I'm landing to the south, stay back out of the way. That ski might snag and swerve the plane." Jillian said, not seeming very concerned.

I didn't like the sound of that, but did as she suggested and stood back away with the front end loader between me and the airport. I couldn't see her land, but could hear the plane set down, the soft swish of snow against the skis, then a scrape of the plastic bottoms against an ice chunk, the quick burst of power, and then the plane was there in the parking area, as if nothing had happened. Jillian stepped out and examined the ski.

"What happened?" I asked.

"Engine quit on the way home. I was real low and just barely made it into a little clearing. Tundra was pretty rough and it cracked the ski. I lashed it together with some baling wire and a Leatherman. We'll have to take it off and fix it better." Jillian filled me in on the day's events.

"Oh, man! How did you get the engine going again? What was wrong?" I asked. Of all the things I had been worrying about, this wasn't one of them.

Jillian laughed. "I reached over to pull the cabin heater on and accidently pulled the mixture knob instead. Shut the engine off! By the time I figured it out, I was already on the ground. That sure made me pay attention! I'm not so tired anymore, nothing like an engine quitting to wake you up!"

I gasped. "How did you get back out of there?"

"It was a pretty small clearing, but I was so low, I had to take what was in front of me, not many options. After I fixed the ski, I taxied around a corner in the trees and took off in a little bigger opening, but it was still pretty tight. Good thing I was on skis! If I had been on wheels, the plane would have flipped on that tundra." Jillian explained.

"Well, I'm glad you're OK! Did your dad's medicine come in the mail?" I asked, hoping that it had, and Jillian hadn't risked her life for nothing.

"Yes. And there was a letter from Iowa. I didn't recognize the address. Maybe it's someone applying for the PCA job." She said.

It was late and starting to get dark, so we decided to fix the ski later. We went home and did our evening chores. Jillian did not tell her dad about the mishap with the airplane. It was needless to make him worry. He seemed to be recovering now from his recent illness. Max was curled on his bed near him and purring contentedly as Harry stroked his soft fur. Our cat always seemed to know where he was needed the most.

After we fed Harry, we brought in the small TV and VCR and showed Harry his favorite John Wayne movie. Since the wind had picked up, our little wind generator had charged the bank of 12 volt batteries, and we had power to run the TV. We had installed the wind generator about ten years ago, on a pole attached to our house. It was a small, inexpensive unit, but efficient and maintenance free. We've learned how to ration electricity to have enough for our needs. While Harry was watching his movie, Jillian and I sat down to read our mail. The letter from Iowa caught my eye. I was almost afraid to open it, almost afraid my hopes would be shattered.

"Open it. Come on, I want to know!" Jillian insisted.

And there it was, a lovely card and a resume from a woman in Iowa! Anne was a retired nurse with a lot of experience caring for elderly patients. She sounded professional, adventurous, and compassionate. It just sounded too good to be true! She was the only person that had applied in the many months of advertising, but she sounded perfect for the job.

I called Anne the next day. She agreed to come up the first part of May. Both Jillian and I were pretty excited. Jillian would be able to go firefighting this summer after all! Harry and I needed the help, and were especially pleased that Anne had a nursing background. She waded through the mountain of paperwork and Jillian bought her a ticket. Things were starting to look promising for us after all.

# Chapter Thirty-Seven

I looked forward to Anne's arrival with nervous anticipation. Would she like it here, or would the accommodations be too primitive for her? Would she embrace the solitude of the wilderness, or would it become too overwhelming for her? Would Harry accept her care? What if he didn't like her, or she didn't like me? The probability of everything going perfectly seemed unlikely. A woman I had never met was now going to be living with us for the summer. It had to work out; there were no other options. There were no other applicants, and Harry desperately needed her professional care.

A week before, I had strained my back getting Harry set up in bed to eat his food. Even bending over was painful. The thought of having to pull Harry upright by myself made me cringe. A few days later, Jillian did the same thing. She was just days away from having to take her physical test for the smokejumpers. I hoped she could do her pullups and pushups, or she wouldn't have a job. Finally, the 'Hoya lift' we had ordered came in the air cargo plane to Bethel, and Jillian brought it to White Bear. She also crammed a folding hospital bed into the Cessna on another trip, and a wheelchair. It seemed that now we were set up with better equipment for Harry's home care. All we needed was a knowledgeable assistant.

When Anne stepped out of Jillian's Cessna 172, I liked her immediately. She was a petite woman, about my age, bright and optimistic. It was the early part of May, and the trail to the house was knee-deep with wet slushy snow. The snow was too deep for the four-wheeler, and too soft for the snowmachine. We all trudged to the house, nearly two miles away. Anne remained cheerful despite the difficult toil up the steep trail through the deep snow. She introduced herself to Harry, and settled into her room.

"You might have a little roommate." I warned her, pointing to Max. He was sniffing her curiously.

"That's fine! I love animals." Anne assured me.

Jillian left for firefighting the next day. Things looked as if they would work out after all. Anne was an incredible help with Harry. She was very knowledgeable and compassionate, and Harry seemed to be at ease with her. She and I got along like long-lost sisters. I listened with rapt interest to her stories about her grandchildren, and her current dilemma over where she would live if she left her husband. Anne listened with similar interest, and even cried when I told her of our battle with the Chalista corporation to save our home.

"Way out HERE? So far from any village? I can't believe they are trying to steal this from you, after all the work you've put into it!" Anne said incredulously.

"First, they filed for the entire valley under 14(h)(8) so it could be available for developing as a mining area. They relinquished the 'cemetery historic site' in favor of that selection. So obviously the hotsprings wasn't of 'traditional' value to them, as they were planning to mine it anyway. The BLM knew it wasn't available to Chalista under 14(h)(8), but they sneaked it in with other land selections, hoping no one would appeal it, and Chalista could get away with it. BLM begged us to withdraw from our appeal, because they knew their selection was in error. When it went to the Board of Land Appeals, the BLM had no choice but to withdraw it. So then Chalista went back to the 'cemetery historic site' application that they had previously rejected, and NOW they want to make a big stink about how this is such an important Native usage area, AFTER they rejected it in favor of mining the whole valley!" I explained.

"They're going to take away all of my hard work. Everything I worked for. All I want is to live out my days here and be buried next to Eddie." Harry interjected. A tear rolled down his wrinkled old cheek.

Anne brushed away her own tear and said, "Sounds like a lot of corruption going on! What a horrible corporation. There has to be something we can do to bring it to light."

"I've written hundreds of letters. Chalista is a giant entity. They have their headquarters in Anchorage, instead of Bethel where the majority of their shareholders are. They don't represent their people at all. It's all about the money. The CEO makes a salary of $283,000 plus all his perks. He gave himself a $400,000 annual bonus for the past five years! All this while shareholders in the villages are starving!" I informed her.

"Have you written to the Senator about this?" Anne asked.

"Yes." I said. "She was very helpful at first and made several inquiries to the BLM. Then, as election time came around, she had to be careful, as Chalista donates a large sum to her re-election campaign. So now she says she can't get involved at all."

"Dolly has written letters to just about everyone! They don't care what's right or wrong. Chalista gets what they want because they are Natives. They can take away everything from us without having to follow any rules." Harry said.

We went on to a different conversation, so as not to upset Harry any more. We tried not to discuss things that upset him.

"Tell me about Tootsie!" Anne said.

"She lived way down the valley to the north, back in the 1930's. She built her own cabin there, and people say she grubstaked the miners." I started.

"Tootsie was a black prostitute." Harry interrupted.

"She was said to be a large, very beautiful woman. People said she was a prostitute, who had moved down from Fairbanks to get away from the trade, but I don't know if that was true. People got jealous of ambitious women back then, and made up stories. Life was surely difficult for a black woman in those days. Tootsie must have loved these mountains as much as I do. She was an amazing woman, worked hard for a living, and didn't hold out her hand for anything from the government." I said.

"Sounds like Chalista could take a lesson from her!" Anne said just loud enough for me to hear. "She didn't act like she was entitled to everything because she was a minority. She actually WORKED for what she had, maybe harder than anyone else."

"Yes." I agreed. "I wish I could have met her. I think we would have been good friends."

Much later, after we had put Harry to bed, we sat up talking of hopes and dreams for the future. Anne was at a crossroads in her life, not enjoying the town she was living in, far from her family, married to a man she was no longer in love with. Her grandchildren were in Anchorage and she missed them terribly.

"This is the perfect job for me." Anne said." It gives me time to think, to sort things out and decide where I want to go from here. It is so peaceful and healing here. Dolly, what do you want to do after this is all over?" She meant, delicately said, after Harry passed on.

"I want to live here as long as I physically can. This is my home. I want to die here, and be buried with my family." I told her.

"Yes, I can understand that. This is a beautiful place to live. Have you ever thought of making it into a lodge, to make a little more money for repairs?" She asked.

"Harry and I tried that long ago when we first built the place. Neither of us liked catering to demanding clients. No, it wasn't worth the money, I would never do that again. I wouldn't mind bringing friends up once in awhile, or helping out veterans struggling with Post Traumatic Stress Disorder, but I don't want strangers in my home, especially not people who think they are entitled to everything." I said.

"That's a great idea, helping out veterans. Having a place away from all the hustle and bustle really helps get one's life back in order. I'm living proof of that. I wish we could start something. Maybe there's some program we can join to help people out." Anne sounded excited.

"We would have to choose clients very carefully. I wouldn't want to be stuck up here with someone that was violent or anything. And I only have one extra bed, so people couldn't just drop in whenever they wanted to. The whole reason I live out here is for the privacy and peace." I explained.

"Maybe there's a program, with Medicaid or something, that would pay for a vet's expenses to come up here for a few months, to heal their soul, away from everything. It might be nice for you to have some company, too, you know, while Jillian is gone firefighting in the summer, after Harry is gone. Do you want me to look up information when I get back to Iowa?" Anna asked.

"If you want. But you know how all this government bureaucracy is! It would be a mountain of paperwork to wade through. Even if there are programs out there, it would be difficult to qualify for them. Remember how hard it was just to get Medicaid to hire you to come here, and how much paperwork we all had to fill out?" I said.

"I sure do!" Anne emphasized. "I almost gave up on it too! I just can't believe this agency! To quantify a patient's care in a level of minutes spent on certain activities is just ridiculous! We are talking about human beings! I just don't understand where all the money goes. It sure doesn't go to the caretakers, or the patient."

"It passes down through all the office people and managers and paper-pushers before it even reaches the caretakers. The people who need the money or the care never get it after it filters through the upper management." I said.

"I'm disgusted with the whole health care system. I'm going to write some letters about it when I get home." Anne stated.

"Good! Maybe you will stir things up and get some results." I agreed.

In late May, Harry's health took a turn for the worse. He woke often in the night, shouting in terror at the phantom Chalista agents.

"Get back! Dolly, they're going to shoot us!" He would yell.

Anne and I would rush in to console him. Harry would awaken and we comforted him and told him that, no, Chalista was not here, they were not taking anything away, he was safe. Harry fell back asleep and a few hours later he woke himself, shouting, "NO, NO,NO! Get out! Get away!"

I held him gently and told him, "No, Chalista is not burning down the house. It's OK, everything's fine. Hush now."

"They'll burn us out, just like they did our cabin at the lake! You know they burnt Ronnie's cabin, too, over by Holy Cross!" Harry said.

Then he cried softly, and I held him and cried too.

Anne was furious with Chalista. "You should sue them for mental anguish. Lord knows, of all the people who file phony lawsuits every year, this one is real. Look at the suffering it has caused Harry alone!"

"We can't afford to sue." I sniffled. "Besides, we aren't that kind of people. We are hard-working Americans, not people who are trying to make an easy buck."

Harry continued to grow weaker, and more anguished daily. Jillian took time off work and came home to try to console her dad. It continues to break my heart that my husband spent his last days agonizing over the injustices of the greedy corporation.

## Chapter Thirty-Eight

Harry passed away on Memorial Day. It was both a great tragedy and a small relief that his suffering was over. But who was to say that one's suffering was over after they had passed, I thought. Death was such a waste of life. Harry had been an incredible, ambitious, hard-working man who did things most people only dreamed about. We had been partners in an amazing and magnificent adventure. We had been through hell and high water together. I missed him terribly already.

The spring storm hit hard, and plans for family and friends to fly up to help with the burial had to be cancelled for safety's sake. Henry had spent the day building his dad's coffin and now it looked as if we wouldn't be able to get it to White Bear. The next morning the storm was still raging, but we had decided we needed to go ahead with the burial soon. Tom volunteered to fly the coffin and one person to White Bear in his helicopter, which could handle the strong winds safer than an airplane. A young man who worked for Henry came up with Tom. He brought a jackhammer along to help dig the grave through the permafrost. After a long, tearful goodbye, Anne caught a ride back to Bethel in Tom's helicopter.

We spent the day chiseling through the frozen ground, and laying Harry to rest besides Eddie. His grave is on the hill overlooking our home, next to our son. It was a difficult, emotional time for Jillian and I, but we managed. The next day the winds had abated, and Jillian flew Ray back to Bethel. A few days later, we had a memorial service for Harry in Bethel. It was beautifully put together, a slide show of Harry's life, the planes he had flown, the building of White Bear, an entire life of hard work in one short video. There wasn't a dry eye in the church at the end, when it showed the clip of Denali stepping forward to Harry's grave and using his nose to help us push the dirt over his coffin. At the close of the ceremony, I was presented a flag from the VFW, signifying Harry's service to his country.

A few weeks later, Jillian went back to work. Over the summer, my sister and brother visited, and I got frequent letters from Anne. She had left her husband and moved to a town near her family. She had no luck yet finding a program where we could help out veterans by offering a short stay at my peaceful wilderness home. I mentioned the idea in a letter to Jillian, and shortly after she came home in the fall, she formed our own non-profit corporation called Wilderness Retreats For Vets.

"Once we get it going, we can get people involved all over the country. Villagers could take vets out to their fish camps for a month, you know, to get away from the city and get back to the land. But right now, we can just have a guest here whenever we can afford it. It will be nice to help people out, to do something for the veterans who risked their lives to protect us." Jillian said.

"I don't know if we can afford to feed another person. I definitely want to help vets, but we don't have much money, you know." I reminded her.

"I know. We will just do what we can afford. I filed for non-profit status, so that should help. Once we get that, we can do fund-raisers and raffles to help more people." Jillian explained.

Henry called my sat phone one day with big news. "You're going to be a great-grandma!"

At first I wasn't sure what I was hearing. Kayla, my little granddaughter, who used to sit on my knee, was having a baby?! I had to remind myself that she was now a grown woman. My, how time sure does fly!

On Christmas Day, Jillian and I went up to the graveyard. A tiny black-capped chickadee followed us, and sat on Harry's cross, singing to us.

"Oh! How precious!" I exclaimed.

"It's a messenger from another world. You should talk to it, tell it the things you wanted to tell Dad, and it will carry the message back to the other world for you." Jillian said seriously.

"Really? Where did you hear that? What religion is that from?" I asked.

Jillian giggled. "It's not. I just made it up right now. But it sounds nice, doesn't it?"

The next day Jillian had the chickadee eating bread crumbs out of her hand. I heard her talking to it softly out my window.

"Mama, do you want to feed it?" she asked one day.

I put out my hand the way she showed me and held the finely crumbled bread. The chickadee flitted from bush to bush, and then landed on my finger. I held my breath. I had never seen a chickadee so close before. Every feather was a finely crafted detail. It regarded me with bright black eyes, and then set to work on the crumbs. It was so tiny and light and fragile, I couldn't understand how it survived the harsh winters.

For more than a month, the friendly little bird visited me several times daily. Even in the strongest wind, I would see it, flying low to the ground, its tiny body struggling through the gales that threatened to blow it away. I knelt down on the snow and held the food low, so it wouldn't have to climb in the strong wind. Somehow, I felt deeply connected to the little chickadee. It was as if I saw myself in the bird, a tiny, fragile being surrounded by harsh, sometimes hostile elements, not just surviving but thriving in its environment. I found myself talking to it, telling it my troubles. It seemed as if a huge weight had been lifted from my shoulders. The bird, whom Jillian had dubbed 'Dee-Dee', listened attentively. And then it was gone, and we never saw it again. At first, I was very sad at the loss of my new-found friend.

"Mama, Dee-Dee had to go back to the other world to deliver the messages. His Visa expired. Maybe he will come back again, in another form." Jillian suggested.

"I just hope nothing happened to it." I said. "Isn't it strange that we never saw it around before, and then suddenly it's very tame, and now it's gone?"

"Yeah. But you know what they say, 'strange things happen under the midnight sun'." Jillian agreed.

In late January, my great-grandson was born. A month later, Jillian flew me to Bethel to meet him. Kayla gently handed me her newborn son, and as I took the tiny baby into my arms, I felt a strong bond to him. He was perfect and healthy and adorable. I just couldn't take my eyes off of him. Here was the great-grandson of the late Chief Eddie Hoffman, and he was also my great-grandson. He is the future of a blended Alaskan people. It seemed to make sense, that life had come full circle.